CHA⊙S

and

BEY⊙ND:

The Best of Trajectories

CHA⊙S

and

BEY⊙ND:

The Best of Trajectories

MOSTLY BY

RoberT Ant⊙N Wilson

with guest appearances by

Arlen Wilson

D. Scott Apel

Barbara Marx Hubbard

Timothy Leary, Ph.D.

Linus Pauling, Ph.D.

Robert Newport, M.D.

Edward Kellogg III, Ph.D.

Peter Russell

George Carlin

and Ed McMahon

International Standard Book Number:
1-886404-00-3

Library of Congress Catalog Card Number:
94-68465

First Edition, August 1994

The Permanent Press
P.O. Box 700305
San Jose, CA 95170

Manufactured in the United Snakes of America

DEDICATION

To
Robert Shea

1933 - 1994

ConTentS

ChApTeR SEVEN

chaPTEr Eight

CHApteR NIne

chapter TEN

OUTroducTion

PREFACE

Owner's Manual
by D. Scott Apel

Hello! And congratulations on your purchase of *Chaos and Beyond: The Best of Trajectories*™ anthology, Version 1.0. We're sure you won't regret your choice of *Trajectories*™ brand futurism and heresy (with the secret miracle ingredient "RAW"). In order to enhance your enjoyment of *Chaos and Beyond: The Best of Trajectories*™ (Version 1.0), we recommend you read this Owner's Manual before attempting to operate this volume.

SPECIAL FEATURES OF
Chaos and Beyond: The Best of Trajectories™ **Version 1.0**
- The best features from the first five years of
  *Robert Anton Wilson's **Trajectories** Newsletter*
- New-to-this-volume 1994 Updates

WRITING CREDITS
- All uncredited pieces were written by Robert Anton Wilson
- All notes in parentheses and italics which begin with *(Note:* and end with *—Ed.)* were written by D. Scott Apel

TRAJECTORIES : THE NEWSLETTER
- Robert Anton Wilson and the Permanent Press publish a quarterly newsletter from which the contents of this volume were drawn. A subscription form for *Robert Anton Wilson's **Trajectories** Newsletter* can be found at the back of this book.

WARRANTY
- The manufacturers of *Chaos and Beyond: The Best of Trajectories*™ (Version 1.0) take no responsibility for any incidental or consequential mind-bending (or spoon-bending), whether express or implied, resulting from the use, misuse, abuse, accident, neglect, mishandling, misapplication, alteration, modification, proselytization or commercial use of this product, or damage that is attributable to acts of any Deity, Sub-Deity, Anti-Deity, Professed Deity, or Force With Which Man Was Not Meant To Tamper.
  Reading this Warranty invalidates this Warranty.

INTRODUCTION:

How I Learned to Stop WOrrying and LOVE

CHAOS

by

Robert Anton Wilson

Sometime in my late 'teens—i.e., in the early Paleolithic age, around 1948 or '49—I found a book called *Science and Sanity* in the Brooklyn Public Library. The book has nearly a thousand pages, much of it containing heavy mathematics, and I had never heard of the author, Count Alfred Korzybski. Nonetheless, gazing over the text, reading a paragraph here, a chapter title there, I gradually got hooked on what seemed to me, and still seems to me, one of the most radical books of the 20th Century. I may not have felt exactly like Keats on first looking into Chapman's Homer, or even like Balboa on the peak in Darien, but I felt the whole universe shift into a new perspective around me.

Everything I have written, however improved or disimproved by my own wisdom or idiocy, begins from the shock of taking a book off a library shelf and encountering the world of Alfred Korzybski.

Science and Sanity, in fact, although published in 1933, upsets conventional Occidental ideas so thoroughly that even though many of its concepts have directly or indirectly influenced virtually every branch of social science, it still remains, in 1994, somewhat controversial—and painfully confusing ("unreadable") to many specialists.

Perhaps I found Korzybski easier to navigate than many learned persons because I had not yet specialized in anything when I read him—and even at 62 I still haven't specialized in anything. I suspect that perhaps I suffer from intellectual Don Juanism. I love too many reality-tunnels to give my heart entirely to any one of them. I agree with Korzybski's friend, R. Buckminster Fuller, who once said, "If nature wanted us to be specialists, we'd be born with one eye and a jeweler's lens attached."

Or perhaps I found Korzybski congenial because I read his book over and over, perhaps two dozen times in the first ten years after discovering it, many times under the influence of marijuana, a herb which makes it easy to understand Korzybski's major thesis, which holds that *our seemingly-immediate perceptions of an seemingly external "reality" contain as much guess-work, abstraction, induction, deduction, outright "gamble" etc. as any of our slower, more "conscious" ideologies, belief systems, religions, sciences etc.* All science and philosophy that follows its own method logically will eventually end with relativity, uncertainty, and zeticism because the sense-data from which we start remains wobbly and unsure.

i

The same year Korzybski published this Agnostic Manifesto, 1933, John von Neumann published a more technical proof, known as von Neumann's Catastrophe of the Infinite Regress, demonstrating that even if we add infinite instruments correcting instruments that correct instruments. . .etc. . . that correct our raw sense-data, we still have some remaining instrumental uncertainty. Korzybski merely drove the last nail in the coffin of Certitutude by showing how the same uncertainty infests every act of seeing, hearing, smelling, tasting etc. Whether you look at a Picasso, a UFO or a member of the opposite sex, your perceptions contain your whole world-view.

Korzybski demonstrated that each individual act of human perception contains that individual human's whole biography and, so to speak, the history of their family and tribe, back to the dawn of humanity, because our language habits (neuro-linguistic reflexes) shape and give form and "meaning" to the raw data received when electrons, photons and other energies impact upon our brains. We each co-create the reality-tunnel we experience.

Loyal readers who have battled their way through five or more of my books know well that this perspective—learned from Korzybski and confirmed by marijuana—appears in both the form and the content of all I write. It shapes my fiction and explains the "deliberately annoying"[1] assaults on all dogmatism that appear in my nonfiction.

I owe an even greater debt to Korzybski for his theory of *time-binding*. This metaphor holds that a sharp break—a quantum jump—exists between humans and other animals. This sounds alarmingly non-Darwinian to many, but Korzybski did not embrace Creationism. Far from it, he fervently espoused evolution. But he believed that the development of the linguistic centers of the human brain placed us in a different *umwelt* or reality-tunnel from that of any other primate—a semantic environment which, growing and changing, causes *us* to grow and change in ways impossible to nonlinguistic animals, thus creating what we once loosely called "progress."

---

[1] I forgot who first used this term for my prose, but it delighted me. When one reader feels seriously "annoyed," it means I have provoked him or her almost to the edge of a thought, which suggests that my books have actually driven others all the way into the experience of actually thinking.

In Count Korzybski's odd terminology[2] he classifies plants as *chemistry-binders,* because they bind-up chemical energy from the sun, air, earth, etc.; prehuman animals as *space-binders,* because they move about to seek prey and play, sex and food, etc. by searching in space; and humans as *time-binders,* because language allows us to communicate across generations. (I can receive signals sent by Thales of Miletus over 80 generations ago.)

About the same time I discovered Korzybski's *Science and Sanity,* I also stumbled upon Shannon and Weaver's *Mathematical Theory of Communication.* This introduced me to a concept much more precise and measurable than Korzybski's "time-binding"—Shannon's mathematical definition of information. For our purposes here, without the math, we can say that *information consists of that part of a message which you cannot predict in advance.* (Thus, in the famous metaphor of Norbert Weiner, political speeches, made up almost entirely of clichés, contain low information, and great poetry consists of very, very high information.)

Shannon and Weaver also demonstrated that information tends to increase more rapidly as time passes—i.e. the vague idea of "progress" derives from humanity's experience of finding itself, every generation, in possession of new information of all sorts; and this leads to new ideas, new Ideologies, new sciences, new technologies, new arts and the dizzy sense of continual revolution that has become more and more familiar to us in recent decades.

These ideas from Korzybski, Shannon, Weaver and Weiner (and Schrödinger, the quantum physicist, who influenced all of the above) do not quite mean the same as the 18th Century French notion of continual "improvement." They say, less dramatically but much more precisely, that humans, as symbol-creators, generate continual *change,* which can appear as improvement or disimprovement, depending on how we use new information (and which persons or groups judge how we use it).

As a result of these writers, by around 1950-52, I had a rather clear anticipation of what later became known as Future Studies, Futurology, Futuremics, etc. In sum, I had learned to

---

[2] He grew up in a castle where people spoke Polish, Russian, German and French every day, and then in his forties wrote his major works in English, a language new to him...

expect change as the norm in human (symbol-using) animals, and I expected the rate of change to continue to accelerate. I had the concept of "information explosion" before anybody coined that term. Everything I have written, whether labeled Futurism or not, has had, at least as subliminal sub-text, the expectation that the world would change faster in my lifetime than it had ever changed before.

Decades later, in the late 1970s or early 1980s, I stumbled upon the statistical studies of French economist-sociologist, Georges Anderla. Readers of my books have heard this before, so I will here summarize it as briefly as possible. (For more details, see my book, *Cosmic Trigger II*.) Anderla, trying to measure the rate at which information increases in time, used binary notation to convert all human symbol-systems into the "language" computers use. He then calculated the rate at which *bits*—*bi*nary uni*t*s: quanta of information—had doubled since the time of Christ. (This now seems a Western-chauvinist date to take as starting-point, but I guess the "multi-cultural perspective" had not penetrated French academia when Anderla did his work in the early 1970s.)

Taking the information-in-bits available to humanity in 1 AD as his unit of measurement Anderla found that information had increased as follows:

1 AD	1
1500 AD	2
1750 AD	4
1900 AD	8
1950 AD	16
1960 AD	32
1967 AD	64
1973 AD	128

You can "taste" the flavor of this acceleration by comparing the first doubling calculated by Anderla with the last doubling he reckoned—1500 years vs. 6 years. Note also that with each doubling, the world changed dramatically and drastically.

After 1500, we had a series of Protestant revolutions (starting with 1517 in Germany and 1534 in England) that effectively ended Papal domination of the Western world.

After 1750, we had an Industrial revolution that moved millions off the land and into cities and their factories, accompanied by a series of political revolutions that began the long decline-and-fall of monarchy and the rise of democracy.

After 1900, we had the dawn of air travel, two world wars, and revolutions in virtually every science and art-form. Relativity. Cubism. Uncertainty. Surrealism.

After 1950, TV remade the advanced nations into a new "global village," as McLuhan said. And after 1960, we had ten-to-fifteen years of youth revolutions everywhere...

About 1988, I heard Dr. Jacques Vallee say in a lecture that information acceleration had reached the point where information then doubled every eighteen months. It has probably increased to a yearly doubling in the last 5 years. (At least!)

In 1989, at the annual meeting of the World Future Society, I heard Theodore Gordon present a mathematical proof that as information flow increases, "chaos" also increases. "Chaos" in mathematical theory does not necessarily mean riot, war or "anarchy": it means totally *unpredictable* social change. Gordon's proof shows that, *not only will technology and science change faster than ever, but so will society as a whole, and we cannot predict these changes in advance.*

In 1989, a few months after I heard Gordon speak, the Berlin Wall fell, and the Cold War came to a sudden, totally unexpected end.

Shortly thereafter, the all-white government of South Africa released Nelson Mandela from prison and began negotiating power-sharing with Mandela's African National Congress and other black groups.

By 1993, progress in South Africa had, despite wobbles and set-backs, reached the point of an interim multi-racial government supervising preparations for the first multi-racial elections in that country. Mandela called off the liberal world's sympathy-boycott of South African products, signifying his conviction that the changes meant real progress, not mere tokenism. (As I write this, Mr. Mandela serves as South Africa's first black president. Who expected that, even after 1989?)

The same month, the leaders of Israel and the Palestine Liberation Organization, which had denounced each other as terrorists for 40 years, signed a peace treaty and began negotiating a nonviolent settlement of their remaining conflicts. The Palestinians now have a state of their own. (What next? The I.R.A. signing a peace treaty with England? Why not?)

Most astonishing of all, the very same month that Rabin and Arafat shook hands on the lawn of the White House, the United States finally took its first steps in joining the rest of the civilized world in providing a national health plan for all its citizens.

In this wild and crazy century, the earlier social shocks—the rise and fall of fascism (1922-45), the rise and fall of Communism (1917-1989)—had not quite prepared us for the "creative chaos" we have now entered. "Future Studies," once the eccentric interest of a few specialists, has become the most important area of concern to any educated person having a leadership position in politics[3], business, art, entertainment, science etc. We cannot predict the next five revolutions, or the next ten, but we can draw trajectories indicating the most probable vectors of change, giving us some guidance and illumination along the way.

Compare the "merely social" changes discussed above with the equally unpredictable (or unpredicted) scientific break-throughs in my lifetime-to-date.

In 1932, the year of my birth, science found the 92nd and last of the natural elements. For the first time, as Bucky Fuller says, we had an inventory of the building blocks of Universe.

In 1945, the atom bomb ended a nasty war in the nastiest way possible. We entered an Age of Anxiety (as Auden called it) as the cold war seemed ever on edge of boiling over into nuclear holocaust.

In the later 1940s, goiter, a disease which once disfigured millions of women, disappeared, conquered by new medical information.

In 1948-50, the basic theories of computer science appeared, mostly at M.I.T. and Bell Laboratories.

In the same few years, TV entered the majority of American homes, killing off the once rich field of radio drama, and introducing a whole new way of experiencing the global township.

In the 1960s, smallpox disappeared and polio began to disappear.

In 1969, Neil Armstrong walked on the moon.

In 1970-1990, the computer revolution and the space revolution moved much of our communication systems into

---

[3] Our leaders no longer remain totally ignorant of these facts. Vice-President Al Gore served as Chairman of the Senate Committee on the Future and belongs to the World Future Society. President Clinton often uses words and concepts that show a familiarity with the main lines of Futurist studies.

outer space, and the global township became more intimate than the villages of our ancestors 100 years ago.

The rate of change *and stress* in all areas—science, art, political divisions or new political unions—continues to accelerate. Information math and Chaos math both give us strong reasons to expect faster accelerations, and no slow-down.

For these reasons, Futurism plays a major role in all my books, and when I began a magazine, I devoted it largely to the trajectories of future evolution—and Arlen, my wife, intelligently named the magazine *Trajectories*.

This anthology attempts to convey the most important vectors and "trends" that I have spotted in the first four years of *Trajectories*, and to share with you the method I call "guerrilla ontology," which my critics—both friendly and hostile—often compare to French Deconstructionism. Whatever you call this method, I use it in both my fiction and nonfiction and it attempts to de-dogmatize our language constructs—to mockingly and blasphemously reduce all so-called "Revealed" Truths, "Undeniable" Truths, "Objective" Truths, etc., to the mere opinions (and tribal prejudices) that they now seem in the light of modern analysis.

As Korzybski said, 60 years ago, "The map is not the territory." No body of dogma, whether religious, political or "scientific," should become an Idol to which we bow in reverence. Information grows faster every day, and to avoid becoming totally out of touch with the world outside our heads, we need to remember constantly that none of our mental "maps" (ideas, beliefs, theorems, etc.) show *all* the territory; that new parts and aspects of the territory get discovered every day now; and that all our ideas will become obsolete and reactionary if we do not continually revise and update them.

For this anthology, I have updated my updates with a running commentary that attempts to bring what I wrote in 1988-92 in line with the new data I have digested, or tried to digest, in 1993-4.

Needless to say, most of what you shall read here almost certainly will appear ridiculously old-fashioned in about five years. Nevertheless, I offer it with the hope that some of it will help you navigate those five years with less anxiety and confusion than most of our fellow citizens currently suffer.

▲   ▲   ▲

Chapter One:

Bad News for CSICOP

Psychic Smites CSICOP

Many who have observed the increasingly McCarthy-like tactics of CSICOP (Committee for Scientific Investigation of Claims of the Paranormal) will be cheered to learn that one victim has struck back successfully. Ms. Noreen Renier, a practicing psychic who teaches at Rollins College and lectures at the FBI Academy, sued Northwest Skeptics (CSICOP's Oregon affiliate) for libel last year and won damages in the amount of $25,000.

The jury's verdict was upheld by the Court of Appeals of the State of Oregon on 3 February 1988. Meanwhile, another libel suit against CSICOP's Hawaiian affiliate is now before the Courts in the Aloha State.

More Bad News For CSICOP

According to *Mind/Brain Bulletin,* in a study by John Barefoot at Duke University, a negative correlation was found between suspiciousness and longevity. In a sample of 500 older men and women whose health was recorded for 15 years, those who scored high on suspiciousness, cynicism and hostility were significantly more likely to die when compared to all others. The death rate of the suspicious remained higher than others when compared by age, by sex, by previous health and by diet and other lifestyle patterns.

In a previous 25-year study of physicians, also by Barefoot, those scoring high on hostility had 6.4 times the death rate of those with low hostility.

Another recent study by the Yale University Health and Aging Project included 1,139 men and 1,617 women, and determined that those with strong religious experience were less likely to become disabled or to show signs of clinical depression. This better health for the "religious" was equally true whether the respondents were members of organized churches or had their own private and inward mystic sensibility.

▲   ▲   ▲

Trajectories **Interview:**

Dr. Linus Pauling

Conducted by D. Scott Apel

DR. LINUS PAULING is both the most respected and most controversial scientist of our times. The only person ever to be awarded two Nobel Prizes in two different areas—for Chemistry in 1954, and for Peace in 1962—he is the recipient of some 40 honorary doctorates and hundreds of other prestigious awards from around the world, in areas as diverse as chemistry, medicine and world peace. He has published over 600 scientific papers and nearly 200 articles on social and political topics. His text *The Nature of the Chemical Bond* has been cited as one of the most influential science books of the century, and his classic *No More War!* was recently re-released in a 25th anniversary edition. The prestigious British magazine *New Scientist* has named Dr. Pauling—along with Sir Isaac Newton and Albert Einstein—one of the greatest scientists who have ever lived.

Today, at age 88, Dr. Pauling—whose name has become almost synonymous with "Vitamin C"—remains active, controversial, and on the cutting edge of modern scientific research. He graciously took time out from his busy schedule to talk with *Trajectories* Managing Editor D. Scott Apel in his office at the Linus Pauling Institute of Science and Medicine—a maze of offices housed in a nondescript warehouse near the Stanford campus in Palo Alto, California.

Trajectories: Can you give us an overview of the studies on the curative or preventative powers of Vitamin C? I've heard you mention that at least 14 different double-blind studies have been done that indicate its efficacy.

Dr. Pauling: In my new book I list 16, because a couple of others have come out. These relate to the common cold, and they're controlled trials, most of them double-blind, randomized trials, involving rather small amounts of Vitamin C. Usually one gram per day—1000 mg per day. Four of them used considerably less: 200 mg in one or two. The average amount of illness among the Vitamin C subjects was decreased by 34 percent. That's the *average* decrease for the 16 studies. The maximum was about 80 percent, I think. And there were a couple others of 78 and 63 percent.

4

Trajectories: So there's no question that this is statistically significant, then, even with the wide range.

Dr. Pauling: Yes. Different populations, different circumstances; so different results are not surprising. And there were different amounts of Vitamin C. Illness declined 40 percent for the one gram a day group, and 32 percent, as I recall, for the studies that were only about 200 milligrams a day.

Trajectories: Then there's a direct correlation between the amount taken and its effectiveness, too?

Dr. Pauling: That's right. And of course I say that one gram a day isn't enough; that adults perhaps ought to take three or four grams a day. Especially if you start feeling that you're coming down with a cold, take two or four or six grams. If you feel like you have some symptoms, do that immediately. If you still have symptoms an hour later, take *another* slug, and just keep taking it until you stop the cold. Almost every worker in this field—there are a few who hold out still—but almost every worker in the field says Vitamin C may not cut down the number of colds very often, or stop the viral infection, but it almost always decreases the number of signs and symptoms, and the severity. There's no doubt that Vitamin C controls colds.

The other big argument is about cancer. My associate, Dr. Cameron, who is the Chief Surgeon of a 400 bed hospital in Loch Lomanside, Scotland, treated several hundred patients with advanced cancer, usually by giving them 10 grams of Vitamin C a day, all of their lives, starting at the time when they were pronounced terminal, or untreatable—or as soon as he could get them onto it. He usually gave it to them by intravenous infusion while they were in the hospital, but started it by mouth, too, and then continued by mouth until they died, or until the present time. Some of these terminal cancer patients of 14, 15, 17 years ago are still alive. One that I've gone to see several times was expected to die in four months in the spring of '72, I think. And she's still alive, 16 years later, taking her Vitamin C. And in general, they feel better. They lead a good life. They have energy. They don't feel miserable, but feel good, lively. Their appetites come back; they don't suffer from anorexia. And on the average, the mean time of survival is several months longer for the terminal cancer patients. Perhaps more important, as Cameron says, a few fortunate individuals— about 10 percent—just live on and on, for five years, or ten years, or 16 years, on the Vitamin C.

Dr. Morishiga, in Japan, became interested when I went to Japan and talked about this, and invited me to his hospital. He has repeated these observations and gets essentially the same results with Japanese patients with cancer who take 10 grams of Vitamin C or more—often he gives them more—compared with those who got no Vitamin C, or only a little Vitamin C.

Trajectories: So you're moving away from anecdotal evidence into more controlled studies and repeatable experiments?

Dr. Pauling: Well, it's difficult to carry out a controlled trial. I talked with Cameron in 1974 there in Scotland about doing a randomized control trial. He wouldn't do it. He said his ethical principles would not permit him to withhold Vitamin C from any of his patients. But in the same hospital were doctors who were *not* using Vitamin C for the same kinds of patients, and there was a sort of randomization in the process of admitting and assigning patients. On the days when Cameron was on duty and a patient came in, it was his patient from then on. If another doctor was on duty, then it was the other doctor's patient. So they were randomized in that way. Even though it wasn't a double-blind trial, the patients that came in for these other doctors had the same mortality that they'd been having the preceding ten years. But Cameron's patients had much lower mortality.

It was like Semmelweis, in Vienna. 15 percent of the women who came in to give birth died of puerperal septicemia. Semmelweis said that the doctor was carrying the infection, and required his interns to wash their hands in sodium hypochloride solution before they went in to see a patient, and in between patients. The other doctor, the head of the department, refused to do that. So during the next year, the head of the department had 15 percent mortality, and Semmelweis had *no* mortality—and got fired!

So with cancer, there's no doubt that Vitamin C has much value, as Dr. Cameron and I say, *as an adjunct to* appropriate conventional therapy. We say, don't give Vitamin C as a *substitute* for appropriate conventional therapy, but *as an adjunct to* conventional therapy, *if the therapy is appropriate.* And by that we mean if it is known that the conventional therapy benefits patients with that kind of cancer, then they should get it.

Trajectories: Your opponents usually cite a study done by the Mayo Clinic, but I believe you have objections to that particular study. Isn't that correct?

Dr. Pauling: The Mayo Clinic study was carried out with a 100 patients with advanced colorectal cancer, considered to be untreatable. And in their paper, the Mayo Clinic doctors said they were justified in withholding chemotherapy because this kind of cancer doesn't respond to chemotherapy. Before their trial was over, they had given chemotherapy to 58 of the 100 patients, even though they know it was not appropriate. And, of course, chemotherapy makes the patient miserable—if he or she is not taking Vitamin C. Vitamin C helps control these side effects of nausea and hair falling out, and so on. So every doctor "knows" that the Mayo Clinic showed that Vitamin C has no value against advanced cancer. That's what they say in their paper. In that paper, they report that they gave 50 patients 10 grams of Vitamin C a day. We're skeptical about that, but that's what they say. And the controls got a placebo. And there was no difference. They say. They gave the Vitamin C for a median time of two months and a half and then stopped it. None of their patients died while they were getting the Vitamin C. They died after it was stopped. Dr. Cameron and I had said in our book, you shouldn't stop Vitamin C for cancer patients; it may be dangerous. They began dying rapidly when the Vitamin C was stopped.

Trajectories: The conclusion you would draw from the Mayo Clinic study, then, is not that it's dangerous to give Vitamin C to terminal cancer patients, but that it's dangerous to stop.

Dr. Pauling: Yes. It's dangerous to *stop* giving it. In fact, they had no justification for their conclusion. They might have said, "It is our conclusion that giving Vitamin C for two months and a half to patients with advanced colorectal cancer has no value." Even that might be debated, but they might have said that. But just to say, "Giving high-dose Vitamin C to patients with advanced cancer"—all kinds—"has no value," is just completely improper, you see? We haven't been able to get *The New England Journal of Medicine* to publish our letters pointing these things out.

Trajectories: The common cold, cancer, longevity...you claim they are all subject to manipulation by Vitamin C. Some of the criticism you've come under is this proselytization of Vitamin C as a panacea. Do you think this has affected its acceptance in the medical community?

Dr. Pauling: The American Medical Association says that a "quack" is a person who says he has something that's good for you no matter what's wrong with you. By that definition, I'm a quack.

Trajectories: Would you go so far as to say that Vitamin C. is some sort of immune system builder?

Dr. Pauling: Oh, yes! That's right; we *do* say it, and point out in what ways it's known that Vitamin C stimulates what aspects of the immune system. You have evidence about infectious diseases, from Dr. Morishiga—who began getting interested in Vitamin C about the same time I did—and from Dr. Cathcart, here in Mountain View. In my book *How to Live Longer and Feel Better,* I give arguments and some evidence about heart disease, especially that high-dose Vitamin C cuts down the cholesterol level, and everyone believes—all the authorities agree, I think—that there's a very good correlation between cholesterol level and incidence of death from heart disease. So probably the main thing that Vitamin C in the high doses does is to potentiate the body's natural protective mechanisms—the immune system and other protective mechanisms.

Trajectories: Can you tell us a little about your latest studies?

Dr. Pauling: Well, among other things, I'm working on the high temperature copper oxide superconductors. They were discovered only two or three years ago, by two men in an IBM laboratory in Switzerland—

Trajectories: —and within a few months even high school students were recreating their experiments with materials costing a few dollars.

Dr. Pauling: That's right! There was great interest among hundreds—probably thousands—of solid state physicists and metallurgists and others working on this problem. I'd published a paper on superconductivity 20 years ago, in which I discussed two classes of superconductors. So I wrote a paper which was published in August, 1987, on the theory of these high temperature copper oxide superconductors, and I wrote another one recently expanding this theory. It's based on my theory of metals, called the resonating covalent bond theory of metals, which I formulated in 1938 and had written about at considerable length. So several other people have now published papers on a resonating covalent bond theory of superconductors. They don't say exactly the same thing that I say—I don't think they understand these matters so well. You should remember that I've been thinking about these things since...well, 1921, anyway, when I was working as an undergraduate on a research problem that I had invented on my own, dealing with the nature of metals—iron, in particular. Actually a couple years before that, when I had some courses in metallurgy. So it's been—how long?—*69 years* that I've been thinking about this.

Trajectories: I'd say that gives you a pretty good edge.

Dr. Pauling: Well, I have a tremendous body of knowledge about metals. I've just formulated a new idea about how to get still *higher* superconducting temperatures from certain compositions.

Trajectories: At any kind of temperature that might be easily available?

Dr. Pauling: Perhaps even *room* temperature.

Trajectories: That would revolutionize the world.

Dr. Pauling: Yes. But I don't know that it will *work*, you know. I'm in the process of trying to get some company interested in checking up on it. So this is what I've been doing most recently.

Trajectories: Have you been involved lately in any active anti-war work?

Dr. Pauling: 30, 35 years ago, I was devoting half my time to work for world peace, giving hundreds of speeches—that was perhaps the main activity—but writing hundreds of articles, too, and participating in many demonstrations—leading peace walks, and things of that sort. I now pretty much restrict myself to signing statements. I just signed one that was a full page in the **New York Times** in favor of withholding all aid from Israel. I believe in peaceful resolutions of problems.

Trajectories: How effective would you say your work for world peace has been?

Dr. Pauling: Well, the Nobel Committee felt it might well be that there wouldn't have been the bomb test treaty if I hadn't been making up petitions and giving all these lectures and writing my book and so on. It may be that they're right; nobody knows, how much effect this had. But the Chairman of the Nobel Committee said he believes that if there hadn't been someone doing what I did, this treaty would never have been made. They awarded the Nobel Peace Prize to me on the day that treaty went into effect: the 10th of October, 1963. There's probably a more direct connection between my activities and the bomb test treaty than anything else.

Trajectories: That's a pretty good connection...

9

Dr. Pauling: Other people have been more effective in keeping the peace movement going. There are hundreds of people who work pretty vigorously in the peace movement now.

Trajectories: What would you suggest to average citizens who really don't have the prestige to carry a lot of weight or the time to devote full-time to peace work? How can they make a contribution of importance?

Dr. Pauling: Well, I say, *do what you can.* Don't worry about how effective your contribution will be. Just go ahead and do it. Write letters to the editors of newspapers supporting peace activities; whenever there's a demonstration, if it's possible for you to go participate in the demonstration, do so; especially, vote for peace candidates in local elections, regional and state elections and national elections. Try to get candidates to express themselves on the issue of use of military might as compared with working for world peace and negotiating solutions to problems. So that's my recommendation to people: Do *something.* Don't think that you're not going to be of any value. You might be of great value. Perhaps your contribution will just be of small value. But altogether, if everybody is doing this, it'll be effective.

Trajectories: Thank you, Dr. Pauling.

▲   ▲   ▲

HOLISTIC REMEDY

This is the world that man made.
These are the ills that plagued
The world that man made.
This is the doctor prescribing the pills
That treated the ills that plagued
The world that man made.
These are the plants and labs and mills
That manufactured all the pills the doctor
Gave to treat the ills that plagued
The world that man made.
This is the banker with tellers and tills
That backed the plants and labs and mills
That manufactured all the pills the doctor
Gave to treat the ills that plagued
The world that man made.
This is the general with trumpets and trills
Who made the war that saved the bank that
Backed the plants that manufactured all the pills
The doctor gave to treat the ills that plagued
The world that man made.
Here is the mother all forlorn
Whose one and only child was born
To die in the war the general made to save
The bank that backed the plants that made
The pills the doctor gave to treat the ills
That plagued the world that man made.
This is the angel who blew his horn
To comfort the mother all forlorn
And fired the general and closed the banks
And shut the mills and scattered the pills,
Retired the doctor and cured the ills
And ended the world that man made.

—Arlen Wilson

11

"Mind-Body" Problem Solved?

The Psychobiology of Mind-Body Healing
by Ernest Lawrence Rossi
(1988; W.W. Norton Co.; $25.95)

Reviewed by Robert Anton Wilson

A cancer patient considered terminal is experimentally given a new anti-cancer drug and within days his tumors have shrunken to half their previous size. Febrile, bed-ridden and considered near death before the drug, the patient is now walking around the ward and chatting happily with everybody.

Obviously, the new drug was responsible, right?

Not at all. The patient—"Mr. Wright," as he was called by Dr. Philip West, who first recorded this case—was the only one who responded so favorably to the new drug, Krebiozen. Doctors eventually decided the chemical was virtually useless. It appears that Mr. Wright got better because he *believed* he would get better.

A South Seas shaman points a "death bone" at a tribesman who has angered him. The victim is given the best medical attention by sympathetic white physicians, and appears normal and healthy in ordinary tests, but within days he is dead. He seems to have died of the belief that "death bones" and curses can kill people.

A remarkable new book, *The Psychobiology of Mind-Body Healing*, by Ernest Lawrence Rossi, begins with careful documentation of these two cases and then cites extensive medical literature to show that such "magical" healings and slayings are far, far more common than we generally realize. If that was as far as the book went, it might leave a certain number of readers—e.g., those who really grok Ramtha and Shirley MacLaine—convinced that metaphysics has more to offer us than science.

But although Dr. Rossi—a professional hypnotist trained by the great Milton Erickson—has seen many similar cases in his own experience, he is not satisfied with vague explanations about "mind" miraculously taking command of "body." He wants to know what the hell is actually going on, concretely, in hypnotism, shamanism, Christian Science, and the ever-

12

perplexing "placebo effect" illustrated by Mr. Wright. Astonishingly, Dr. Rossi seems to have found a large part of the answer.

But first, to show how commonly this mysterious "mind-body" link appears, let me cite some double-blind studies quoted by Dr. Rossi. In six careful double-blind studies, placebos proved 56 percent as effective as morphine; in nine double-blind studies, placebos were 54 percent as effective as aspirin; in three double-blind studies, placebos were 56 percent as effective as codeine. ("Effectiveness" in these studies was measured by decrease in pain.) In short, *for more than half of all patients, belief that one has received a pain-killer is just as helpful in reducing pain as an actual application of one of the three most common pain-killers would be.*

My own books, especially *Prometheus Rising,* have numerous examples of how so-called "positive thinking" produces positive effects in such psychological phenomena as social relationships, general happiness, etc.; but everybody (in our society, at least) feels there must be something "spooky" happening when a belief system actually vanquishes physical pain and disease. This seems to be because our culture has never recovered from the Christian split of "soul" and "body" and the subsequent attempt to harmonize this with science by means of the unwieldy Cartesian philosophy of "the ghost in the machine."

As K. Bowers wrote in 1977, "The tendency to split etiological factors of disease into either psychic or somatic components... perpetuates, at least implicitly, a mind-body dualism that has defied rational solution for centuries. Perhaps what we need is a new formulation...that does not presuppose a formidable gap between the separated 'realities' of mind and body. One way of reformulating the question involves the concept of information... " (cited by Rossi, pg. 23).

The "mind-body" dualism has "defied rational solution," Rossi suggests, because any questions asked within that framework are scientifically unanswerable and probably (in the Wittgensteinian sense) meaningless. However, if we drop the "mind-body dualism" from our thinking and ask questions in terms of Information Theory, none of the data of placebo effects or faith healings seem intractable or inexplicable at all.

A basic concept of Information Theory is *transduction,* the translation of form from one information system into another. For instance, when I speak on the phone, the transmitter transduces my sound waves (speech) into the isomorphic

13

system of electrical impulses; at the other end of the line—if I'm lucky and the phone companies are not screwing up again—the receiver transduces these electrical impulses back into sound waves which are heard as speech by the listener.

Similarly, while I sit here at my word processor, the console is transducing my words typed on the keyboard into binary units coded on the disk, and also transducing those binary units back into English words on the screen, so I can correct them at any time. Later—if I'm lucky and the computer is not screwing up again—the machine will transduce the bits on the disk into electrical signals to the printer, which will transduce them into words on paper—words you are now reading without asking meaningless metaphysical questions about how the ghostly "essence" of "wordness" can turn into electrical units and then turn back to something as "mental" as words again.

Quite similar processes of *information transduction,* Rossi shows, underlie the ability of the cortex of the brain (which contains "beliefs," along with other verbal codes) to send signals to the hypothalamus, the ancient little part of the back brain which regulates a variety of neurochemical and hormonal processes.

Among the most important chemical systems regulated by the hypothalamus appear to be the *neuropeptides,* including the now-famous endorphins, which act as natural pain-killers.

Neuropeptides have a strange duality about them which reminds me of the photons of quantum mechanics. Photons, as you have all heard by now, act like particles some of the time, but also act like waves some of the time. Neuropeptides just as Taoistically act like neurotransmitters part of the time and also like hormones part of the time. The little blighters never heard of Aristotelian either/or logic, I guess.

Acting like neurotransmitters, neuropeptides perform many functions in the brain, but seem most important in this context because they allow the opening of new neural pathways and "networks." This means, existentially, that with increased neuropeptide activity you are likely to have new ideas and probably also new perceptions. You might say neuropeptides are mild natural psychedelics. When new neural circuits form, this increased "creativity" (perception/conception) and its accompanying sense of novelty appears to be a large part of the "rebirth" process in most systems of non-medical healing.

When they leave the brain and start acting as hormones, neuropeptides interact with all the major systems of the body, including the immunological system. Increased neuropeptide

14

activity, therefore, usually leads to increased "resistance" to disease and correlates with an inner sense of "feeling better" and becoming more hopeful.

It is probably no accident that the new mind-machines being used as pain-killers in many hospitals—and also as aids to deep meditation by many New Agers—all have definite effects on the hypothalamus and all seem to increase and maximize neuropeptide activity, especially in the brain and immunological systems.

A short review cannot do justice to the richness of detail and complexity of material handled so elegantly and coherently by Dr. Rossi. Some highlights seem worth mentioning, however:

* Those who respond best to placebos seem to be especially alert to synchronicity; those who respond least seem "rigid and stereotypic" in their thinking. It almost appears that a hard-core materialist would rather die than be cured by something that looks to him like "magic."

* Memory appears to be mood dependent. While happy, people remember more positive experiences; when sad, they remember more negative experiences.

* "Reassociating"—changing the categories of one's thought, or forming new reality-tunnels—seems as important in healing as the specific neuropeptide boost to the immunological system.

* The brain does not remember like a tape recorder or repeat like a parrot. "Reassociating" or reframing or updating goes on constantly; we remake our past continually. Rossi even suggests that what witnesses are expected to do in courtrooms—tell one story and stick to it—may be totally unnatural for the human brain.

* The traditional hypnotic suggestions to relax and close your eyes serve to trigger a shift from the *sympathetic* ("outer-active") nervous system and *beta-wave* dominance to the *parasympathetic* ("inward-passive") nervous system and *alpha-wave* dominance. This again correlates with increased neuropeptide activity.

* It is becoming increasingly possible to reformulate and unify biology and psychology into the framework of Information Theory, with neuropeptides serving as the main transducers between such subsystems as the semantic circuitry (cortex), the autonomic nervous system and the endocrine and immunological systems. Materialist skepticism about "mind moving molecules" becomes irrelevant when we speak less metaphysically and more scientifically about transduction of information between brain circuits and body circuits.

* Since the neuropeptides are transmitted through virtually all the body fluids (blood, lymph, cerebrospinal fluid, etc.), as well as between neurons, the neuropeptide system acts more slowly but more holistically than the central nervous system.

One of the charms of this highly technical book consists in Dr. Rossi's practical turn of mind. Not only is every general idea in the text documented from recent neuroscience, but each is also illustrated with simple exercises the reader can use in order to experience directly the transductions being described.

If you sit still for a few moments, for instance, you will notice that one nostril seems less "open" or slightly more "clogged" than the other. Experiment with this, and within 90 minutes you will find a time when the right nostril seems the "clogged" one. Lie down on your right side and passively observe your mental processes. If this works as well for you as it did for me, you will have a quicker and more thorough "right-brain" experience than with most techniques of meditation taught by Gurus. Any positive thoughts about health in that state seem likely to transduce into better health shortly. Try it and see!

Conversely, if you think you might lean toward too much right-brain dominance—the gaga state called being a "bliss ninny" in California and a "mere ecstatic" in Sufi literature— reverse the above. Wait until the left nostril feels more clogged, lie on your left side, and observe how naturally you move into analytical and linear modes of perception/thought.

Rossi concludes that the brain constantly seeks "the high information value of an improbable event." Information Theorists have known since Shannon that such high information is mathematically reciprocal to negative entropy. Improbable events (or interpretations) counteract the tendency of material systems to "run down" toward entropy and formless chaos, i.e., that Fundamentalist Materialist equivalent of the Apocalypse, the "heat death of the universe." Information Theory suggests that information as negative entropy runs upward against this Doomsday scenario.

In other words, all our reframing, reassociating, "creativity," etc., amount to a continuous search to feed the brain more information: to decrease mental entropy, and thereby decrease physical entropy. This concept ties psychology more intimately to information theory than ever before, and might also explain the frequent link between boredom and illness (and between synchronicity and placebo effectiveness). Rossi's speculations on this crucial issue remarkably echo and expand quantum physicist Erwin Schrödinger's famous insight that life may depend upon its own ability to generate and regenerate negative entropy. Bucky Fuller expressed the same idea by saying that the human brain seems designed to oppose entropy by acting as an improbable local problem-solver.

If you've ever wondered how something as ghostly as "mind" can influence something as "gross" as, say, the lower intestine, Rossi should help you understand why that metaphysical (and meaningless) question can never be answered, and why it is more profitable to ask operationally and existentially how the semantic system in the cortex influences the endocrine and other systems that control the intestine.

Perhaps the final word I can offer on this wonderful book is simply to say that I have "understood" these general principles for over 20 years, but only in a "right-brain" way: vaguely and incoherently. After reading Rossi, I begin to feel that I really have started to understand neurosomatic wholeness in a clear, crisp and scientific manner.

▲   ▲   ▲

1994 Update

The notion of multiple information systems, which probably still seems either mystical or incomprehensible to some readers, served as the plot basis for the most popular film of 1992—the one that grabbed an Oscar, at last, for Clint Eastwood—*Unforgiven.*

In this "anti-Western" (as some have dubbed it) Eastwood plays Will Munny, a retired gun-slinger trying to make a living as a pig farmer, and not doing too well. Persuaded by a group of whores (and a fee of $1000—a lot of money in those days), Munny undertakes to assassinate three sadistic men who scarred the face of one of the ladies. Alas, most of his skills have disappeared during his years of respectability and, even when asked about his most famous exploits, Munny can only answer, "I was so drunk then I can't remember what happened." When he arrives in the village of the three whore-bashers, Will gets beaten up and run out of town by the sheriff and his hired goons.

At the climax, Munny finally gets drunk again, and completes his mission, killing so many men so quickly that I lost count of the victims—not all of whom seem guilty of anything. Munny staggers off, shouting semi-coherently that if anybody tries to shoot him in the back, he'll return and burn down the town "and kill your wives and children, too."

An anti-alcoholism parable? Partly. The key fact stands out: the audience believes in the sudden transformation from the conscience–ridden sober Munny who has forgotten how to use a gun effectively back into the criminal sociopath who kills as efficiently and emotionlessly as a robot. The shoot-to-kill information and its associated outlaw "personality" exists in other brain networks than the "decent" pig-farmer who has internalized normal social rules. In other words, all of us understand, intuitively and unconsciously, what Philip of Macedonia meant when he said 24 centuries ago "Philip Drunk is not Philip Sober." We understand this, but *only* intuitively and unconsciously, until Dr. Rossi stated this intuitive understanding in clear, conscious terms.

In an ambiguous afterword to the Eastwood film, we learn that "some say"—all great folk-legends have variant or uncertain endings, as Levi-Strauss documented—that Will Munny sobered up again and went to San Francisco where he "prospered in the dry goods business." This makes perfect sense in terms of the

Rossi model of many information systems and many latent "selves" within each brain.

We cannot understand faith healing, hypno-healing, etc., without this "many selves" concept. We also cannot understand most of the real oddities of psychiatry—MPD (multiple personality disorder), Munchausen's syndrome (surgery-addiction, usually combined with compulsive lying), schizophrenia, bipolar disorders...and most of the astounding things we "normal people" do ourselves that make us exclaim, an hour, a week or a year later "What the devil got into me? Why, I wasn't myself at all!"

In short, modern neurology increasingly confirms Buddha's claim that the "self" does not exist — except as a phalanx of temporary and ever-shifting sub-selves. We will soon have to junk all psychology *and all social institutions* based on the block-like "self" imagined in Aristotelian logic, putting them all on the back shelf labeled "Discarded Myth," along with the flat earth, the "infallible" pope or Perfect Master, and the National Debt. This will mean a bigger social revolution than space colonies, nanotechnology, Virtual Reality—or the emerging DNA engineering that already makes *Jurassic Park* seem more plausible than most viewers guess.

▲   ▲   ▲

(hapteR Two

Who Owns the Jesus Property?

by Timothy Leary, Ph.D.

I've been trying to make sense out of the current flap about *The Last Temptation of Christ*. Why are Fundamentalist Protestants attacking this movie inspired by a novel penned by a tormented Greek Catholic, adapted by a guilt-ridden Protestant screen-writer and directed by a moody Italian Catholic? Since they all claim to be sincere Christians why all the rhubarb?

Here's my theory:

What we have here is a typical bunch of quarreling Christian sects—exactly the same noisy cast of characters who have been profiting from similar theological battles for two millenniums. They've bickered, century after century, about the trinity or the virgin birth or that always explosive topic, the personality, the habits, the human/divine endowments of Jesus.

The sides in these well-publicized debates are usually drawn along geographic lines. In general, the people from North Europe tend to define Jesus and the women in his life as less emotional than people from the Mediterranean do. The Nordics want a Jesus like themselves, cold and repressed. The Southerners want a passionate, volatile Jesus—again, like themselves.

There is a fascinating parallel here with Islam. The angry born-again Fundamentalists picketing Universal City are much like the Shiite Moslem Fundamentalists in Iran; the liberal studio Protestants and the Greek and Italian Catholics are like the moderate Sunni and Saudi Arabs who are just trying to make a buck on the Mecca tourist trade and the oil wells, but who are forced to band together to resist the highly impractical Iranian militants.

This relativistic speculation cheered me up. It showed me, once again, how far our American Christians (and American Jews and Moslems) have evolved from their pesky counterparts in the Old World. In the Middle East these theological differences are still being fought out with tanks and bombers and poison gas; in Northern Ireland, the dour Protestants and passionate Catholics have at each other with guns and gelignite. Just like the Middle Ages, except for improved weaponry.

23

But here in the U.S. our sectarian Christians merely quarrel like talent agencies disputing who owns the screen rights to the Jesus Christ story. We're hassling over the ownership of one of the most valuable Properties of all time. Look at the script: The birth in the manger. The walking on water. The loaves and fishes. The scourging of the money-lenders from the Temple. (Well, on second thought, let's not stress that scene.) The betrayal by Judas. (I wouldn't mention the 30 pieces of silver, to spare Jerry Falwell's feelings.) The crown of thorns. The ever-popular Crucifixion Climax. The surprise-ending Resurrection. It beats Indiana Jones, doesn't it?

Our Fundamentalists and Television Evangelists under-standably insist that they have a monopoly on the Jesus Property. Of course, there's no shred of evidence to support this in any court. There's not a single paper anywhere that says the Christ family signed away these valuable docu-drama rights to North European Protestants and their descendents in the right wing of the Republican Party. Hey, man, these Johnny-come-lately Protestants didn't appear on the scene until *15 centuries* after the death went down. To be absolutely frank, the ancestors of these bad-tempered Bible thumpers were running around bare-assed in bearskins, sacrificing virgins to Thor the Thunder God, when the original Christ script was penned.

The TV Evangelists are obviously worried that their alleged monopoly on the billion-dollar-a-year Christ Market will be threatened by passionate Latin and Greek versions which attribute Mediterranean humanity to Christ in contrast to the pale, blonde, Plastic Doll version which they are peddling. The primordial Greek-Latin image of J.C. is too "human" and emotional for dogmatic Jerry Falwell or shy, onanistic Jimmy Swaggart or sexually naive Jim Bakker.

In my scenario of these events Jesus and Mary Magdelene and Peter the Fisherman and the rest of the gang would be laughing their haloes off at this grubby wrangling for the screen rights to their story. After all, the Jewish Jesus, or Yeshuah-- the prototype, even older than Greek-Latin versions--seems to have been an easy-going Liberal Rabbi with a sly sense of humor.

Anyway, if the Writers Guild takes an interest, they should demand residuals for Matt, Mark, Luke and John, those four hard-working, ink-stained wretches who penned this eternally interesting and controversial script.

▲   ▲   ▲

More on Vitamin C

Dear Editor:

Dr. Linus Pauling's work on peace and Vitamin C may not be so divergent as might be thought. Vitamin C has so many functions in the metabolic factory of the body that to live without almost surplus amounts of it is to live with a body that is ill, in almost as many ways as are possible. Every major organ system is serviced by Vitamin C, including the nervous system and the brain, and it is little wonder that tension, irritability, low frustration tolerance, poor impulse control and madness in many forms and degrees can and do result from insufficient amounts of C.

Dr. Irvine Stone, a long time friend of Dr. Pauling and author of *The Healing Factor: Vitamin C Against Disease,* believed that almost all humans were suffering from "hypoascorbemia" (lack of sufficient Vitamin C) and that many of mankind's chronic ills were caused by this condition. In my own experience as an orthomolecular psychiatrist, almost all of my depressed and angry patients benefited to some degree by so-called "mega" doses of Vitamin C. This is not to say that Vitamin C is a cure-all, and by itself it doesn't usually cure depression, but as an adjunct it is indispensable.

A warring world is not reflecting the well-being of healthy citizens; rather, the pathology of the citizens is manifesting through war. People are manipulated through their fear and tension into bellicose anger by leaders who are themselves driven by fear or greed or both.

Frequently the medical profession assists in this scenario via monopolized support for medical mystification, thereby perpetuating everybody's fear and sense of helplessness, and it may have been this attitude which has made Dr. Pauling "controversial" rather than being lauded for the truly great man that he is.

Robert R. Newport, MD
Santa Cruz, CA

1994 Update

The dispute over Vitamin C (and other non-allopathic herbs, vitamins and nutrients) has grown even more heated in recent years.

In 1992, the FDA raided the office of Dr. Jonathan Wright— a fully qualified MD with his degree from the University of Michigan Medical School—and terrorized the staff with drawn guns and other terror tactics similar to the Gestapo or the Drug Enforcement Administration. (For further details on this raid, see *Trajectories* #12, Spring 1993.) The FDA has not yet charged Dr. Wright with any crime; his offense consists of using chiefly non-allopathic methods in treating his patients. Dr. Wright, however, has filed suit against *them*.

The FDA currently sponsors legislation that would permit such raids, and suppress most "alternative medicine"—leaving physicians like Dr. Wright unable to sue even in the most terroristic raids, and depriving many of us of vitamins and herbs that we believe have helped heal illnesses or prevented illnesses before they start.

Opposing the FDA's power-grab, Sen. Orrin Hatch has sponsored Senate Bill S 784, which would prevent the FDA from forcing one type of medical theory on the whole country. S 784 would guarantee in law our liberty to choose. You can add your name to a nationwide petition supporting S 784 by writing to Bonnie Miller, Box 528, Gainesville, VA 22065.

Meanwhile, the largest-ever study of Vitamin C, involving 11,348 men followed over a ten-year period concludes that "Men whose Vitamin C intake was the highest...had a 42% lower risk of death from heart disease, and a 35% lower risk of death from any cause." (*Epidemiology*, Enstrom: 194-202, 1992.)

Under current FDA rules no manufacturer or seller of Vitamin C may mention this study to a prospective customer— but, amusingly, most history books still erroneously claim that the Holy Inquisition ended in 1819.

Some paranoid persons of Left and Right claim to find significance and complicity in the fact that the same few rich men seem to serve part of their lives as officers of the FDA and part as executives of the major pharmaceutical companies. Often, these men switch back and forth several times between selling expensive (and often dangerous) drugs for Eli Lilly and its competitors, and policing and working toward a total ban on cheap and totally harmless drugs for the FDA. We must not *think* about this, of course, or we might become "paranoid" also. Remember the magic banishing ritual: "Coincidence! Coincidence! Coincidence!" Repeat this word often enough and it banishes all data that makes you nervous...

Meanwhile, the Surgeon General's office reports for 1990, the last year on which we have complete figures, that 360,000 Americans died from tobacco (a subject of no interest to the FDA), 130,000 from alcohol (another unimportant subject) and *18,675 from the hard prescription drugs approved by the FDA.* (A statistic you should forget as soon as possible unless you want to get very, very nervous, and even a little paranoid, yourself.)

Deaths from Vitamin C that year total 0.00—zero, zed, none—curiously, the very same number as deaths from marijuana, another drug from which our government wishes to protect us...

(Surgeon General's statistics quoted from *Grey Areas*, Fall 1992 and *Southern New Jersey Libertarian,* July 1993.)

▲   ▲   ▲

OUR LADY
of
OUTER SPACE

Reach down for the sun, reach down
for the stars, reach deeper for the secret
places of the body of her the stars adorn.
You are lost and found in her embrace.
There is nowhere else for you to fall and
no escaping from her love for she is
black and pulsing source,
her million twinkling nipples
nurse all life,
her jeweled ardent body
twines around you always
and there is no place
to go but
home
to
her

—*Arlen Wilson*

CHAPTER Three

Blinded by *What?*

The latest polemic against the American Medical Association to come to our attention is a powerful piece in the L.A. *Weekly* (Sept. 16-22, 1988). Called "Blinded By Science?", the article by Carolyn Reuben reveals that only 20 percent of established medical procedures have been validated in randomized, double-blind, placebo-controlled trials, according to the Office of Technology Assessment. In other words, doctors are more or less guessing 80 percent of the time.

Nonetheless, Reuben notes, doctors who use alternative therapies are routinely subject to harassment and sometimes Inquisitorial persecutions by the A.M.A bureaucracy. A case in point: a pediatrician, using conventional treatment, failed to cure an ear infection in twin three-year-old boys. The mother then took the boys to Dr. Michael Gerber, who treated them with nutrition and Vitamin A. Despite the fact that the boys then got better, the pediatrician complained to the bureaucracy, and Dr. Gerber, after four years of struggle and investigation of other unorthodox treatments by him, lost his medical license for "gross negligence."

Dr. Richard Ikeda explained to journalist Reuben that gross negligence means using treatments "falling far outside the normal standards of acceptable practice." Reuben says this means that if a doctor cures something with Vitamin A and no other doctors are using Vitamin A for that condition, this can be ruled "gross negligence."

▲ ▲ ▲

31

The "V" Effect and "ESP"

According to Fundamentalist Protestants, all evidence for so-called "ESP" is actually the result of "demons," while according to the Fundamentalist Materialists the same evidence is the result of "coincidences." New research by psychologist Michael Persinger of Laurentian University (Ontario) throws doubt on both these models.

Dr. Persinger has published data (cited in *Omni,* Nov., 1988) indicating that the "ESP" function has a periodicity that reflects almost in a mirror the periodicity of Earth's geomagnetic field. In brief, whenever geomagnetic fields show a V-shaped valley, the measured ability of "psychics" rises, but when geomagnetism again surges toward a crest, "psychics" show less ability.

If Dr. Persinger's data is replicated, the Fundamentalists of both schools will have to explain why "demons" or "coincidences" act in harmony with geomagnetism. The only alternative model, distasteful to both Fundamentalisms, would seek some scientific law expressed in these functions.

Incidentally, Dr. Persinger has a plausible article in the Nov., 1988, MUFON UFO Journal, in which he offers a model that relates UFO "abductee" experiences to abnormal brain functions, sometimes correlated with earthquake faults. Compassionately, he warns that this model should not be used to debunk or humiliate those unfortunates who have had traumatic UFO abduction/rape experiences. The abduction experience, he says, "will be considered real by the experient. Attempts at debunking...will not only be futile but may verge on ethical violations if the experience has been a psychological solution to personal problems."

Twelve years ago, Persinger published *Space-Time Transients and Unusual Events* (Prentice-Hall, 1977) which first tentatively related over 6,000 historical reports of "paranormal" and "anomalistic" events to geomagnetism and earthquake fault lines.

▲   ▲   ▲

The Future of the Future

There was a Fundamentalist Futurist back in the 1890s who demonstrated that New York City would be abandoned as unfit for habitation by the 1930s. His argument was based on projection forward of population trends, and he correctly estimated that population would grow from 4 million to over 7 million in 40 years. (He didn't guess it would reach over 12 million by now.) It was then obvious, he said, that the amount of horses necessary to provide transportation for that many people would result in a public health hazard of incredible dimensions: there would be horse manure up to the third floor windows everywhere in Manhattan.

This illustrates the most frequent fallacy found in Future projections: the "elementalistic fallacy" named by Alfred Korzybski. The elementalistic fallacy, as Korzybski noted, seems to be built into our very language. We can talk about Joe Smith in isolation from his (or any) environment; we can therefore think about Mr. Smith in such fictitious isolation; and in such "elementalistic fallacy," we will almost always draw wrong conclusions, because Mr. Smith cannot exist without some environment. (He will explode in a vacuum, and without a social world his mind will similarly explode—or implode—or at least mutate shockingly, as isolation experiments have shown.)

Projecting population forward without projecting other factors forward has produced numerous elementalistic fallacies similar to thinking of Joe Smith without an environment. Malthus, for instance, "proved" that population will always increase faster than resources, but this was disproven by technological history, and we now understand that "resources" only exist when identified by analysis and each new discovery in pure science shows us new resources everywhere.

One example: the Newtonian system allowed us to tap 0.001 per cent of the energy in a glass of water; 19th Century thermodynamics showed us how tap 0.01 per cent of that energy; we can now tap 1.0 per cent. Nobody knows how much we'll be able to tap in 50 years.

Elementalistic fallacies abound in Future projections (including my own). We are only gradually and gropingly learning to think "non-elementalistically" (in Korzybski's phrase) or "synergetically" as Bucky Fuller liked to say. I have found one quick way to avoid the more obvious elementalistic and Fundamentalistic errors, which is this:

Whenever I project one trend forward, I then re-analyze the situation, projecting at minimum five other trends forward also.

For instance, lifespan and population have both been increasing in the past 200 years. Projecting these trends forward elementalistically (in isolation) has led to some notable Doomsday scenarios in which humanity overcrowds itself to death. An entirely different picture emerges, however, if one projects these trends synergetically along with five other trends, such as:

1. The effect of industrialism on population. As documented by Fuller (in *Critical Path*), a nation's population only rises rapidly in the transition from feudalism to industrialism, then levels off when industrialism is well established in a country.

2. The emergence of Feminism and self-choice among women, beginning with the 18th Century radicalism of Mary Woolstonecraft and now including Women's Liberation movements in all parts of the world—even dawningly in Islamic nations.

3. The movement of communication technology into space, with clear trends indicating that "industrial" (or, more likely, post-industrial) technology will follow, with workers and then families and then schools and grocers and museums, etc., moving into space colonies.

4. The continued improvement in birth control technology and the fading line between contraception and abortion. There is already heated debate, for instance, about whether certain devices—e.g., the IUD—"are" or "are not" abortifacients.

5. The neuroscience revolution (or H.E.A.D. Revolution— **H**edonic **E**ngineering **A**nd **D**evelopment) with its increasing promise that humans in the near future will achieve more freedom from mechanical conditioned reflexes (both "physical" and "mental") than ever before.

Whenever I try to project all five of these trends even 40 years into the future, I find the "overcrowding" problem seems less likely than New York being buried in horse manure. To get a feel for synergetic thinking, try your own projection, "guess-timating" what the next decade will bring in each of these fields, and the decade after that, and so on, to 2029.

For instance: How will encroaching industrialism effect third world birthrates by 1999? How will this interact with the Feminist meme, and space colonization projects, and improved contraception, and brain-change technology, in that ten years? How will all these interact in the 20 years before 2009? In the 30 years before 2019? By 2029?

Another safeguard against Fundamentalistic fallacies in Future projection is to remember the unpredictable.

Millions of people sincerely believe that superior beings from Outer Space are going to land any day now and solve all our problems for us. Whatever one thinks of that New Age faith, one should consider that something equally astounding could happen at any time, throwing all Future scenarios into a totally new Gestalt.

Consider the foremost critic of Fundamentalist Futurism, Sir Karl Popper. In *The Open Society and its Enemies* and *The Poverty of Historicism,* Popper has written an absolutely devastating critique of those classical Futurists (Plato, Aristotle, Hegel and Marx) who thought they could predict the future exactly and in detail. (Historicism was Popper's name for what I call Fundamentalist Futurism.) The strongest of Popper's many arguments against that Fundamentalism can be condensed thusly: even if we collected every possible fact about the past and present, and projected trends with the best statistical techniques, we could not predict those "Eureka" experiences in which a solitary philosopher or scientist suddenly sees a new paradigm which reorganizes all our habitual ideas.

Such "Eureka" insights or creative breakthroughs always change statistical trends. A new philosophic idea may become a political ideology quickly, with earth-shaking results. (Consider what happened when the subtle philosophy of Nietzsche collided with the unsubtle brain of Adolph Hitler, or when Lenin read Marx.) A new scientific idea inevitably leads to new technology—which changes the habits and trajectories of entire cultures even more radically than politics or ideologies.

A million people working in universities or labs (or outside them) are developing new insights every day, and we cannot predict which of these will be the philosophical or scientific type of "Eureka" that will change everything as radically as mass landings of alien spaceships would.

A sane Futurist must think synergetically, not elemental-istically, and must avoid Fundamentalism by remembering the unpredictable nature of the creative process.

Does it begin to sound as if a sane Futurist would avoid making any predictions at all? Not necessarily. Most Futurists have learned to make contingent predictions, or "scenarios." A scenario, like a mathematical proposition, says "If X happens, then Y will also happen." Only experience in time ("existential experience") will tell us if X will happen, but one can very often calculate the probability of Y following X with high precision.

35

If X is the present-day international banking system, for instance, and Y is a domino-like series of defaults by the leading debtor nations, then Y seems to be virtually inevitable, as numerous commentators have noted. This does not mean that the defaults must occur. It is still possible that the banks may change X, the rules of the money-and-debt game, before it is too late, or that some other group or coalition of groups may combine to force the bankers to change the rules. Considering what Roosevelt and Hitler did to the bankers in the 1930s, government intervention again may well occur—or a coalition of governments, such as the European Parliament, or even the United Nations, may act decisively before the default process sets the dominoes crashing.

Still, it seems the current rules of the currency game cannot long continue, without the unpredictable "Eureka" occurring. It is hard to imagine a gimmick that will perpetuate international debt as the cotton gin perpetuated slavery after Jefferson thought slavery was about to be abolished—but some such gimmick may come along. "Doomsday" scenarios or even "October 1929" scenarios about world currencies must always be tentative, not dogmatic. Otherwise, we cease to be Futurists and might inadvertently launch another Fundamentalistic (if Godless) religion like Marxism.

My guess is that the rules of the money-creation game are going to have to be changed. After all, banks only acquired the monopoly on currency issue in the 19th Century: before that, every nation created its own coinage. (Lord Coke even defined sovereignty as "the right to coin money.") The control of money fell into the hands of the bankers, we must remember, only when nations developed such a habit of degrading their moneys that none of them would trust any other for long. Now that the banks have created a world when no major debtor nation can ever hope to pay its debts without Divine Intervention, the rules of the money game will very probably mutate again as they did when control slipped from kings to bankers.

Whether money will become a United Nations prerogative, or we will replace money entirely with computer notations, is not something that can be predicted. Most likely, we will bump and blunder our way into some new system that cannot be predicted in advance.

Here are some other trajectories that seem "high probability scenarios" to me:

Δ *Space Colonization is coming soon.*

There are several thousand reasons for this—e.g., the hundreds of satellites in orbit indicate that the colonization process is already under way; the profits to be made in space seem staggering by any accounting; etc.—but the main reason is that, as Ray Bradbury says, space has become the new religion. There is no hour of the day or night in which there are less than a million people looking at *Star Trek* re-runs somewhere on this planet. A 1970s poll in Europe showed that 80 per cent of all children expect to travel in space when they grow up. Space is to the 21st Century what "America" was to 17th and 18th Centuries—the place to go to try something new and, hopefully, better.

Δ *The process that Bucky Fuller called "ephemeralization" will not only continue but will accelerate.*

That is, every step forward in pure science leads to new technologies that give us "more for less"—more energy output for less human input. Since there are more scientists alive today than in all previous history, and since microprocessors are accelerating research in every area, the "more for less" factor will happen faster and faster.

Δ *Nanotechnology will probably cause a jump in "ephemeralization" that will give us astounding output for very little input.*

We will then either have to start wars to get rid of the surplus, in order to maintain the market (a traditional "solution")—or else, if we realize that we as a species cannot survive large-scale wars with modern weapons, we will have to change the laws of the market. This will be as radical as the upcoming change in the laws governing who creates money (and what they should be paid for making paper into magic tickets for survival.)

Δ *Feminism shows no signs of being a "passing fad" or even "just another ideology."*

It increasingly looks like some kind of evolutionary bio-psychological upheaval in which one half of the human race is demanding more participation in the decisions about which Future scenarios are going to be realized and which discarded. Nobody, not even the leading Feminists, can really predict what this will mean over the next 40 or 60 years, but it contains many "Eureka" factors that will synergetically alter and re-form all other Futurescans.

The interaction of Space, Feminism, radical changes in money-and-debt creation and market economy, the neuroscience revolution with its promise of better mental functioning for all (and its threat of enslavement for all...) and the ongoing longevity revolution can only synergetically produce a total "Eureka" experience for all humanity within 30 years and perhaps within 15 years or sooner.

In my travels, I am often asked what I think of the Cosmic Transformation scenarios of Terrence McKenna and Jose Arguelles. Sadly, I regard that sort of thing as Fundamentalist Futurism and look at it skeptically. Nonetheless, I am bemused by the odd " coincidence" that, working on the basis of mystical theories and in total isolation from each other, both of these prophets fixed on the year 2012 as the time when humanity mutates utterly and enters a new relationship with space-time. I don't believe this literally, but I can't help suspecting that this is a message from the collective unconscious—like the quite opposite "Apocalypse" scenarios of Fundamentalist Protestantism.

Visions of that order of magnitude, I think, indicate that at a deep psychic level people everywhere are beginning to suspect that we are entering the most radical period of evolutionary change since life migrated out of the oceans onto the land. Without being Fundamentalistic about it, I think "Harmonic Convergence" is a metaphoric way of approximating toward awareness of where the remorseless forces of social evolution are carrying us.

The mother or father or 2012, I think, will find it very hard to explain to their children the primitive customs, and even more primitive beliefs, that held sway on this planet back in the Dark Ages of the 1980s...

▲   ▲   ▲

Exo-Evolution

As noted a few pages back, millions of people believe literally that benign extraterrestrials are about to land any day now and solve all our problems for us. A smaller group believes that nasty extraterrestrials have been meddling with our genes, mutilating our cattle and even making Machiavellian deals with our government. Only a tiny minority resolutely insists that there is, as yet, no hard scientific proof that any extraterrestrials have ever come anywhere near this boondocks planet.

Rather than entering this weary, flat and stale debate, I would like to offer a larger perspective on it, in the form of a Taxonomy of the different kinds of theories that have been offered about extraterrestrial factors in our planetary evolution.

1. Life arrived here from extraterrestrial sources by accident.

The first proponent of this notion was a Swedish biologist around the turn of the century named Arrhenius. I know nothing of him, aside from brief references to him by Sir Francis Crick and Dr. Timothy Leary. The Arrhenius model is called Cosmic Panspermia, and it perhaps looks a bit more persuasive today than it did in Arrhenius's day because amino acids and other precursors of life have been found on meteors.

Some ghoulish variations on Arrhenius are found in the novels of William S. Burroughs. *The Exterminator,* for instance, holds that life started here when a spaceship dumped its shit while passing.

2. Extraterrestrials designed the DNA and life here is an experiment by them.

This is the model preferred by Sir Francis Crick, co-discoverer of the DNA helix. Crick's chief argument is that DNA is too "intelligent" to be an accident. Lesser arguments are flaws he finds in orthodox Darwinism. This model is called Directed Panspermia.

I sometimes suspect this is attractive to Crick only because he grew up and lives in a sub-culture where the word "God" is taboo. He also conspicuously avoids any implication that our extraterrestrial Creators have any affection for us, and rather makes it sound as if they regard us the way most scientists regard laboratory animals. Crick was educated when scientists

39

were supposed to be "cold" and "unemotional" (like Mr. Spock, you know) and he projects this onto his hypothetical exo-geneticists.

2A. Extraterrestrials designed the DNA, but not "coldly" or experimentally.

They did it for the same reason we have children: they wanted somebody to love and nurture.

Dr. Timothy Leary defends this in his book *Info-Psychology*. But in the same book he defends the alternative model that we-in-the-future traveling backward in time created the DNA. Leary wants to make us think, not to convert us to any one particular model.

3. Extraterrestrials created the DNA (as Crick claims) but other unearthly influences on evolution have arrived by accident (as Arrhenius suggested)—such as debris floating about with amino acids or whatnot on it.

This is the model preferred by Sir Fred Hoyle, and he argues his case, in my opinion, better than either Crick or Leary. As a matter of fact, while trying to avoid opinions about the unknown, I have been infested by a suspicion that Hoyle has the best model around. Try his book, *Evolution from Space,* and see what you think.

4. Extraterrestrials intervened in evolution 4,000,000 years ago by provoking hominid apes to invent tools.

This is not a scientific model, but a story idea for a movie. Nonetheless, it is the basis of probably the greatest film ever made, *2001: A Space Odyssey*—a film which has undoubtedly influenced more people than Arrhenius, Crick, Leary and Hoyle combined.

When something appears in both art and science, I suspect a Jungian unconscious process is occurring in the whole human psyche; a "shift in the constellation of the archetypes," as Jung would say.

5. Extraterrestrials intervened about 30,000 years ago.

This was put forth way back in the 1950s by a guy named M.K. Jessup who died a somewhat mysterious death and is subject to wild speculation in many UFO journals. In my opinion, the evidence is unconvincing and the logic is lame, but there is so much mystery about Jessup and his associates that I remain curious.

6. Extraterrestrials invaded and enslaved humanity about 8000 years ago and are the origin of the basic ideas of Judaism, Christianity and Islam.

All three monotheisms are actually late reworkings of Sumerian myths which were rationalizations to continue our enslavement.

This chilling notion is ably and persuasively defended by an Israeli named Sitchin whose book, *The Twelfth Planet,* I never finished and Neal Freer, whose book, *Breaking the Godspell,* I did finish. I said this was persuasive; it is far, far, far from being proven.

I detect here overtones of Burroughs' "Nova Mob" and one version of the Illuminati in Volume Two of that nefarious trilogy. As said already, an idea is appearing both in art and "science"— or something that tries to be science. One must suspect a collective unconscious process is afoot.

Update: This enslavement thesis appears again in *The Gods of Eden,* by William Bramley (Avon, 1989), who doesn't seem aware that others have suggested it.

7. The extraterrestrial invaders are still meddling with us, carrying on genetic experiments on "abductees."

Amateur hypnotist and UFO buff Budd Hopkins seems to be the major source of this Horror Story, and he has persuaded many hypnotic subjects, although not the famous Whitley Streiber, that this is the "real" explanation of Altered States of Consciousness they have experienced. This explanation is becoming virtually a new religion (or demonology).

So now we find the same basic idea in science, art, crypto- or pseudo-science and in what looks like a new folk mythos.

I have already hinted that these ideas have surfaced from the collective unconscious, where we are all grappling with new concepts of our position in space-time. But I also agree with Hoyle that orthodox neo-Darwinism has an unconscious "pre-Copernican bias." Thinking about evolution on this planet in isolation from the cosmos as a whole does seem to me a hangover from theological "Flat Earth" ages. We will probably have to come to grips eventually with the idea that Earthside evolution is only one small chapter in Cosmic evolution.

And, now, a sidelight...

About a year ago I was doing an interview on KFOX radio (Long Beach, CA) and arrived an hour early, due to a misunderstanding. In the guests' waiting room, I found an obese, nervous man who wanted to know who I was and seemed afraid I was somebody else than I claimed. When the interviewer arrived, she had to explain again that I was the scheduled guest for the following hour. The man still seemed nervous and unconvinced. Then they went on the air.

The man insisted on having a handkerchief wrapped around the microphone several times, to disguise his voice. He would not give his real name or tell what city he lived in. He was another UFO abductee and told the standard story of being kidnapped, raped by a machine that extracted his sperm, and having some gizmo inserted into his brain by way of his eye. He also showed the interviewer (and me—I was watching through a window) scars on his arms made, he said, when the UFOnauts took tissue samples.

I watched this fellow and listened to him for an hour. My impression was that he was very definitely not seeking fame or notoriety, but actively avoiding them, that he believed what he was saying, and that he was not schizophrenic, although he was obviously suffering from traumatic shock. He had been "treated" by Budd Hopkins.

Budd himself came on the air, by phone from New York, and it seemed to me that some parts of this abductee's "memories" were definitely influenced by what Budd wanted him to say.

Well, last week I was on KFOX again and what do you think happened? I met a non-abductee. This guy worked for the station, and told me he had wanted to meet me ever since reading *Cosmic Trigger*. He said he woke up one night in 1980 and found an 8-foot tall being with pointy ears standing at the foot of his bed. "Go away," he said, "I'm tired." The "alien" or whatever it was then went away...and never came back.

I didn't ask this gentleman if he was sure he was awake when this happened. I just said, "You were lucky to get a tall one, I guess. The short ones don't go away if you tell them you're tired. They drag you out to the spaceship and experiment on you anyway."

On my desk I keep a card so I old that I forget when I got it or who gave it to me. I only remember only that I had it in San Francisco before I moved to Ireland seven years ago and I brought it back across the Atlantic when I returned to The States. It means a lot to me, obviously. This is what it says:

"If you think
you know
what the
HELL
is going on,
**YOU'RE
PROBABLY
FULL OF SHIT"**

▲   ▲   ▲

1994 Update

Terrifying tales of genetic manipulation via UFO abductions have now become part of a much larger, more Apocalyptic scenario, including very similar yarns of incest and of Satanic child-abuse (with such traditional medieval elements as claims of cannibalism and human sacrifice), which have multiplied faster than maggots in the years since I wrote the above.

Since I express my skepticism about this modern demonology in our first *Trajectories* video tape, "Fear in the Night" (see catalog at the back of this book), and we explore one "Satanic" case at length later in this volume, I will here comment only on a few minor aspects of this increasingly nationwide hysteria.

One: As said above, much of this material represents a re-run of similar hysterias in the middle ages. The modern UFOnauts who conduct sexual (and, some claim) genetic meddling with humans have a striking resemblance to the Incubi and Succubi (sex-demons) that plagued the Dark Ages (and usually attacked celibate monks and nuns...). This either means that the little monsters went away for a few centuries and have now come back, or else that similar anxieties again plague the collective unconscious. Such "Shadow" archetypes, according to Jung, indicate the collapse of old systems and the "helpless" feeling that most humans experience before new systems arise and provide new maps of our selves and our worlds. In short, the incest/Satanism/UFO hysteria demarks the psychological aspect of the process defined by Theodore Gordon and discussed in my introduction: information flow has unleashed the "creative chaos" out of which a New Age will evolve.

Two: Since the spreaders of this new mythos consists of a ragtag and disorderly alliance between Radical (i.e., androphobic) Feminism and Protestant Fundamentalism—and since both movements already share a fervid desire to abolish the Bill of Rights in general and the First Amendment in particular—I expect some sort of union of the two as they put their minor differences aside and form a kind of Femdamentalism. I won't feel surprised, some day soon, to see Andrea Dworkin and Pat Robertson on the same platform leading a new crusade against the U.S. Constitution.

Three: The aspect of all this which I have called "apocalyptical" has a reverse-image reflection in many New Age thinkers. For example, Terrence McKenna expects the doubling of information (or "novelty" as he more often calls it) will lead to our "encounter with a Transcendental Object" in 2012; Peter Russell has an equally spectacular, but less metaphysical, notion about the "awakening" of Earth when planetary population, around 2012, reaches 10 billion—the number of cells in the human brain; Dr. Timothy Leary expects humanity to undergo total transformation very soon due to the triple impact of Space Migration, Intelligence Increase and Life Extension; and so on. I suggest that both the dark Fundamentalist scenarios and the sunny New Age scenarios both register the fact that the "creative chaos" of our time will break down all our historical assumptions about humanity's position in space-time.

We may even have to learn that we do indeed have starry ancestors as the Crick, Hoyle and Leary models suggest...

▲   ▲   ▲

Old Woman on the Beach

I sit crosslegged under the moon
Unto myself
Complete.
My substance went out
    a few men
A few women
    certain children
Now it is back with me.
I sit crosslegged under the moon
Unto myself
Now.
I am back where I have been
Always
No better
    no worse
        no different.
So.
I like the smell here
It roars in my nostrils.
The salt
    the rot
        the sweetness
All the mess of birth
    afterbirth
And death
    aftermath
All equal and
Dissolved.
Its breath
    my breath
In
    out
        in
Out.

—Arlen Wilson

CHApTER Four

The Chalice and the Blade
Our History, Our Future
by Riane Eisler

(Harper and Row; paperback edition, 1988)

Reviewed by Arlen Wilson

It is a common misconception to think that women have always been subordinated, restricted to the private, purely domestic sphere, or to the lowliest kinds of work, and that they are only now beginning to emerge into full human beings. There is now great historical and prehistorical evidence for woman's crucial role in early public life. What we are seeing now is not the emergence of woman but her re-emergence—and none too soon, given the conditions that prevail.

Exploring back through the mists of history and prehistory to a time before women became the "second sex," Riane Eisler sets the record straight on several accounts in her book *The Chalice and the Blade*. One of the main misapprehensions she tackles, so typical of either/or thinking, is the notion "If it wasn't a patriarchy it must have been a matriarchy": that is, if men did not rule exclusively then women must have ruled exclusively. There is no evidence whatsoever for this. There is, however, an increasing amount of evidence for a long period, during the early formative phase of all the great civilizations we know of, when women were in a position in society quite different from the one to which they were later relegated.

Many scholars believe that humankind first conceived of the deity as Mother; that the idea of a male deity or male deities was a subsequent development. If this is so, women would be perceived as Goddess's earthly representatives. Whether this is true or not, it is clear that women were molders and co-determiners (to say the very least) of the shape and structure of those early societies, and that they continued their role well into the early phases of these civilizations in a way that seems remarkable today. The role of female intelligence is becoming more recognized in the invention of all the "arts of peace" upon which civilization depends: the domestication of animals; horticulture and agriculture; the technologies of food and fabric;

the design of buildings; social institutions; the administration of justice; in human language itself.

The female psyche suffers in a "man's world," but the male psyche suffers as well. Neither sex can function at its best except in a linkage, a full and complementary partnership situation. Linkage and partnership are key words in Eisler's admirable work.

The evolution of human intelligence obviously entailed the evolution of both its male and female components. Any species with a gaping differential or a serious alienation between the intelligence of its two halves would surely be headed for extinction. Granted, there are differences in male and female intelligence, but these very differences must have been adaptive devices for the survival of the whole race. Not allowing both the similarities and the differences full play has got to be maladaptive in evolutionary terms.

(One very evident difference, which may have had some important survival advantage, is the fact that the brain of female humans, as in other higher mammals, has a much larger *corpus callosum* than that possessed by the male. The *corpus callosum* is that passageway which allows communication between the right and left hemispheres of the brain. Those who are intrigued by contemporary neurology can conjecture about this.)

Though I differ with her slightly here and there, I am lost in admiration for what Eisler has done in this book. The Chalice is what gives life; the Blade is what takes it. The Chalice nourishes us all, and the Blade, all too often glorified, is what threatens all of us. Both are obviously at work in human life as we know it.

Drawing as it does on history, prehistory, recent archeology and paleoanthropology to increase our sense of the range of human options, this book is far more than just another philosophical treatise or some kind of cranky feminist tract. It has to do with the whole human condition. Ashley Montagu calls it "the most important book since Darwin's *Origin of Species*". Fritjof Capra calls it "pathbreaking...perhaps a key to our survival". I would agree with them.

Of course I must admit that one reason I liked the book was that it validated a lot of things which I and some women friends discovered during our own slapdash if enthusiastic researches back in the early days of the Women's Movement. Needless to say, Eisler has done it far better and far more impressively, with more detailed scholarship and more relevant scientific findings than we could possibly have managed back in the late '60s and early '70s with the limited resources we had. Still, the sense of recognition was sweet. We managed to come up with a scenario very similar to that of *The Chalice and the Blade*.

*   *   *

It was almost twenty years ago that I was asked to teach a class in Women's History at a funky, low-rent women's center we had set up in Chicago. I took it on for the lack of anyone else willing to do it, the field at that time being nonexistent as a separate subject for classwork. There were no texts, or books on women's history then, although there were plenty of eager students. All the treasures of "herstory" were hidden in books on other, more general, topics. I managed to come up with a somewhat eccentric but workable bibliography, however, and an outline of the subject matter, some of which surprised me as much as anyone. With no proper qualifications as a historian (but also with no one to tell me what to do or what not to do), I decided to make an adventure of it, to take the subject back as far as I could possibly get—to the caves; maybe even to the trees—and to show the relevance of the whole history of the world to the current women's struggles and street demonstrations we were involved in then. It was a mad, impossible enterprise, of course, but those were heady days, and I had an exciting time of it, rushing from rallies to libraries, sometimes only getting lecture notes put together minutes before the class was to begin.

Other women in the group caught the bug and began bringing in their own discoveries to share. We pondered those prehistoric "Venus" or "Goddess" figurines from 25,000 years ago. Were they no more than fertility talismans? We gleaned what we could from the archeology of early human settlements. (Much more evidence has come to light since then.) We watched with our mind's eye the rise of the earliest temples with their priestesses who were also craftswomen, businesswomen and administrators. We glimpsed women in the earliest city-states functioning as lawyers, physicians, administrators, scribes, merchants. We found that the clay tablets of ancient Lagash in the Middle East showed that little girls were educated in temple schools and learned not only reading and writing but the extraction of square roots along with little boys. And we uncovered many another womanly wonder from what we decided to call "Phase One" of civilization.

51

At whatever civilization we looked, if we looked back far enough, the tantalizing pattern was there. The distinct traces of this early phase were all there in the books for anyone to see, even then. But hardly anyone had ever bothered to look. We had certainly never "had" it in school, this amazing period of human social and political development involving both sexes during civilization's long dawn—so different from what came later, as far as womankind was concerned. Only retroactively did men become "boss." So what happened back then to interrupt and change a state of affairs we're only just beginning to return to now?

According to our giddy explorations back then—and Eisler's far more detailed, thorough and convincing work—this Phase One of civilization, with its balanced gender participation bit the dust as a result of repeated onslaughts by the Bad Guys, the ones the books referred to only as "nomadic herdsmen." Starting about five thousand years ago, these "cowboys" periodically swept down on every single peaceable, advanced human center of culture, trade, learning and wealth. Eisler calls the main villains the Indo-Europeans, but we found similar phenomena in places as far apart as China and Peru.

Each fresh wave of male-dominant marauders set up an new class of overlords more ruthless and authoritarian than the last. They had to be that way to conquer the territory. And this is about where history as we are usually taught it officially begins: the thugs have already won, and all that remains is for them to slug it out with each other. The technology of destruction, of armed rule, had invaded civilization and become established and prestigious. The arts begin to turn to a glorification of battles, of bloodshed.

Everywhere and always as civilization "advanced," the position of women fell. Their earlier status became buried, hidden, blotted out, though traces of it did persist for many centuries here and there in the subsequent patriarchal period in such places as Egypt, very notably in Crete, and even in Greece with its powerful goddess figures. Not only in art and folklore did this earlier state of affairs linger on in some places. When the resplendent Incan Empire was conquered by the Spanish, for instance, a powerful guild of women still had an absolute, state-backed monopoly on the production and distribution of all liquor and textiles. Naturally, the latest wave of rapacious invaders put a quick end to that unwelcome anachronism.

Little has been known of this early, promising, hardly utopian but definitely more gender-balanced phase of civilization. A few men have known of it; even fewer women, at least until recently. As has been remarked before, history does tend to be written by the winners.

From the viewpoint of the interrelationship of intelligent men and women and in the light of today's knowledge, it seems as if human civilization, starting in the late Stone Age, got off to a long, slow but good start. Then came the cowboys. These unsavory characters are still very much among us, threatening at present to bore us all literally to extinction. But the last five thousand years—encompassing what Eisler calls "the androcratic detour"—aren't such a long time in relation to the time span of human evolution. Amid the terrors and tragedies of the present age there are at least a few hopeful signs that we may be getting back on course, so that men and women together—really together in a workable way—can get on with finding out what human life is all about, and what we can make of it.

▲   ▲   ▲

Get It?

by Peter Russell

Paul is at home when the phone rings. He picks it up.

Paul: "Hello, this is Paul."

Voice: "Wow, how amazing!"

Paul: "Why?"

Voice: "I was just thinking of you."

And the line goes silent.

What do you think is the best continuation for this story?

1. Paul says "Hello?. . .Hello?. . .Hello?" and then hangs up with a shake of his head and a tut-tut.

2. He runs into the kitchen saying, "Jane, Jane, I have just had another amazing synchronicity!"

3. He sits down and begins to ponder the questions, "Why did he say that? What could have been his purpose?"

4. He waits a while before putting the phone down, and then spends the rest of the evening keeping one ear open for it to ring again, waiting for the explanation, the sequel, the sales pitch, or whatever. He cannot believe there is nothing more to come.

5. He thinks about it for a while; picks up the phone and calls a few friends to ask them what they think it means; talks about it at dinner parties for several months. And for the rest of his life cites it as "one of those strange things that happened to me once."

6. He rushes out into the street screaming...only to find that everyone else is doing the same.

7. He goes back to the book he was reading and within half a minute the whole incident is forgotten...except that he begins to have recurring dreams of a city wrapped up in telephone lines, with a haunting voice saying "I was just thinking of you."

8. He leaves the phone lying on the table, walks into the kitchen and says, "It's for you, Jane."

9. He becomes depressed and worries that the surrealists are taking over after all.

10. He goes out to the kitchen and tells Jane what happened, asking her opinion. She replies, "Don't bother me now, honey, I'm feeding the kids."

11. He leaps up and down in glee, embracing cushions and dancing on furniture, shouting "There is somebody alive after all!"

12. He shouts, "I've had enough of your obscene phone calls. This line is being monitored and they've got you traced by now, my friend."

13. A smile creeps across his face, and he says to himself, "I...get...it. Beautiful!"

14. He shouts "Same to you!" Drops phone and lurches across the room, bottle in hand, muttering, "Shtupid ferking intellecshals."

15. He picks up the phone again and dials Alcoholics Anonymous.

16. He asks uneasily, "How long ago did we take that stuff?"

17. He says "Far out! Too much! I mean a-mazing, man! Wow! That's just...incredible. You got me there, man! Far fucking out! Great!" And never smokes another joint in his life.

18. He fumbles in the dark to put the phone back on the hook, turns over and goes back to sleep. Five minutes later he sits bolt upright exclaiming, "WHAT?"

19. He puts the phone down and calls out "Okay, God. You've got me cornered. I give up."

20. He puts the phone down, but picks it up again. Dials a number at random. When a voice says "Hello, this is Peter," he cries out, "Wow, amazing...I was just thinking of you." And then hangs up.

21. He decides life on Earth is fun and signs up for another incarnation.

22. Glances at the article he has been reading entitled "Get It?" and exclaims, "What a coincidence!"

23. He whistles three notes into the phone. There is a click and a computer voice says, "This is Sirius FBHQ. There is a 347 on the STRD. Come in immediately."

24. Ponders, walks over to his desk and begins writing a piece entitled, "Get It?"

25. He puts the phone down with a look of puzzlement. Almost immediately it rings again. He picks it up and the same voice says, "Get it?"—and hangs up immediately.

26. He puts the phone down and exclaims, "Great! Another pataphysicist!"

If you're not sure which is the best answer, you know how to find out...

Chaos and Beyond: The Best of Trajectories

Postscript by RAW: *Another variation on this game: Try to figure out how the scene would develop in a film directed by Hitchcock, or one by Fellini, or Bergman, or Orson Welles, or Woody Allen, etc.—or in a novel by Kafka or Douglas Adams or Joyce or Chandler or Flann O'Brien...*
Get it?

▲   ▲   ▲

1994 Update:
An Introduction to
"The Great Brain Machine Debate"

In early issues of *Trajectories,* I wrote quite a bit about brain machines. Most of what I wrote now seems archaic, almost medieval; this technology has advanced so rapidly that all my comments now sound like earnest propaganda for the airplane written before the Wright Brothers got off the ground.

However, the following exchange from our letters column still seems topical—and introduces another topic of great importance to me.

Brain-change machines employ sound, or light, or electromagnetic pulses to "slow" the brain from its usual rapid beta waves to alpha (relaxation) or to theta (deep meditation) or even to delta (dream/vision.) Some models now on the market use only sound; some use only light; some use sound and light together; some use other combinations. Some appear to work better than others, in scientific tests, and some appear so ignorantly or carelessly made as to pose a real danger to users. Instead of giving my own personal evaluation of all the models currently on the market, I recommend the magazine *Megabrain* (PO Box PO Box 2744, Sausalito, CA 94965) which provides up-to-date reviews of the scientific literature.

I temporarily stopped all experiments with such machines a while back, because it became impossible to judge which results I should attribute to the "new, improved" machine some inventor just sent me, and I had used three times in a week—and which results more probably derive from long-term brain-training by all the machines I've tried to date—-and which results from other brain-change gimmicks I tried before or after the machines...

However, I definitely feel that among the machines I've used some cumulative good effects have occurred: meditation, for instance, has become much easier, and sometimes I even find myself entering a meditative state without consciously trying. I also found, on delta frequencies, easy entrance to realms which otherwise I had only experienced in dreams and on LSD—but the delta state produced by the better machines lends itself to rational observation and quick learning.

You can only accomplish this inner learning with years of practice when using the tools of consciously insightful drug exploration and/or training in lucid dreaming. But the drugs remain illegal, while lucid dreaming remains hard for most people to learn. Thus, I foresee a large future for brain machines.

After all, America (and, especially its ruling elite) has never regarded machines with the same paranoia it has toward chemicals.

And now, a debate between the brilliant Dr. Ed Kellogg and myself...

The Great Brain Machine Debate

Part I:
Dr. Kellogg Writes

Dear Editor:

I wish to take exception to the general view expressed in "Have Fun With Your New Head" (*Trajectories* #2). This view essentially classifies biofeedback devices as obsolete "brain trainers" as compared to the now available "brain tuners" that use light and sound and/or electromagnetic energies to entrain the user into different brain-wave states. In this you appear to have made a fundamental error, which I'll try to explain as best I can.

First, "brain tuner" devices work very much like drugs, in that they forcibly entrain the brain from the "outside in," taking the locus of control from the user to the device. Essentially, this can put the user into a dependent state, where the user sees her/himself as needing the machine to change consciousness. Like chemical drugs, electromagnetic drugs may allow the user to easily and effectively access states of consciousness not normally experienced, and in this I see their main value. But they also share many of the disadvantages of chemical drugs, including the fostering of dependency, and the possibility of serious side effects (such as accelerating the growth of cancer cells—see Becker's *The Body Electric* for more details.)

Biofeedback devices work on an entirely different principle, as they simply supply information to the user. One might liken their effect to that of a mirror, or of removing a blindfold, as they allow the user to bridge the gap between normally conscious and unconscious processes. Biofeedback devices like the Mind Mirror allow the user to change consciousness from the "inside out," bringing about a state of in-dependence for the user. They don't do anything to you, but they allow you to do something to yourself. The locus of control moves from the outside world to your own volition. Such skills, once learned, no longer require a machine, as the user has integrated conscious-unconscious processes, and has changed fundamentally in this regard.

Brain-tuners belong to the realm of the newly burgeoning field of "Electronic Pharmacology," and may soon supersede chemical drugs for both therapeutic and recreational uses. Biofeedback devices, however, operate through an entirely different mode that allows users to make fundamental changes from within, bringing them to an increased state of inner, rather than outer, dependence.

E.W. Kellogg III, Ph.D.
Ashland, OR

Part II:
Robert Anton Wilson Replies

My article did not intend to present an either/or choice between "tuners" and "trainers" or to reject biofeedback devices as "obsolete," and, in fact, I specifically included the Mind Mirror, which operates on biofeedback, as one of the newer devices that arouse my enthusiasm.

Your rather Aristotelian distinction between "brain trainers" and "brain tuners" (which also "entrain") seems too metaphysical for my comprehension. In my experience, most people, whether "trained "with biofeedback or "en-trained " with light and sound waves or electromagnetism, soon learn the knack of entering altered consciousness without the machines. In three years of traveling widely to lecture on these machines and meet researchers and users, I have not yet heard of a case of dependence on these machines—even in the metaphoric sense, in which some critics claim that computers or TVs have created dependence. The general pattern appears that users employ any brain machine for a few months, learn how to enter alpha or lower brain frequencies at will, and stick the machine in a closet or give it to a friend.

This, of course, must be classed as an anecdotal and impressionistic report (like your letter); we will only have hard data when placebo-controlled double-blind studies have been published and replicated.

As for Becker's book, unless my myopic eyes missed something, he only deals with cancers correlated with voltages around 100,000 times greater and frequencies 100 times greater than those to be found in any current brain machine. Many uncritical inferences must be accepted before one makes any predictions from his data to the low millivoltages and very low frequencies in these machines. To me, worry on this score seems like giving up peaches after discovering they contain trace amounts of the prussic acid that in much higher doses acts as a poison, or fearing a doctor's X-ray because nuclear radiation can cause damage.

However, new technologies always contain possible negative effects, and I certainly think we should all keep this in mind. As I wrote in the article under discussion, "(E)lectromagnetic fields may have side effects that will prove most unpleasant...Everybody will divide on this issue according to the usual temperamental modes created by early imprints—the neophiles will do the research and take the risks (if any); the neophobes will worry and predict Doom from the sidelines." No such anxieties should arise at all concerning light-and-sound machines, since people have been using light and sound to alter consciousness since the dawn of history with no bad effects ever noted (except for epileptics.)

Meanwhile, my major point remains, not to praise or dispraise any particular existing machines, but to indicate that further research can be expected to produce better brain machines very quickly, now that this promising area has been opened to us. The next five years, I suspect, will produce devices that make all our current "trainers" or "entrainers" seem primitive by comparison.

Afterword

The prose of this letter by Dr. Kellogg contains one unusual feature usually not found in scientific or philosophic writings—or other writings in general. This characteristic of Dr. Kellogg's prose may have great benefits for humanity if it becomes widely copied, according to certain theorists.

Can you determine what this unique feature is without reading the explanation which follows? *Hint*: Sombunall of RAW's prose also contains this structural feature. (And if you don't know what "Sombunall" means you haven't read *The New Inquisition* and shame on you!)

For the full explanation, see the next chapter.

▲   ▲   ▲

Robert Anton Wilson

Sic Transit Gloria Hirohito

Video stores in Tokyo reported a surge in sales and rentals of X-rated tapes the day of Emperor Hirohito's funeral, according to the *Washington Post,* which explained this by saying that many Japanese became bored with the endless TV coverage of the Sun King's life and last rites.

Is The Body of My Enemy My Enemy?

Is the body of my enemy my enemy?
No.

Is it my friend?
No.

Is it neutral?
No.

What then?
It is an organ of your body.

What?
Risen in revolt as in disease.

How to control it?
How is the body already controlled?

By the mind.
Well?

I don't know how.
You'd better find out.

Where and from whom?
Enough has been said.

Thanks.
Anytime.

— *Arlen Wilson*

Chapter Five

How to Publish Heresy in Mainstream Publications

by Timothy Leary, Ph.D.

The French semioticist, Michel Foucault, has demonstrated that those who control the thought-engines (i.e., the mass media) control the minds of the people. The students in China learned how to use TV to *create* history from American dissidents of the '60s; the geriatric male Deng clique learned how to *rewrite* history from the Lee Atwater crowd in Washington.

Like many Outsiders, I have become concerned at the manufacture of "news" by those who control our press and TV. Therefore, for the last few years, I have been experimenting with methods by which the lone individual can insert dissident and libertarian perspectives into the information assembly lines.

For example, the editorial pages of newspapers publish opinion pieces by well-known columnists. These syndicated pundits are selected to give the illusion of a variety of viewpoints, but in reality such columns cover only a narrow spectrum between the extreme right-wing of the CIA-Pentagon fan club and the bland, tame platitudes of the loyal "liberal" opposition.

If somebody like me—or Alex Cockburn or Noam Chomsky or even Gore Vidal—were to submit a truly dissident essay, no matter how convincing the facts and witheringly brilliant the logic, there is very little chance that it would be published.

"Letters to the Editor" is the only section of the paper where far-out opinions are expressed. The publicity wings of various political and religious groups know this and tend to flood the editorial offices with their boiler-plate propaganda. Extreme fascist opinions, which "respectable" columnists dare not mention, can be published this way; and sometimes even Leftish or truly heretical (libertarian) views can also creep into print this way.

In the last ten years I have written hundreds of letters to the Los Angeles *Times*, the L.A. *Herald Examiner* and the L.A. *Weekly*. Letters signed with my own name usually vanish down the memory hole and do not appear in print. However, I have a high rate of success (publication) when I write under pen-names, especially if the social-ethnic flavor of the name fits the content. For example, I invented Mary Alice O'Brien, to question the position of Mother Theresa and the Pope on birth control. I invented I.J. Katz, a retired rabbi, to criticize Zionist extremism. Zachary Chase was a junior high school student who was disturbed by the blood bath mentality revealed in many quotes from Mr. Reagan. Etc.

The most effective info-raid technique, I have found, is to avoid stating dissident opinions openly. Simply adopt the current Establishment line, exaggerate it a bit (in the manner of Voltaire) and "defend" it in the passionate jargon of the true believer. Satire reaches those deaf to logic and evidence.

On the following page, for instance, is one of my current Mary Alice O'Brien missives. Readers are encouraged to experiment with this American method of *samizdat* info-guerrilla journalism.

Dear Editor,

Even flaming liberals agree that scrawling anti-American or anti-religious graffiti on the Washington Monument should not be constitutionally protected. Nonetheless, some card-carrying ACLU lawyers apparently convinced the Supreme Court that a flag bought and paid for by some mental patient is not a national monument.

Surely, now other self-appointed Civil Liberties lawyers will defend the more insidious case of "closet creeps" who will undoubtedly continue to burn flags in the privacy of their own homes, thus evading detection and prosecution even if Bush's proposed Amendment is passed. Can not our schools and police educate children to turn in such parents?

In the current climate of global disrespect for authority and for sacred symbols, should not the right to possess, transport and sell sacred symbols like the flag, the Blessed Sacrament, guns and Bibles be restricted to patriotic and God-fearing citizens whose loyalties are beyond suspicion and who can be counted on not to desecrate in public or in private?

For example, suppose you saw a Jesse Jackson follower like Willie Horton swaggering down the street with a flag in his hand, or a Dukakis follower with a Bible in his hand. Wouldn't it make you wonder uneasily what they might do with these sacred relics when nobody is watching?

Mary Alice O'Brien

▲   ▲   ▲

Medard Gabel
and the World Game

The images flashed across the screen, a montage of the outstanding techno-triumphs and social disasters of recent decades. Quotes appeared between the images: "No man knows enough to be a pessimist."—Norman Cousins. Moon landings... Nuclear missiles..."To make the world work for 100% of humanity in the shortest possible time through spontaneous cooperation without ecological offense or the disadvantage of anyone"—R. Buckminster Fuller... Graphs showing the rate at which smallpox was vanquished in the 1970s... Bigger nuclear missiles... "At Dachau we learned what humanity is capable of. At Hiroshima we learned what is at stake."—Bertrand Russell... Hungry children in a Third World village... Star Wars schematics...

The World Game was about to begin.

I had signed up for a day-long seminar on the World Game, held the day before the annual convention of the World Future Society, and I was wondering who would lead it now that Bucky Fuller, its inventor, was dead. I found the Game was run by Medard Gabel, an astonishingly young looking man whose book, *Ho-Ping: Food for All,* I had read nearly ten years ago. Gabel, I decided, was not as young as he looked—otherwise he must have written that very erudite book as an adolescent; the explanation of his youthful look must be endorphins, as Barbara Marx Hubbard would tell me a few days later. *(Note: Robert Anton Wilson's interview with Barbara Marx Hubbard appears later in this chapter. —Ed.)*

When the Game started I was assigned to represent the Near East (except Israel.) I was given the props to represent that Arab world's share of the planet's resources. Eggboxes represented food, light swords represented energy, and balloons represented weapons. I found I had 3% of the world's food, which was adequate, since I represented 3% of the world's population. I also had 9% of the world's energy, which also seemed adequate. I forgot to count my bombs and money. However, my literacy rate was only 65%. I decided to attempt to raise it to 80% in the course of the Game.

I tried to sell some food, hoping to buy more later. The people who really needed food couldn't pay me. The people who could pay (e.g., the U.S.) didn't need food. I was stumped.

I tried to sell some of my bombs. People were busy with other deals and nobody wanted bombs just then.

I invested $50,000,000,000 of my capital in buying educational equipment and teachers, raising my literacy rate to 75% in the first round. I then got another egg-box, since when literary increases 10%, food production increases proportionally. I now owned 4% of the world's food, and had only 3% of the world's population to feed. I tried again to sell some food, but the hungry couldn't pay and the wealthy weren't hungry.

I decided to give some food away, to Africa. This earned me a Good Will certificate, which meant I could collect something from Africa eventually. I gave away some more food to South America, and got another Good Will certificate. With that much Good Will, I felt secure in investing another $50 billion in education — and got a bonus light-sword, since energy production increases when literacy rises.

Quickly, I sold my light sword to South-East Asia and bought more education. Things were getting exciting: Players were shouting, trying to hurry deals before the time limit ran out. I gave away some more food, bought more education, and got a bonus in food production to bring me back to the 3% that I had started with.

When the Game ended, I still had 3% of the world's food, 9% of its energy, a lot of good will from Africa and South America, and had raised my literacy rate beyond the 85% I had aimed at, to a full 100%, meaning that food and energy would increase in the next round (if the Game had continued.) I was down $100 billion in cash, but with 100% literacy and food and energy production increasing, I thought I would earn that back fairly quickly. Besides, I still had all my bombs, so even Reagan could not say my strategy was wimpy.

Why haven't the Arabs followed this Game plan? I guess they've been too busy trying to destroy Israel, or defend themselves from Israel, or whatever they think they're doing.

Because of my "generosity" to Africa and South America, infant mortality declined in both places, meaning that the birth-rate would also decline soon. (Birth-rate always drops when most children who are born live past their first two years. Most excess births are "insurance" against high infant mortality.) Of course, although I'm a "bleeding heart liberal" emotionally, I'm a

71

libertarian intellectually: I had given the food away, for Good Will, since I couldn't sell it, and getting Good Will seemed "smarter" that just letting the food rot. I hadn't realized I was also causing the world's birthrate to drop...

I was beginning to get an idea of the sociological meaning of Fuller's concept of synergy, which previously I had understood largely as a mathematical concept.

The World Game, I decided, operates just like the World, only faster. You can cheat in it, I think, but the pace is such that the results will bite your ass very damned quickly, instead of coming back to afflict your grandchildren long after everybody has forgotten how that chunk of Flying Bad Karma got into orbit.

There are now 50,000 thermonuclear weapons on Earth. Gabel carried us through an alternative scenario, in which all 50,000 weapons were used in a global conflict. Each weapon was represented by a red plastic chip about the size of a dime. On the World Map, each chip covered the area that would be destroyed when a nuke was dropped. The 50,000 chips were spread across the map...and covered every square inch. No part of Earth was not blown up totally, in this scenario. If any humans survived in that script, it would be coal miners working in very deep mine shafts. Very deep indeed.

"This only represents the immediate effects of the blasts," Gabel told us. "We're not even considering fall-out and nuclear winter and other long-range effects."

I suddenly felt, with terrible embarrassment, that I was about to weep and make a spectacle of myself. Then I noticed that all the other players were showing signs of the same internal battle against tears.

John Lennon's "Imagine" suddenly began to play on the stereo. Medard Gabel and his associates cleaned up the red plastic "bombs" and the Earth was clean and alive again. We would have another chance to avoid Doomsday and try again to make the world work.

Since each of us players had been representing only part of the planet, Medard Gabel now gave us some statistics on the whole picture. We (as a species) now produce enough food to give each human 4.7 pounds of food a day—enough to create a world-wide obesity problem. *Starvation does not exist because of scarcity but because of the rules by which nations currently play the World Game.* A child in Costa Rica currently has better health care than a child in the U.S. To raise American child health to parity with Costa Rica would cost only a sum equal to 8 days of our yearly military budget.

A computer was brought in and we began receiving the latest statistics on all major variables involved in the World Game. Working as teams, now, we tried to develop plans to manage the planet so that Fuller's goal—"advantaging all without disadvantaging any"—could be accomplished as rapidly as possible. It was exciting and exhilarating. Some of our plans began to seem feasible when we checked them against the computer statistics. We were making the World work!

*   *   *   *   *   *

I had a chat with Medard Gabel later and asked him how he had gotten involved with Bucky Fuller and the World Game.

"I was majoring in English," he told me, "and then Martin Luther King, Jr., came along. I dropped out, and went to Selma to work with him. Later on, I was active in the anti-war movement, too. Then I heard Bucky speak, and I decided he had the best, most practical approach to solving the problems facing us."

Gabel returned to college, got a degree in Comprehensive Planning and Design, and went to work for Fuller.

"Sometimes it was chaotic," he says. "We'd have ten projects underway, and Bucky would have another brainstorm and we'd be working on twenty projects the next day."

From 1969 until Fuller's death in 1983, Gabel worked on the World Game, and has continued it on his own since then. In addition to the work involved in amassing up-to-date statistics (the Game must be accurate to be meaningful), he somehow found the time to write *Ho-Ping: Food for All*, *Empty Breadbasket*, *Energy, Earth and Everyone* and *Design Science Primer*.

The World Game, meanwhile, has mushroomed rapidly in the past three years. Gabel did 33 World Game workshops in 1987, 55 in 1988 and 92 this year.

"I'd like to see it in every high school on Earth," I said.

"Well," Medard said, smiling, "we'll have it in every high school in Westchester next year. Each student there will have 5 days work on the World Game in April, 1990."

The Game—which I tend to consider the greatest learning device since the alphabet was invented—could spread much faster, Gabel said, but he wants to make sure it is not oversimplified or misused. He will franchise it to others, but only after they've spent three months in training.

"And we can't have any Fundamentalist preachers running it and ruining our reputation," he said. "It must remain scientific and accurate. It can't become a tool of Republican propaganda or Communist propaganda, or anything like that."

The statistics in the World Game computer come from the most reliable and up-to-date sources possible: The United Nations Statistical Yearbook, The UN Yearbook of Energy Statistics, the World Development Report, the CIA's World Factbook, the World Bank, the Center for Defense Information (Washington), etc.

34 Congresspersons and 80 Congressional staff members have played the World Game. Congresswoman Patricia Shroeder arranged to have the Democratic Party officials of Colorado play the Game recently. Ten top American businessmen will be playing it with 10 European and 10 Japanese executives this September.

People are really motivated to win the Game—to make the world work—after the Death Of Earth scenario is enacted, Medard says. At the Colorado Democratic Party session all 280 players openly wept when the planet was destroyed before their eyes.

I switched the conversation back to Bucky Fuller himself and asked what it was like working with him.

Bucky had too many ideas, Medard said. "We couldn't work on every project that he conceived. We eventually developed a rule: If he mentioned it twice, he was serious and we should start working on it."

The next step in the evolution of the World Game will expand it beyond seminars and workshops. Medard has developed software, compatible with Apple Computers, that will allow people to play the World Game at home. Using the characteristic Apple icons, any user can zoom in on one country, or on one ecological system, or on the whole globe, or whatever challenging area he or she wishes to confront that day.

"Then we start networking and comparing solutions to various problems," Medard said. "Every year we'll give a prize to whoever comes up with the best solution to a local or planetary problem—but it's not the usual prize. The money we'll award must be used to move the solution one step further in the following year—to do more detailed research on the problem, to communicate the solution to all those who should be concerned with the problem, or to do whatever makes the Game work as real problem-solving tool."

Medard grinned at the possibilities. "Some year the winner might be a high school student. A Minister of Agriculture. A housewife. Who knows?"

"How much will the software cost?" I asked, envisioning myself abolishing world hunger at my Mac Plus keyboard.

"We're trying to keep it cheap," Gabel said. "I had hopes of making the price around $50. Now...well, it may cost $100 or $120."

That doesn't seem much to invest to have a chance at doing something about world problems instead of just complaining about them.

For more information on the World Game and its software, write Medard Gabel, World Game Institute, 3215 Race St., Philadelphia, PA 19104.

▲   ▲   ▲

Trajectories Interview:

Barbara Marx Hubbard

Barbara Marx Hubbard founded the Committee for the Future and now serves on the board of the World Future Society. Once described by Buckminster Fuller as "the best informed human" in the field of Future Studies, Barbara was a candidate for the Democratic Vice Presidential nomination in 1984. Her best-known book is the lyrical account of her search for meaning, The Hunger of Eve. *Barbara recently formed Global Family and acts as its coordinator.*

Robert Anton Wilson interviewed Hubbard at the Sixth General Assembly of the World Future Society, held in Washington, D. C. July 16-20, 1989.

Trajectories: You've been involved with the World Future Society a long time. How fast has the WFS been growing?

Hubbard: It started out as mimeographed newsletter, printed by Ed Cornish in 1967. He had been with *National Geographic*, but he felt we needed a journal of Future Studies, so he started it on his own. Now we have 30,000 members worldwide.

Trajectories: A reporter from NBC was telling me yesterday that the World Future Society has become less "visionary" in the 1980s and is more into "nuts and bolts" analysis. Have you gone through a similar evolution?

Hubbard: I tried, but it didn't suit me. It has been a challenge to me, as a visionary, to manifest my vision concretely. I've spent a lot of time in the last seven years trying to put my ideas into scientific and replicable form.

What I've come up with is a kind of sociological experiment—a phalanx of core groups founded on what I call "the heart." That is, groups based on mutual trust and the acceptance of diversity. All the groups are united under the title of the Global Family. We have hundreds of core groups now, mostly in the United States, the Soviet Union and Latin America. If these core groups can manifest real social change, I'll have demonstrated how a new form of society can emerge from the old systems.

Trajectories: Are you working on any new books?

Hubbard: I'm doing my first novel, *Pole Shift,* in collaboration with Daniel Masiarz. It's sort of science-fiction, I guess. I'm also working on a new non-fiction work called *The Supra-Sexual Revolution.* My thesis is that the Age of Procreation is drawing to an end: we are the last generation that will reproduce to the maximum, since the population explosion has become a clear menace. What will become of the reproductive drive, then? I think it will mutate into a creative drive. You can see this happening especially among women, where it appears chiefly as discontent with traditional roles. You can see the trajectory in my own family. I had three daughters. None of them has reproduced to that extent. One of them has two children, but the other two have one child each.

Trajectories: There are lots of women around who are in their '30s and haven't reproduced yet...

Hubbard: The symptoms are everywhere. The creative urge now wants to synergize genius, not genes. It wants to produce not progeny, but projects.

The drive for Self-Actualization, as Maslow called it, is increasing in both sexes, because the procreative drive is being transmuted. Evolution is shifting from within. I've lived through it. When Vocational Arousal strikes, you are transmuted, sometimes painfully. You thought you were doing fine before, but suddenly you find you are discontented and need something else. My God, I thought I was *sick*, at first. And in my case, the new drive didn't get channeled into Feminism, because I had too much sympathy for men. It took me years to realize I was seeking a role as a Co-Creator of the future.

Feminists mostly want to join the existing society, but I want to make a better society than has ever existed. It was Riane Eisler who finally gave me the words: I am looking for a way out of the Dominator system into a Partnership system.

Trajectories: She gave a lot of us the words. For years I talked in terms of Libertarian versus Authoritarian, and I was always misunderstood. Now I talk in her terms: Partnership society versus Dominator society.

Hubbard: Eisler is brilliant. (*Note: See the review of Riane Eisler's* The Chalice and the Blade *in Chapter Four.—Ed.*)

Trajectories: What do you think of the backlash of the Reagan-Bush years—the "bombs and Jesus" movement? You know, what Hunter Thompson calls "the White Trash Revolution?"

Hubbard: My metaphor is that we're all new-borns. The 1960s were the birth of a new humanity. Now we're in the stage of post-natal torpor. The most important fact about Earth, as Bucky Fuller always said, is that it came without an Operating Manual. We have to create our own instruction book. The best minds of the 1960s saw that they had to start with themselves, with their own brains, and disappeared from public view while they worked in the Human Potential movement and personal growth and so on. Visionaries like you and me and Tim Leary and F.M. Esfandiary didn't communicate to the general public, we didn't articulate well enough, so there was a Vision Gap. The moralists came to the fore. They were people who knew what we had to stop, but had no idea of what new social forms we had to create. Moralists always operate on the fear-guilt-pain circuits. So we had two opposite groups of moralists working those circuits. The Environmentalists worked mostly on fear, the Fundamentalists mostly on guilt, but the whole fear-guilt-pain syndrome was activated by their joint activities. The Fundamentalists got a bigger public, because their lines was, "What does it matter if Armageddon is coming? God planned it that way. Besides, I'm *saved!*" That line has always been popular in our culture. It says we have no need for scientific research or creativity to solve our problems: once the world is destroyed, the "saved" will have eternal bliss in Heaven. Reagan rode on that wave, and also offered the Vision of the Shining City on the Hill—America could be saved, and could be wonderful again, and all we needed was to take on the highest military budget in the world. Salvation through faith was the pure Fundamentalist line; Reagan adapted it to salvation through bombs.

Trajectories: I left the country for six years after Reagan was elected...

Hubbard: I went around asking myself "What did I do wrong? Why didn't I communicate better?" Finally, I began to get more evolutionary perspective. A doctor who has delivered over 1,000 babies knows what's normal post-natal development. If we could see 1,000 planets similar to ours, we'd probably find out present state is quite normal at this stage of evolution. What's our basic problem? A sense of separation between people. A sense of separation between us and our environment. A sense of separation, in general. That's probably normal in the early stages of evolution.

Trajectories: Doris Lessing, in her novel *Shikasta*, suggests that this planet lacks something all advanced planets have, SOWF. That means "substance-of-we-feeling."

Hubbard: Exactly. I think that's a brilliant book. The Global Family is an endeavor to activate that "substance-of-we-feeling." I think evolution, or the morphogenetic field, is moving toward what I call Co-Creation... Minds joining in a more empathetic way. When we feel with each other, we share in the work of the system Intelligence, or "God." The nuclear threat could have been an Evolutionary Driver, forcing us to higher consciousness, but it was part of the old system; it divided us further. The Greenhouse Effect may be the ultimate Evolutionary Driver, and it's scientifically demonstrable; it will unify us. 100 times a day we're all being driven to think, "How will this effect the whole system?" Do you use plastic bags or paper bags? Every little decision becomes important. We have to get beyond every little local "we" and think in terms of the total "we." Humanity needs experience in working together and the Greenhouse Effect may be just the teaching device we required.

Trajectories: Before we conclude, I can't help noticing that you still look as young as you did ten years ago. What's your explanation of that?

Hubbard: I think it has something to do with creativity...and its relation to endorphins. Doing work you enjoy unleashes endorphins, doesn't it? I call creative work a Natural High and Safe Sex.

▲   ▲   ▲

Feminist Vector

According to Cetron and Davies' **American Renaissance,** women's salaries continue to move closer to men's. The trajectory: 1960, women earned 61% of what was earned by men in comparable jobs; 1980, 64%; 1986, 70%. Leaving out the states south of the Mason-Dixon line, women have advanced even further: outside the Confederacy, women now earn 87% the salaries of male counterparts.

"Just Asking..."

by *Arlen Wilson*

On George Bush's recent visit to Hungary, our President volunteered our Peace Corps to go in there and help them with their problems...a heartwarming gesture. On a recent visit to Hollywood, our President came to mind again when I discovered that under the bushes beside a freeway on-ramp there was a colony of children and teenagers sleeping in the daytime... children with no beds, day or night; the so-called street kids. Lulled by the noise and the fumes, they try to sleep by day; some of the lucky ones even have blankets. The night streets of Tinsel Town provide them with a modicum of food and drugs in return for their bodies or other services.

There is no census of this invisible population which is in the process of becoming visible in more and more American cities. Combined with the adult homeless, we have here a real "growth sector" in our country.

There are free and prosperous countries in Western Europe where this kind of thing does not happen—where the situation here, if it were known, might prompt some of their privileged and idealistic young people to brave the terrors of our primitive urban terrain. Such idealistic young Europeans would train and organize, doubtless pray and take vows and sign pledges before they crossed the ocean. They could then set up encampments in our cities and teach us Americans technologies known to the advanced nations of the world, such as how to put children into beds.

This may be a distant hope, but surely sooner or later a compassionate consortium of the sane will emerge from concerned folk abroad who care about the preventable suffering due to underdevelopment in the USA. It may be time for a Reverse Peace Corps. Why not?

Just asking...

Quiet Lady

I am not sure these rumors are about
A place that's real or not, nor is it likely
I will ever know. Inquiring out loud
About such things would be a mark
Of. . .what? Ingratitude. Come closer though.

> They say that ordinary women there
> Could walk outside at night without fear.
> I try to imagine what it would be like
> To see the moon through branches
> While my heels click down a street.
>   I cannot finish the thought.

I know our dangers are the price we pay
For freedom. This has been explained to me.

> Then on the other hand they say
>   This far-off place has freedom
>   But no maddened poor.
I know
This isn't right. That's not the way
We're made. It's lies.
            Still just to see
                How it would feel I think yes
                    I would like to go there once
                        Before I die.

—Arlen Wilson

E-Prime

The First Annual *Trajectories* Puzzle Contest has a winner: Mr. Jeffrey D. Raess of San Jose, CA, whose letter reached us sooner than any other. Mr. Raess correctly identified E-Prime—standard English minus the "is" of identity—as the salient feature of Dr. Kellogg's prose.

Others who correctly identified E-Prime include Mary Jane Waxler of Fairfax, CA; Tim Freeman of Pittsburg, PA; David Smith of Albany, NY; and James Conroy of China Spring, TX—but their letters arrived later than Mr. Raess's. (Nobody thought of beating the crowd by sending us a telegram...) Eric Wagner of Tempe, AZ, who did not recognize E-Prime, but observed correctly that Dr. Kellogg "treats his observations as possibilities rather than absolutes" deserves Honorable Mention, and Jack Beiler of Irving, TX, gets another Honorable Mention for observing that Dr. Kellogg "has definite opinions about the issue but uses a socially relativistic tone to express them. He does not say 'You are wrong; this is how it is.' By saying 'You appear to have made an error,' he admits that he is not omniscient."

So why did I offer this challenge to our readers, and where did E-Prime come from, and why do I think this should be discussed further?

E-Prime, abolishing the "is" of identity, originally appeared in *Science and Sanity* by Alfred Korzybski; the name "E-Prime" arrived later and seems to have been coined by David Bourland. Many have urged that all scientific papers be written in E-Prime, to avoid the infiltration of unacknowledged metaphysical assumptions; among others, Dr. Albert Ellis re-wrote the second edition of his *Guide to Rational Living* entirely in E-Prime. Korzybski himself felt that all humans should be trained in E-Prime from grade school on, as "semantic hygiene" against the most prevalent forms of logical error, emotional distortion and "demonological thinking."

To understand E-Prime, consider the human brain as a computer. (Note that I did not say the brain "is" a computer.) As the Prime Law of Computers tells us, GARBAGE IN, GARBAGE OUT. (GIGO, for short.) The wrong software *guarantees* wrong answers. Conversely, finding the right software can "miraculously" solve problems that previously appeared intractable.

It seems likely that the principle software used in the human brain consists of words, metaphors, disguised metaphors and linguistic structures in general. The Sapir-Whorf-Korzybski Hypothesis, in sociology, holds that a change in language can alter our perception of the cosmos. A revision of language structure, in particular, can alter the brain as dramatically as a psychedelic. In our metaphor, if we change the software, the computer operates in a new ways.

Consider the following paired sets of propositions, in which Standard English alternates with English-Prime (E-Prime):

1A. The electron is a wave.
1B. The electron appears as a wave when measured with instrument-1.

2A. The electron is a particle.
2B. The electron appears as a particle when measured with instrument-2.

3A. John is lethargic and unhappy.
3B. John appears lethargic and unhappy in the office.

4A. John is bright and cheerful.
4B. John appears bright and cheerful on holiday at the beach.

5A. The first man stabbed the second man with a knife.
5B. The first man appeared to stab the second man with what appeared to me to be a knife.

6A. The car involved in the hit-and-run accident was a blue Ford.
6B. In memory, I think I recall the car involved in the hit-and-run accident as a blue Ford.

7A. This is a fascist idea.
7B. This seems like a fascist idea to me.

8A. Beethoven is better than Mozart.
8B. In my present mixed state of musical education and ignorance, Beethoven seems better to me than Mozart.

9A. That is a sexist movie.
9B. That seems like a sexist movie to me.

10A. The fetus is a person.
10B. In my system of metaphysics, the fetus must be classified as a person.

The "A"-type statements (Standard English) all implicitly or explicitly assume the medieval view that has been called "Aristotelian essentialism" or "naive realism." In other words, they assume a world made up of block-like entities with indwelling "essences" or spooks—"ghosts in the machine." The "B"-type statements (E-Prime) recast these sentences into a form isomorphic to modern science by first abolishing the "is" of Aristotelian essence and then reformulating each observation in terms of signals received and interpreted by a body (or instrument) moving in space-time.

Relativity, quantum mechanics, large sections of general physics, perception psychology, sociology, linguistics, modern math, anthropology, ethnology and several other sciences make perfect sense when put into the software of E-Prime. Each of these sciences generates paradoxes, some bordering on "nonsense" or "gibberish," if you try to translate them back into the software of Standard English.

Concretely, "The electron is a wave" employs the Aristotelian "is" and thereby introduces to the false-to-experience notion that we can know the indwelling "essence" of the electron. "The electron appears as a wave when measured by instrument-1" reports what actually occurred in space-time, namely that the electron was constrained by a certain instrument to behave in a certain way.

Similarly, "The electron is a particle" contains medieval Aristotelian software, but "The electron appears as a particle when measured by instrument-2" contains modern scientific software. Once again, the software determines whether we impose a medieval or modern grid upon our reality-tunnel.

Note that "the electron is a wave" and "the electron is a particle" contradict each other and begin the insidious process by which we move gradually from paradox to nonsense to total gibberish. On the other hand, the modern scientific statements, "the electron appears as a wave when measured one way" and "the electron appears as a particle measured another way" do not contradict, but *compliment* each other. (Bohr's Principle of Complementarity, which explained this and revolutionized physics, would have been obvious to all, and not just to a person of his genius, if physicists had been writing in E-Prime all along...)

Looking at our next pair, "John is lethargic and unhappy" vs. "John is bright and cheerful," we see again how medieval software creates metaphysical puzzles and totally imaginary contradictions. Operationalizing the statements, as physicists since Bohr have learned to operationalize, we find that the E-Prime translations do not contain any contradiction, and even give us a clue as to causes of John's changing moods. (Look back if you forgot the translations.)

"The first man stabbed the second man with a knife" lacks the overt "is" of identity but contains Aristotelian software nonetheless. The E-Prime translation not only operationalizes the data, but may fit the facts better—if the incident occurred in a psychology class, where this experiment has often been conducted. (The first man "stabs," or making stabbing gestures at, the second man, with a *banana*, but many students, conditioned by Aristotelian software, nonetheless "see" a knife. You don't need to take drugs to hallucinate; improper language can fill your world with phantoms and spooks of many kinds.)

The reader is invited to employ his or her own ingenium in analyzing how "is-ness" creates false-to-facts reality-tunnels in the remaining examples, and how E-Prime brings us back to the scientific, the operational, the existential, the phenomenological —to what humans and their instruments actually do in space-time as they create observations, perceptions, thoughts, deductions and General Theories.

I have found repeatedly that when baffled by a problem in science, in "philosophy," or in daily life, I gain immediate insight by writing down what I know about the enigma in strict E-Prime. Often, solutions appear immediately—just as happens when you throw out the "wrong" software and put the "right" software into your PC. In other cases, I at least get an insight into why the problem remains intractable and where and how future science might go about finding an answer. (This has contributed greatly to my ever-escalating agnosticism about the political, ideological and religious issues that still generate the most passion on this primitive planet.)

When a proposition resists all efforts to recast it in E-Prime, many consider it "meaningless." This view has been promoted by Korzybski, Wittgenstein, the Logical Positivists and (in his own way) Niels Bohr. I happen to agree with that verdict (which condemns 99% of theology and 99.999999% of metaphysics to the category of Noise rather than Meaning)—but that subject must be saved for another article. For now, it suffices to note that those who fervently believe such Aristotelian propositions as "A piece of bread, blessed by a priest, *is* a person (who died 2000 years ago)," "The flag *is* a living being," or "The fetus *is* a human being" do not, in general, appear to be talking sense by normal 20th Century scientific standards, and such people often appear to act in the fanatic and frenzied manner typical of the medieval theologians, whose logic consisted entirely of "is-ness" statements.

▲   ▲   ▲

1994 Update:

E-Prime

This article contains a major error. When Bourland invented E-prime, he intended the term to mean a subcase of English abolishing all forms of "is" or "be" or their synonyms, not just the "is of identity" criticized by Korzybski. [1]

Frankly, I have not decided whether I consider removing all forms of "isness" as important as I consider Korzybski's goal of just removing the Aristotelian "is" of identity. Meanwhile, I have experimented with E-prime extensively—removing all forms of "isness" from my prose.

I have even written a whole book, *Quantum Psychology* entirely in E-prime. Experimenting, I have discovered that E-prime "works" (helps clarify the otherwise obscure, removes reification and "demonology" from discourse, and banishes common fallacies), not only in dealing with the scientific issues in a book like *Quantum Psychology*, but even in such unexpected areas as film criticism. (I have done studies of both Orson Welles's *Touch of Evil* and Jonathan Demme's *Silence of the Lambs* in E-prime, and the results appear to me better— clearer, and closer in "style" to their cinematic subject-matter— than if I had written those articles in ordinary English.)

---

[1] Korzybski considered the "is" of identity particularly pernicious, not only because it has created endless confusion in science—see our previous discussion of "the electron is a particle" and "the electron is a wave"—but because it plays a pivotal role in motivating fanaticisms of all sorts. (For instance, note its use in "All Jews are usurers," "All men are rapists," "All Oriental religion is Satanic," etc.) Bourland and other proponents of E-prime point out that other uses of "is: have their own built-in flaws; e.g., "The grass is green" overlooks the fact that the grass "is" many other things (a chemical structure, a sweet smell, a particular botanical species, a food for herbivores, etc.) and that the green-ness does not reside in the grass but in our eye/brain system and their *relation* to the grass. In general, "is" statements medievalize our thinking by implying Aristotelian stasis and essence, while avoidance of "is" forces us to modernize—relativize and existentialize—our brain programs.

I have also used E-prime in several bits of political satire, evading a great deal of unwanted and unintended dogmatic "tone" without losing any "bite" or sarcasm....

Everything I write for *Trajectories*, I now (1994) write in E-prime, although I do not enforce this on Scott or Arlen (who have their own opinions about the value of this discipline).

Curiously, people of strongly dogmatic temperament often do not notice E-prime at all, and write rebuttals as if I had used "is" in its most Aristotelian and medieval manner, even when I have scrupulously avoided any form of is/be/being and their cognates. It seems that, just as the sad man lives in a sad world, the angry woman in an angry world, etc., the dogmatic see absolute statements even where the writer has carefully shunned absolutism and relativized every sentence.

(This habit of seeing absolutes even where I avoid them appears most notably in Christian Fundamentalists, the few remaining Marxists and members of CSICOP.)

Once, many years ago, I tried an ancient Cabalistic exercise—abolishing the pronoun "I" from my speech for a week. I found the results of this exercise shocking, painful and extremely illuminating. (For further details, see my *Cosmic Trigger I.*) E-prime, by comparison, seems free of shock and pain (although it does induce certain stress at first) and even more illuminating that getting rid of "I."

Those who have tried to remove "sexist" terms from their language already know that such semantic reforms can have dramatic results. ("A change in language can alter our appreciation of the cosmos," as Benjamin Lee Whorf once wrote.) E-prime changes a hell of a lot more of our habitual neurolinguistic-perceptual patterns than replacing "mankind" with "humankind," believe me. And with only a little practice you can handle it without going to such bizarre extremes as the certified saints of sanctified Politically Correctness who write "personhole cover" or "genitalroach."

Of course, the Radical (or male-bashing) Feminists (e.g., those of the Andrea Dworkin-Robin Morgan-Valerie Solanus school) will probably resist E-prime more than any other group. After all, with every sentences beginning "Men are..." removed, most Radical Feminist books will say virtually nothing at all, or nothing coherent—much like a Hitler speech with all sentences beginning "Jews are..." excised from it.

In E-prime all group stereotypes (anti-Jew, anti-male, anti-plumbers or whatever) become impossible, and one can only say, loosely, "I think I've observed that many plumbers do so-

89

and-so" or, more scientifically, "In this study, 45 per cent of the red-headed persons did so-and-so, 20 per cent did thus-and-such and 35 per cent behaved in various other ways."

In brief, if the Korzybski hypothesis[2] has any validity, a future social scientist reading *Mein Kampf,* without any knowledge of 20th Century history, could predict that Auchwitz would occur if that book became popular—just by counting the uses of the dogmatic "is" applied to a large and non-homogenous group of miscellaneous eccentric individuals (all the Jews in Europe, of whom Hitler could not have met and judged more than about 0.001%)

I leave it to the reader to decide if one could also predict the John W. Bobbitt case—the man who literally got his penis chopped off—from reading Andrea Dworkin and counting the uses of "is" in general and the Aristotelian "is" of identity in particular applied to another large and miscellaneous group (all the males currently on the planet, of whom Dworkin cannot have met and judged more than about 0.0000000001%).

Incidentally, I can't leave this subject without a comment on ETC., a magazine ostensibly devoted to extending the work of Korzybski (and Bourland, and others.) ETC. has never reviewed my *Quantum Psychology,* and when I attempted to learn why this black-out had occurred, a staff member told me, off the record, that the editor would never allow any review of any book of mine, because he bitterly resented my skepticism about CSICOP. Of course, I do not know if this report tells the whole truth or consist only of gossip and rumor. Nonetheless, I find it both curious and amusing that readers of ETC., a group with great interest in E-prime, do not yet know that a book about quantum physics and psychology written entirely in E-prime actually exists in this country and still remains in print.

▲   ▲   ▲

---

[2] Sometimes called the Korzybski-Whorf-Sapir hypothesis after the two researchers who suggested it at about the same time as Korzybski—linguist B.L. Whorf and anthropologist Edward Sapir.

Feedback

Letters From Our Readers

Mrs. Trajectories
Permanent Press
PO Box 700305
San Jose, CA 95170

Warning! Warning! If you're holding the winning number but are not going to return it on time MRS. TRAJECTORIES IS ABOUT TO LOSE TEN MILLION DOLLARS!

Dear **Mrs. Trajectories,**

One of two things is certain if one of the numbers that you're holding in your hands right now is the one preselected as the grand prize winner: **Mrs. Trajectories** will be the new $10 MILLION DOLLAR WINNER...or **Mrs. Trajectories** will be the new $10 MILLION DOLLAR LOSER the moment when I award the American Family's giant prize on national television.

I've been right there, center stage, when people have WON their MILLION DOLLAR prizes and I've been there when people have LOST their MILLION DOLLAR prizes.

You see, **Mrs. Trajectories**, what most folks don't know is that— for every MILLION DOLLAR WINNER we've had in the past, there has also been a MILLION DOLLAR LOSER.

Someone like you had received the winning number, but then failed to send it in. Maybe they were just too busy. Maybe they didn't believe they could win so big a prize. Maybe they were just too lazy to collect the ONE MILLION DOLLARS, or the TWO MILLION DOLLARS, or the TEN MILLION DOLLARS that could probably have changed their lifestyles. I'll never know what made each of these people throw away their millions. But I know that I'd be very sorry to see you make the same mistake, **Mrs. Trajectories.** And that's why I'm now urging you to return the enclosed Entry-Order Card today.

> *Ed McMahon*
> *American Family Publishers*

RAW Replies:
Has Johnny got you smoking those funny cigarettes again, Ed?

Dear Bob,

I thoroughly enjoy *Trajectories*, but I must correct a factual error which appeared in the Spring issue. In "The Last Temptation of Mohammed," you refer to "...the nine forbidden words" while discussing Pacifica Radio and its troubles with the FCC. May I humbly point out (since it was my record they played on the air precipitating the trouble in the first place) that there were only seven words involved in that case. They are: *shit, piss, fuck, cunt, cocksucker, motherfucker and tits.*

The original routine, "Seven Words You Can Never Say On Television," appeared on an album called "Class Clown" in 1973. My next album ("Occupation: Foole") included a sequel piece entitled simply "Filthy Words." It was this second routine (album cut), played on the air by a Pacifica station, WBAI, New York, which brought a Declaratory Order from the FCC forbidding the broadcast of such language "at times of day when there is a reasonable risk that children may be in the audience." Naturally, they did not specify which times of day these might be, nor did they in any way define "children."

Pacifica appealed the order to the District of Columbia Circuit Court of Appeals and won a reversal. The FCC then appealed to the U.S. Supreme Court and they were upheld, thus forever inscribing "shit, piss, fuck, cunt, cocksucker, motherfucker and tits" in the official, recorded, legal history of the United States of America. (Please, no applause.)

Additionally, toward the end of "Filthy Words" I noted that I had left three very obvious candidates off the original list: *fart, turd* and *twat*. I cannot imagine why the FCC and the Court neglected to outlaw such gross indecency, especially since "twat" is a precise synonym for "cunt."

Such logic! Such law!

Anyway, thanks for all the good stuff of yours I've read, watched and listened to in the past couple of years.

George Carlin
Los Angeles, CA

chAPTteR SiX

☛ The Global Energy Grid

☛ The Great Drug Debate

☛ Preview
   of Coming Attractions

☛ H.E.A.D. Research

☛ Gender and Terrorism
   The Demon Lover:
      On The Sexuality of Terrorism
      by Robin Morgan
   Reviewed by Arlen Wilson

☛ Conspiracy
   and Demonology Update

☛ 1994 Update

The Global Energy Grid:

I. Coming Soon?

The American Society of Mechanical Engineers will hold a conference on Buckminster Fuller's proposed Global Energy Grid in Anchorage, Alaska, early next year, and Peter Meisen, leading proponent of the Grid, has been invited by the Soviet Union to discuss the Grid at their January conference on "The New Relationship: Joint Projects for the Third Millennium."

The ASME conference in Anchorage will include Americans, Russians, Japanese and Europeans from both the areas of science and finance, and probably represents the greatest single step toward achieving the Global Energy Grid since Fuller first proposed the idea in 1969.

Alaska has been chosen for the meeting because experts agree that integrating the American/Canadian/Soviet electrical networks across the Bering Straits seems the most logical first step in constructing the World Grid.

The first inklings of the Grid came to Fuller in the 1920s, when he observed that electrical networks were growing larger at an accelerating rate. Calculating the growth factor, he predicted that networks of 1,500 miles would appear by 1960. (They actually appeared in 1961.) Fuller did not develop the idea further until after the 1,500-mile networks existed, but then he began envisioning a world electric network, and by 1969 had a practical proposal he felt ready to talk about. (Bucky had an almost religious aversion to proposing new technologies until he had all the details clear in his head and could demonstrate their working principles operationally—an inner discipline unknown to the critics who liked to dismiss him as "Utopian".)

Basically, Fuller's World Grid envisions the hook-up of all existing electrical networks into one synergetic system, as in the map on the next page.

95

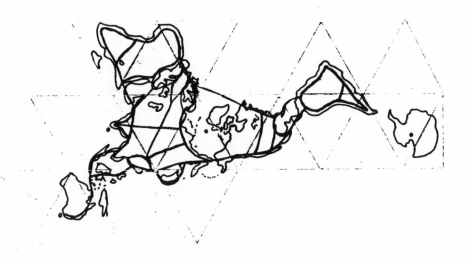

Dr. Fuller's Dymaxion Map with global energy grid system.
A dymaxion map has minimal land mass distortion
and displays the world not as a separate East-West world,
but as a connected North-South island.

In such a Grid, he realized, the normal peaks-and-valleys of electrical usage ("peaks" in the daylight hours when most people work; "valleys" at night) could average out to maximum cost-effectiveness for each member nation—a massive win/win situation. This would at least double the energy available to all humans, thereby fulfilling his principle that Design Science should "advantage all without disadvantaging any."

In other words, a world-wide electric grid would allow poor countries to sell electricity to rich countries during the night and buy electricity during the day. Or it would allow any area anywhere to sell electricity during any "valley" (period of low usage) to any other area that suddenly required more kilowatts than normal—any unexpected "peak." The sociological and ecological results that might result from this, as Fuller calculated them, seemed so promising that he announced, "The global grid is the World Game's highest priority objective."

In the 1970s, Canadian Prime Minister Pierre Trudeau expressed keen interest in Fuller's Grid, and the Soviet Academy, after investigation, pronounced the idea "feasible and desirable." Fuller devoted his last years chiefly to publicizing and popularizing the plan—an uphill battle in a world where many literary intellectuals oppose all technology, and the "cold war" made plans for global cooperation seem unlikely to succeed.

Peter Meisen, the organizer of GENI (Global Energy Network International) and the man who will explain the Grid at the Soviet "Joint Ventures" conference in January, has listed the following advantages which Fuller expected to result from the creation of the Grid:

1. Increasing everyone's standard of living
2. Reducing fossil fuel demand and its resultant pollution
3. Relieving the population explosion
4. Reducing world hunger
5. Enhancing world trade
6. Promoting international cooperation and peace

The claim that the Grid will raise everyone's standard of living rests on the fact that as electrical networks have grown larger, the average standard of living has improved measurably in those parts of the world having such networks. Also, Fuller and associates have shown that many chronic Third World problems could vanish quickly if cheap energy becomes available there, as will happen once the Grid exists.

The Grid will lower pollution levels for the following reasons:

a) We will need fewer new generating plants as areas buy energy from adjoining areas;

b) Non-polluting energy sources, such as solar collectors and windmills, can easily join the Grid

c) Some ecologically dangerous practices might cease—for example, the Brazilians might cut down less forest to pay their national debt if they can make more money selling electricity to other members of the Grid.

The Grid will lower world population, Fuller argued, because population has consistently shown the same pattern: it increases steadily in agricultural economies, and it stabilizes in industrial and post-industrial economies. (His book, *Critical Path*, contains graphs showing birthrate and kilowatt hours generated in various nations, illustrating his point: as energy increases, birthrate always drops.) It appears that under-developed countries overbreed because so many children die in infancy there. (Also, industrialism always brings an upsurge of Feminism, as documented in my GAIA articles in issues #4 and 5 of *Trajectories*; and Feminism always gives women a greater sense of multiple options.)

97

The Grid will reduce world hunger, Fuller argued, because of its effect on lowering population as discussed above and also because industrialized nations do not have the massive resource problems faced by agricultural nations.

The Grid will enhance world trade because it creates a model of non-zero-sum or win/win economics, in contrast to our traditional zero-sum win/lose models—models created in an age of scarcity and surviving in age of abundance only due to inertia, ignorance and greed.

(For further details on win/win economics, the reader should consult Fuller's books and also the works of Hazel Henderson and Barbara Marx Hubbard.)

Finally, the Grid will advance the cause of world peace by demonstrating, on a global scale, that we will all profit more by cooperation than we ever have from traditional imperialist conflict and its ever-more-destructive wars. With benefits reaped daily from the Global Grid it will not make sense for any nation to blow up the other end of "their" energy system.

As Peter Meisen summarizes, "Electricity is the problem and the solution." Lack of electricity creates endless struggle between "haves and have-nots"; adequacy of electricity will creates a world of abundance.

Actually, the Global Energy Grid seems inevitable to many who have studied Fuller's proposal. As noted, networks have steadily grown larger every decade, and 26 countries already share grids that cross national boundaries. With the coming unification of Europe in 1992, the thaw in the cold war, the increasing exchange of electricity and gas between Europe and Russia, and so on, the World Grid looks like a logical next step and not the "Utopian dream" some called it when Fuller first began promoting the idea 20 years ago.

II. GENI Update

Global Energy Network Scores in USSR;
Kuwait to Sponsor New Conference

In our last issue, we reported on the growing support for Buckminster Fuller's Global Energy Network, but the pace of events has accelerated even more since then:

° In the USSR, the presentation of Fuller's world-wide grid by GENI (Global Energy Network International) inspired warm support from the Energy Department of the USSR Academy of Sciences, and the Global Grid received nationwide exposure on Soviet TV, reaching over 100,000,000 viewers. (GENI representatives say this means more Russians have heard of the World Grid than any other people on Earth.)

The most pointed question asked by Soviet scientists: *Why has the Grid received more attention in the USSR than in the US?* GENI spokespeople replied that the potential linkages (and benefits) for the Soviets exist on all sides and seem obvious as soon as anyone mentions them—e.g., Soviet electrical networks can easily hook up and synergize with Eastern and Western Europe, the Mid-East and China. The US, on the other hand, has only two immediate neighbors (Canada and Mexico) and still thinks of itself as isolated by two oceans. The advantages to the Grid to the US may only appear obvious when one looks at the linkages on a Fuller Dymaxion map, instead of a Mercator map. Then the proposed Grid seems intuitively obvious.

° The Global Energy Network has also received major coverage on TV in Greece and Zimbabwe.

° East and West Germany have already agreed to connect their electrical grids.

° The GENI team have an invitation to return to Moscow for further discussions and planning.

° The Kuwait Institute for Scientific Research has offered to host a conference on a proposed Mid-East grid, probably covering Turkey, Syria, Jordan, Iraq, Egypt and Libya.

° The Department of Energy in Washington has at last shown interest, saying "further analysis" and "full consideration" will be given to the Fuller grid.

GENI, meanwhile, plans a conference on a Central American grid, as a first step toward a North-and-South American grid, saying, "What seemed politically impossible just a few months ago can now be discussed in earnest."

When all the pieces of the global energy network come into linkage, according to Fuller, we will obtain a worldwide increase in *everyone's* standard of living, a model of the kind of technology that "advantages all without disadvantaging any," a reduction of fossil fuel usage and its associated pollution, and a reduction in world population and starvation. For evidence to support these claims see Fuller's *Critical Path* (St. Martin's Press.)

(For additional information, including a short video presentation of the GENI proposal, write GENI, P.O. Box 24455, San Diego, CA 92124; and/or GENI Alaska, P.O. Box 100296, Anchorage, AL 99510)

"There is no Energy Shortage.

There is no Energy Crisis.

There is a Crisis of Ignorance."

— R. Buckminster Fuller

▲　　　　▲　　　　▲

The Great Drug Debate

As the 1980s end, we have seen a sudden increase in distinguished persons urging an end to "Drug Prohibition," declaring it has failed as totally as Alcohol Prohibition did 1919-1933. Among the voices urging legalization or decriminalization:

• Conservative columnist and TV star William F. Buckley Jr.

• Nobel laureate economist and free-market theorist Dr. Milton Friedman

• Former federal prosecutor Kurt Schmoke (now mayor of Baltimore)

• Former Secretary of State George P. Shultz

• Former NY police commissioner Patrick Murphy

• Astronomer Dr. Carl Sagan

• Professor Gene Stephens of the College of Criminal Justice, University of Southern Carolina.

Peter Reuter of RAND Corporation says, "There is an enormous closet elite interest in legalization. I address a lot of groups of the educated elite around the country...and this is the central question they want to discuss."

Meanwhile, at the opposite pole from Reuter's "educated elite," columnist Ann Landers, has asked her readers for their ideas on how to handle the drug problem, and recently devoted two full columns to their answers. As you might expect, one of Ms. Landers' readers urged the death penalty for all (illegal) drug merchants; two more vaguely urged "tougher" laws, but without explicitly mentioning the death penalty; two urged better education; one suggested that the President should make the "problem" our number one priority; one offered no solution, but bitterly claimed drug abuse results from child beating and the other violence endemic in our "sick society"; one explained that "we have strayed from God's ways" and should "pay attention to the Scriptures;" but even in this audience, two readers urged an end to Prohibition. Two out of ten is 20 percent...

It certainly appears that decriminalization, an idea that seemed to have died with the '60s, has now made a return into the arena of respectable debate. Naturally, Bush administration officials have hit back against this upsurge of Heresy. White House Press Secretary Marlin Fitzwater declared that Shultz, who served in both the Reagan and Nixon administration, "has been out on the West Coast too long" and is "starting to say strange things." Drug Czar William Bennett has offered a equally philosophical rebuttal, calling the dissenters "intellectuals... with an ignorant sneer." (Wouldn't you love to have a group photo of Buckley, Dr. Freidman, Dr. Sagan, Secretary Schultz, Commissioner Murphy *et.al.,* all standing around with ignorant sneers?)

The day after Bennett's blast, U.S. District Judge Robert W. Sweet joined the voices calling for an end to Prohibition, saying drugs make up an industry worth $150 billion per year and should be taxed and regulated. The press did not note whether or not Judge Sweet had an ignorant sneer at the time.

A few days later, attorney William Kunstler also called for decriminalization, saying 23 million Americans use illegal stimulant drugs (crack, speed, etc.) and we don't have enough police to handle such a problem. Professor Ronald Siegal of UCLA Medical School has estimated the number of marijuana users at 44 million, so the total of illegal drug users, adding our 2 million junkies to the 44 million pot-heads and the 23 million stimulant freaks, seems at least 79 million. (Most experts regard all these figures as low, since obtaining accurate statistics on clandestine behavior seems impossible.) And, of course, this "guesstimate" does not include all those Straight Citizens strung out on legal drugs such as alcohol, nicotine, caffeine, tranks, etc.

Without mentioning legalization specifically, Dr. Stanley Korenaman of UCLA Medical School recently published an article pointing out the failure of the police state apparatus we have developed and argued that addictive drugs should be approached scientifically. Noting that three already-known drugs—carbamezepine, desipremine and buprenorephine—seem to block some kinds of addictive behavior, Dr. Korenaman suggests a search for chemical antagonists to each of the major addictive type drugs, which would (he argues) cost much less than the ever-growing budget of the "War on Drugs." Once such vaccines against addiction become available, he says, doctors will quickly cure drug-dependencies and their side effects— which no laws, however Draconic, have yet significantly altered.

I find no record of whether or not Dr. Korenaman had an ignorant sneer when he wrote that.

Prof. Ronald K. Siegel (previously mentioned), also of UCLA Medical School, takes yet another approach in his recent book, *Intoxication: Life in Pursuit of Artificial Paradise.* Siegel, a long-time consultant to the Drug Enforcement Administration, documents with encyclopedic and sometimes hilarious thoroughness that all animals seem to get intoxicated, doped, stoned, inebriated or generally zonked as often as they can, both in the wild and under laboratory conditions. His book, which we highly recommend, has hundreds of amusing, tragic and instructive stories about drunken elephants, opium addicted insects, hallucinating cats, cattle poisoning themselves with compulsive tobacco eating, etc. and seems to demonstrate well his dual hypotheses that all living creatures have four basic drives: hunger, thirst, sex and the need to get high periodically; and that the last drive can easily turn into addiction if the animal happens upon an addicting drug or plant.

Siegel seems to have a certain closet sympathy for decriminalization, but says that our society does not appear ready to consider that alternative. He suggests a scientific search for "safe highs"—drugs that provide the periodic "lift" all animals seek but have no addictive or unhealthy side effects. (He does not examine the claim that a few such drugs already exist and have been mistakenly included in the list of substances forbidden by our government. One feels at a loss in trying to guess if Dr. Siegel never heard that claim or just doesn't think it prudent to discuss such Heresy.)

The best and most succinct argument for decriminalization we have seen appears as a two-page broadside by Marshall Fritz, a Christian Libertarian. The first page, addressed only to Christians, gives Biblical reasons for nonviolent, noncoercive approaches to deviant behavior; but the second page gives 19 pragmatic arguments, addressed to believers and nonbelievers alike.

Fritz's 19 points:

1. People would be safer under decriminalization; addicts would commit few or no crimes when a Free Market brings the price of drugs way down from its present inflated Black Market level.

2. Prison crowding would be relieved.

3. Police would have more time to deal with violent crimes.

4. Decriminalization would unclog the court system.

5. It would reduce corruption of police and others in the justice system.

6. It would save tax money.

7. It would cripple organized crime.

8. Users would be safer from contaminated drugs and needles.

9. This would slow down the spread of AIDS.

10. Decriminalization would partially reverse the erosion of Constitutional liberties, which have suffered much from our "War on Drugs."

11. Some foreign countries would be safer to visit.

12. Decriminalization would repair relations between the U.S. and some other countries.

13. Jobs in the inner city would increase as businesses were less afraid to locate there.

14. Downtown areas would be revitalized as businesses moved in and shoppers felt safe.

15. Inner city youths would not see drug dealers as role models of quick success.

16. Female addicts would not need to resort to prostitution to support the high price of illegal drugs.

17. Decriminalization would decrease elitist and racist attitudes of white suburbanites. (Racist attitudes often determine which drugs we make legal and illegal.)

18. It would reduce the incentive for addicts to sell to children.

19. Decriminalization would raise the national living standard by stimulating productive activity now diverted to spying, entrapment, punishment, etc.

(***Sources:*** Los Angeles *Times* Nov. 20, 1989; Santa Monica *Outlook* 14 December 1989; LA *Times* 15 December 1989, *Christian Science Monitor* 15 December 1989.; LA *Times*, December 18-19, 1989; LA *Times* 7 Sept. 1989; Ronald Siegel, Ph.D., *Intoxication* (E.P. Dutton, New York, 1989); Marshall Fritz, Advocates of Self Government, PO Box 5039, Fresno, CA 93755)

H.E.A.D. Research

Three scientific studies of the brain machines recently discussed in *Trajectories* have come to our attention. As we go to press, we have details on only one of these studies, but we will be printing news of the other two in our next issue. All three studies, however, tend to support the "entrainment" effect of the new technology.

At Temple University's Stress and Research Biofeedback Laboratory, 17 persons with drug abuse problems received two sessions with tapes manufactured by Acoustic Brain Research (Durham, NC). Although these tapes, designed to remove drug cravings, should be used daily according to ARB's protocol, the 17 subjects showed clear improvement after only two sessions. The improvement occurred in the areas of drug usage (decrease) and sense of self-control (increase); Temple researchers did not attempt to measure self-esteem, which ARB also claims will improve with use of their tapes.

A randomized pre-post Control Group design allowed accurate measurements of differences before and after the tapes, and between those who received the tape therapy and the Control Group which did not. ARB tapes employ frequencies that entrain the brain to alpha and theta rhythms, together with verbal material employing Ericksonian and NLP positive suggestions, based on the work of Dr. Ernest Lawrence Rossi.

(Note: For further discussion of Dr. Rossi's work, see the review of his book in Chapter One; for more on the H.E.A.D. revolution, see "H.E.A.D. Hardware" in Chapter 8. Or perhaps you would rather be kept in the dark! —Ed.)

▲　　　　　▲　　　　　▲

Preview of Coming Attractions

In December, 1988, the World Future Society released its annual list of "Top 10 Forecasts"—the ten most plausible scenarios published during 1989. Their choices:

1. Cash will soon become illegal for all but very small transactions. Whatever you do involving more than $10 in value will leave a paper trail for government snoopers.

2. "Electronic immigrants"—people who live in one country but work in another, via computer—will become commonplace.

3. Within 50 years, robots with human intelligence, or higher than human intelligence, will be in wide use.

4. Prisons will be phased out as government resorts to chemical and electronic implants to monitor and control "criminal" behavior.

(Will this include political "crime" and Thoughtcrime? O brave new world that has such implants in it...!)

5. Future furniture will get "smarter" and communicate with householders.

6. Many U.S. citizens will migrate to northern Canada as the Greenhouse effect creates favorable working conditions there.

7. Replacing defective genes with healthy substitutes will be common by 2010.

8. "Smart" cars with built-in computers will do all the driving (as in the old science-fiction joke about the airplane of the future, which has a pilot and a dog: the pilot is there to feed the dog, and the dog is there to bite the pilot if he or she touches anything.)

9. Two-generation geriatric families will increase in the 1990s; that is, 60-to-70-year old "children" caring for parents in their 90s.

10. Genetically engineered gardens will have plants that can be programmed to change colors, or even to change species.

(**Source:** *The Futurist,* December, 1989)

▲   ▲   ▲

Robert Anton Wilson

Gender and Terrorism

The Demon Lover:
On The Sexuality of Terrorism
by Robin Morgan
(Norton, 1989)

Reviewed by Arlen Wilson

With its provocative title and its cover design of utterly helpless, abandoned, and sexually-inviting fillet of female, complete with demon crouching on her midsection, this book will be picked up by many a curious male. Most of them will probably be turned off somewhere along the way and not finish it. This is unfortunate, since the effect is cumulative and the most important parts are toward the close.

Robin Morgan's evolution from a 60s violent revolutionary (albeit married and pregnant) to a post-leftist divorced militant feminist, to a lesbian post-revolutionary anti-militarist feminist is a colorful saga of our times. (Sorry, but these somewhat pompous labelings are unavoidable in considering her chronicle.)

For anyone interested in a counter-cultural recap of the past twenty-five years from a unique and intensely involved personal perspective, the book is worth reading in full. However, be warned: it's an arduous, painful and often repellent trip. You will learn more than you want to know — or perhaps even need to know — about men's increasingly documented inhumanity to women on a global scale. The terrorist's cynical use of "his" women (the theme suggested by the title) is only an extreme case. Even the "up" parts of the book, the "post-tragic" vistas toward the "Beyond Terrorism" section at the end, may seem rather eerie. Besides noting her impressive (and sometimes defective) scholarship, one needs to remember that along with the list of descriptive labels given above, Morgan is also a formidable poet. As such, she may be what Shelley called one of the "unacknowledged legislators" of the future, and on that score deserves a portion of our attention, however ambivalent, and at times horrified, the quality of such attention might be.

Waftings of rumor about Robin Morgan's recent evolutionary thinking had reached my ears from other women, and I looked forward to this book as perhaps a transcendence of the "Us versus Them" divide. (I like the subversive Partnership Model of co-evolution myself.) But "Us vs. Them" it is for Morgan, and more ferociously so now than ever, though she does admit there are some differences among men when it comes to violence toward the helpless. To me this latter truth deserves a hell of a lot more then a cursory nod—something more on the order of a few billion dollars for research, development, and encouragement. Health is ultimately even more fascinating and mysterious than disease. However, my friends, *The Demon Lover* is a vast overview of disease for your delectation—if you have the stomach for it.

▲   ▲   ▲

Robert Anton Wilson

Conspiracy and Demonology Update

Robin Morgan's *The Demon Lover* presents the latest in Radical Feminist theory. While I have learned a great deal from Feminist writings (and from living with a Feminist for a long time), I must admit "Radical" Feminism scares the blue Jesus out of me. I do not claim to understand it in any rational sense, and I especially stipulate that I do not understand Morgan's demonology, since she—a poet and a political activist—writes in a style that mingles fiery poetry and even more fiery polemic.

Such poetic/emotive prose seldom descends to the level of philosophical logic or ordinary discursive speech, and cannot be grasped by the critical mind. I do not believe one should even seek rational or analytical meanings in either poetry or Ideology, since the former transcends reason and the latter ignores reason, but I think Morgan does communicate something of importance, and I wish I had some faith in my ability to comprehend it.

Despite these semantic reservations, I think I grasp some kind of thesis in *The Demon Lover*. The thesis seems to hold that Terrorism results from a defect in the male brain. (Female terrorists have all been misled by males, she claims.) "Men" "are" violent, or contain "violence demons" in the medieval sense, or "violence genes" in the sociobiological sense, or something of that sort. I have tried and tried to find clarity, but I still find myself unable to decide if, in Morgan's semantics, "men" intends to signify "all men" (Aristotelian meaning) or "most men" or "some men" (statistical or scientific meaning).

Ezra Pound, by comparison, remained a model of clarity even in his most frenzied moments: his rage aimed itself at "some Jews," not at "all Jews," and he always made that clear. (He tried to make it even clearer by mentioning his favorite villains by name, but the libel laws and his publisher's lawyers prevented that.) Hitler, in contrast, said and meant "all Jews" in his polemics. Whatever one thinks of the rants of these two, one knows what they mean. Pound hated some Jews; Hitler hated all Jews. I cannot decide if Morgan hates all men, most men, or just some men.

Since reading Morgan makes me feel like a Jew reading Pound or Hitler, and since I dislike all Ideologies based on hate, I leave further comment in the competent hands of my esteemed

109

co-editor, who informs me that I missed a sentence in which Morgan did indicate that she meant "most men." I pass on to a work that lacks the poetic spirit of *The Demon Lover,* but at least makes up for that in specificity and clarity, *Inside the "Men's Club": Secrets of the Patriarchy,* by Hawthorne Abendsen (A-Albionic Consulting and Research, Ferndale, MI; 1989.)

Mr. Abendsen believes that "men's clubs"—the all-male secret societies found in most primitive tribes—underwent a radical change at the beginning of the Bronze Age, when war, slavery and the subjugation of women began. These "clubs" have dominated history ever since, he claims. The most powerful of these secret societies have gradually amalgamated into one international lodge which, he says, now rules the world: the Priory of Sion (which, despite its name, includes both Jews and gentiles). Other all-male secret societies appear, if I understand Mr. Abendsen correctly, as either fronts for the Priory of Sion, or as recruiting grounds, or as small bands of bungling amateurs trying to compete with the Priory.

Mr. Abendsen claims to know the inner secrets of the Priory of Sion—not as an ex-member (as in many anti-Masonic polemics), but as a student of history who has logically deduced what these inner secrets "must be." These inner secrets, according to Abendsen, consist of two fundamental points:

1. The earliest god in the Old Testament—El Shaddai, the god of war—remains the true Judeo-Christian god to the initiates of the Priory. Later, softer pictures of divinity (e.g., the "god of love") serve only as myths to deceive the rest of us: those who have not been admitted to the Priory of Sion. Service to the god of war consists in making war (of course) and also in the bloody rituals which Fundamentalists currently blame on a "Satanic conspiracy." The conspiracy does not worship Satan, according to Mr. Abendsen: it worships the primordial Old Testament god who demands animal sacrifices regularly, human sacrifices occasionally, and total war on all who do not belong to his cult and worship him.

2. The inner rituals of the Priory of Sion involve homosexual acts, as charged in polemics against Masonry and the Knights Templar.

In other words, Abendsen's thesis holds that our world has been governed for 3000 years by a group of homosexual (or bisexual) Jehovah-worshippers who kill animals in ritual, regard war as a sacred duty, and hide these secrets from the rest of the men in the world, and from all the women.

Damn! I suggested something of this sort in *Illuminatus!,* but I thought I was writing satire. Mr. Abendsen appears totally serious.

A-Albionic Consulting and Research, the publisher of *Inside the Men's Club,* does not endorse Abendsen's theory. Rather unique among Conspiracy Researchers, A-Albionic publishes a variety of literature presenting a variety of "models" of how ruling elites operate—and, yes, they actually use the scientific metaphor "models," and do not insist that any one model explains everything. Curiously, they have even changed their own favorite model recently.

Until this autumn, A-Albionic's newsletter, *The Project,* had a masthead proclaiming "The British Empire is the Central Phenomenon of World History Since the Decline of the Vatican," and their editorial comments stressed the model which holds that the British ruling class gained control of the world in the Elizabethan age and has held control, behind the scenes, even as British power has seemingly declined. Now, in their Summer-Fall-Winter issue 1989-90, the masthead reads "The Overt and Covert Organs of the Vatican and British Empire are Locked in Mortal Combat for Control of the World," and an editorial explains that the Vatican, in alliance with various fascist groups, now has regained enough power to struggle effectively against the British overlords.

Actually, the A-Albionic models have been somewhat oversimplified above (as in their own mastheads). The "British" conspiracy they more fully describe as "Comsymp-International Banker-Judeo-Masonic-British Labour Party-British Intelligence -Socialist International-Social Democrat-Fabian-AFL/CIO/ UAW-KGB," and the "Vatican" conspiracy as "post-WWII Pope Pius-Vatican-CIA-Fascist International-Georgetown Jesuits-McCarthyite-Buckleyite-Knights of Malta." But they leave no doubt that the British nobility controls the first alliance (or "affinity group") and the Pope controls the second.

Both versions of the A-Albionic model, you will note, reduce the US and the USSR, allegedly the super-powers battling to control the world, to a much less impressive role either as dupes of the British (first model) or as tools in the British vs. Vatican war (second model).

I cannot resist giving you a sample of A-Albionic analysis: "Already we see the heavy hand of Catholic thinking eroding legal protections for the individual under the color of 'war on drugs,' limiting abortion, scapegoating occultists and Jews, promoting cultural conservatism and Fundamentalism, etc. The

111

suspicion must be revived that AIDS and the resultant homophobia have served the Church's new counter-reformation well."

Double damn! On my lecture tours, I frequently get asked about the theory that the CIA created AIDS. I always answer that I have seen no good evidence to support that, and that if I were to suspect anyone, I would suspect the Vatican, since the AIDS terror has most of us acting like Catholics. But once again, I thought I spoke satirically.

Incidentally, I recently had some correspondence with A-Albionic. I told them frankly that some of their literature sounds paranoid to me. They replied with a courteous letter, suggesting a most sophisticated new model, proposing that what appear as conspiracies might better fit the category of Sheldrake's morphogenetic fields. I'm still trying to get a handle on that idea.

But returning to the Priory of Sion: this appears to exist (in some sense) and consists largely of French aristocrats, with some associated Swiss bankers, and has been the subject of many conspiracy theories quite different from that of Mr. Abendsen. For instance, according to Gerard de Sede's *La race fabuleuse,* the Priory's inner circle consists of men descended from intermarriage between ancient Israelites and extra-terrestrials from Sirius, while according to Baignet, Lincoln and Leigh's *Holy Blood, Holy Grail,* the Priory serves as a knightly defensive order protecting the descendants of Jesus Christ and Mary Magdelene (who had a son who emigrated to France). Swiss journalist Matthieu Paoli, in *Undercurrents,* more prosaically claims the Priory of Sion merely wishes to restore monarchy in France. He does indicate that the Priory heavily infiltrated the de Gaulle government, but does not claim it controls the world.

On the other hand, Michael Lamy's *Jules Verne: Initiate et Initiateur,* claims the Priory serves as a front for the infamous Illuminati of Bavaria and has an alliance with immortal superhuman beings who live inside the (hollow) Earth. (Jules Verne, Lamy argues, knew about this and hinted at it in several of his novels.) More mysterious, *The Cult of the Black Virgin,* by Eon Begg, a Jungian analyst and former Dominican monk, claims the Priory erected the mysterious statues found in many European churches in which the mother of Christ appears black or Negroid; after that promising (and puzzling) beginning, Begg wanders off into esoteric hints about Mary Magdeline and the Egyptian goddess Isis, links between the Priory and the Sufi mystics of Islam, the symbolism of alchemy and the Tarot, etc., and leaves the reader guessing about What It All Means. More explicit and much more incredible, *Genisis* (a deliberate pun, invoking Isis), by David Wood, traces the Priory back to Atlantis and claims Satan—an extraterrestrial, not an angel—created humanity as a genetic experiment. He also asserts that members of the Priory amputate their penises, as a sacrifice to Isis, which clearly contradicts Abendsen's lurid vision of homosexual orgies in the Priory's lodges. (Or can men have orgies without penises? I don't know everything about sexual oddities...)

Baigent, Lincoln and Leigh, incidentally, charge that de Sede himself belongs to the Priory and that his books deliberately intend to deceive outsiders. That made me wonder in turn about Baigent, Lincoln and Leigh—and all the other authors of Priory exposés...

My co-editor, Arlen, on learning that Jean Cocteau once served as Grandmaster of the Priory of Sion, offered yet another theory: the Priory started as the last and greatest surrealist joke, and intends to puzzle and provoke the curious until we all learn to think outside the categories of our conditioned definitions of reality and poetry. I like that.

Fundamentalist Christians, meanwhile, continue to circulate numerous books and pamphlets attributing the violence of the world to the well-known, if ill-documented, Satanic Conspiracy. They have even persuaded many police chiefs to credit this theory and most American occultists have developed an acute suspicion that they are under police surveillance as possible Satanists.

In conclusion, sociologists agree that most violence, everywhere, has been perpetrated by one group of males: certain individuals between 18 and 25 years of age, making up about one-half of one percent (0.5%) of the total male population. Nobody has ever produced convincing scientific-type evidence that these goons all belong to any secret society or have anything in common except a statistical tendency toward the psychological profile called Hostile Weakness by Dr. Timothy Leary or "I'm Not Okay, You're Not Okay" by Dr. Eric Berne. And—*pace,* Robin Morgan—the other 99 percent of all males remain mostly nonviolent all their lives (except at football games).

And most secret societies (I have investigated quite a few) have no secrets beyond a few techniques to alter consciousness, none of them quite as effective as the psychedelic drugs used by the earliest Stone Age "men's clubs."

1994 Update

In retrospect, I wonder if Mr. Abendsen consciously intended his melodramatic little booklet as a parody of the Radical Feminist brand of "historical revisionism" (or Feminist demonology, as some skeptics call it)...?

A-Albionic, on the other hand, seems to me definitely serious about their *two mega-conspiracies* model of "modern" (post-1600) history. They appear to sincerely believe that virtually nothing has happened from the time of Elizabeth I to that of Elizabeth II that didn't result, at least in part, from the titanic struggle between the English crown (and its dupes) and the Vatican (and its dupes.) I have exchanged subscriptions with them for four years, and I think I know enough about satire to recognize it after that long, if it exists. They do not intend their work as satire.

Since I first became famous (or infamous) for a novel parodying conspiracy theories, some simple souls, or Aristotelians, think I reject all such notions. Other simple souls, including one gent from CSICOP, think I believe all and every conspiracy theory. As usual, I do not see things in such Simple Simon either/or terms.

Conspiracy theory, whether in the most rudimentary forms (such as the Nazi "the Jews did it" panchreston or the Dworkinoid "the males did it" bromide) or disguised in the more sophisticated and complex sociological abstractions (e.g., the Marxist "the capitalists did it, but Iron Laws of History compelled them to do it") always seems over-simplified to me; but the notion that conspiracies do not exist seems to me equally unconvincing. We have laws against conspiracy, in every nation I know anything about, because conspiracies do occur, not occasionally but continually. As Prof. Carl Oglesby of the University of Boston once said, "Conspiracy is the normal continuation of normal politics by normal means."

I think we can best comprehend conspiracy by analogy with the atheist, polytheist and monotheist models in cosmology. In this metaphor, orthodox historians and the corporate media take an "atheist" position—everything in history happened by accident. In the classic, or paranoid, conspiracy theories, a "monotheist" model—or a monoSatanic model, more precisely—prevails: everything results from one dominant but malign Intelligence, which does not intend any good for you or me or any ordinary folks.

I reject both the "atheist" and "monotheist" models because I do not see either the utter chaos that the first implies or the sense of order and predictability that the second suggests. I see periods of order followed by chaotic change followed by new, higher degrees of order. This suggests the work of a committee, as H.L. Mencken argued a long time ago, in choosing polytheism over both atheism and monotheism.

Bringing the metaphor back to history and politics, I see evidence of conspiracies, plural, but no evidence of one "controlling" conspiracy, or even of a "war" between *only* two conspiracies. I see evidence of many "committees" in Mencken's sense, all of them plotting against each other, and all of them at times at war within themselves.

Curiously, when I explained this multi-conspiracy model to Dr. Timothy Leary, about twenty years ago, he said, "Yes, yes—I recognized 24 'gangs' fighting over the turf when I taught at Harvard. Later I recognized the same 24 gangs at war in Folsom prison. The ones at Harvard spoke better English, of course."

I don't know if Leary had actually counted 24 or just grabbed a number from the air, but, oddly, the same number came up several years later in a conversation during a seminar I taught at Esalen. A man who had served as DA. in a small California coastal city said he had observed that at least 24 cliques battle over control of any city, and most of them eventually descend to the kinds of deception and fraud covered by the criminal conspiracy laws.

The literary world, similarly, operates entirely on the basis of "affinity groups," and everybody not admitted to the inner sanctum of the dominant affinity group regards it, with some justice, as a god-damned conspiracy. I believe the same applies to the art world, the theater, films...

If you try to find out who owns the land in the city or town where you live, you will come upon evidence of clandestine economics (conspiracy) very quickly. In most cases, you cannot trace large areas further than anonymous syndicates, which might conceal the Mafia, the Arabs or the Martians for all you will ever know for sure. If the city announces a new highway, which will increase the value of some land and decrease the value of other land, conspiratorial behavior flourishes to the extent that indictments for bribery often appear by the end of the battle.

Conspiracy plays a major role in von Neumann and Morgenstern's epochal *Theory of Games and Economic Behavior*—one of the most important mathematical treatises on economics ever written. Von Neumann and Morgenstern simply do not use the word "conspiracy," since this *awful word* makes you sound like a nut in academic circles; but they discuss, at great length, the two major principles of successful competition—collecting accurate information for your coalition, and feeding inaccurate information ("disinformation") to the competing coalitions. The former practice does not differ much from spying, and the latter differs even less from deception; and spying and deception virtually define the parameters of conspiracy as a human survival tool.

So, then: I assume that, to quote Prof. Oglesby again, "a multitude of conspiracies contend in the night." I also think that, jointly and severally, each acts as a check on the others, which prevents any one of them from becoming as all-powerful as the more ardent conspiracy buffs imagine. (However, at some specific times, one single conspiracy may control a city, or a nation, or several nations, for a while...but only until the competition sharpens up and gets on the ball again...).

But I also think conspiracy buffs sound like real "conspiracy nuts" so much of the time because they remain wedded to the Aristotelian logic of the medieval monks, a bad habit they share with most Ideologists. In other words, they too often argue as if their speculations, or guesses, rank as *hard proof* in some sense—and anybody who remains dubious about their latest dogma gets classified as a "dupe" of their favorite conspiracy, or an "agent" consciously working to confuse sincere researchers.

I recognize several types of *hard proof*, in different areas. A "hard proof" in mathematics remains almost "eternal," or as close to "eternal" as the reasoning mind itself, simply because pure math refers to nothing but the symbolism (game rules) it has itself created. (As Einstein said in this connection, "As far as the laws of mathematics refer to reality, they are not certain; and as far as they are certain, they do not refer to reality.")

A "hard proof" in the physical sciences, on the other hand, always has about it as element of relativity and uncertainty. Most physicists today, for instance, do not talk about "true" theories at all, but only about "the theory that seems best at this date." Some insist on avoiding the word "theory" entirely because of its associations with the medieval ideas of "a true theory" and "a false theory." They speak of *models,* which reminds you that any human map has a limited application for a limited time. The most popular philosophy in the hard sciences, indeed, has the name "model agnosticism" and parallels directly the guerrilla ontology in my books or the work

116

of the French Deconstructionists. But to establish that one model works best *at this time* requires more hard work than most conspiracy buffs can imagine...

A "hard proof" in law has even less certitude. Many men have later proven innocent after juries condemned them to death. I, therefore, cannot believe in the "infallibility" of twelve citizens picked at random (a doctrine which sounds, except to the most ardent fans of capital punishment, as medieval as the alleged "infallibility of the pope.")

Conspiracy theory, as practiced by radicals of both Left and Right, falls far short of any of these standards of "hard proof," even the very loose legal standard. The judicious will regard it all, like theology, as an entertaining and sometimes exciting field of speculation, or whimsy—at least until the specific charges against some person or group actually result in indictments and trials. And even after a trial, for the reasons just mentioned, I personally retain some lingering doubts. The guilt of Sacco and Vanzetti, or Alger Hiss, or even that raving nut and publicity hound Albert de Salvo remain somewhat less that 100 per cent sure in my mind...

After all, the newspaper convention, whereby they describe a person as "the alleged felon" during the trial and then as "the guilty person," in the cases where the jury votes for guilt, remains *only a convention.* A great many innocent people have perished just because the DA had better oratory than the defense counsel... The guilt of any person remains, to some tiny (or not so tiny) degree, uncertain even on the day they march into the execution chamber, a fact which did not escape the logical mind of Thomas Jefferson and motivated his passionate opposition to capital punishment.

In short, I enjoy the study of conspiracy theory, because most people fear to touch it with the proverbial ten-foot pole and because it shows the eccentricities of the human mind in bold highlights, but I refuse to take any of it as seriously as its True Believers do.

▲   ▲   ▲

**FOR
SECURITY PURPOSES,
THIS PAGE
INTENTIONALLY
LEFT BLANK**

ChApTeR SEVEN

The War On Drugs

"Your body belongs to your country"
—*First of the Ten Commandments of the Hitler Youth*

As the War on Drugs increasingly replaces the Cold War as Washington's major "crusade," the consequences grow more dreadful to civil libertarians. In recent news reports we find:

Clogging The Courts

Many delegates at the February meeting of the American Bar Association believe that drug cases have placed a crushing burden on the Federal Courts, which the system simply cannot bear. Pointing out that drug cases now account for 44 per cent of all criminal trials and 50 per cent of criminal appeals, many lawyers say that this has increased the delay time in getting civil cases before the bar; ABA president Stanley Chauvin estimates that it now takes 3 to 5 years to bring a civil case to trial, and the delays will steadily increase as more drug cases clog the system.

A 15-member ABA panel concluded that "rapid expansion of the federal criminal caseload due to drug prosecutions threatens to overwhelm the federal courts" and recommended turning more drug cases over the State judiciaries. (*Christian Science Monitor*, 2/13/90)

Meanwhile, one State judge has indicated that the States cannot handle this additional burden. California Chief Justice Malcolm M. Lucas in a State of the Judiciary address— he first time the state legislature has asked for such as assessment— announced that the California courts have been overwhelmed by the upsurge in drug prosecutions. Saying drug cases have doubled in five years, Mr. Justice Lucas bluntly stated, "Drug-related cases are swamping the courts. The system has begun to take on so much water we are close to foundering. Too often, civil cases get drowned."

Lucas pointed out that criminal cases receive priority in the courts and that the increasing delays in hearing civil cases has long postponed "significant and complex cases that affect the environment, civil rights and other important aspects of our lives." (*Los Angeles Times*, 2/13/90.)

The Bush Administration, unmoved, continues to escalate the War.

121

Gutting The Fourth Amendment

Under the heading "Tough measures put Fourth Amendment rights in jeopardy," the conservative *Christian Science Monitor* (2/2/90) quotes several legal scholars who claim the "War on Drugs" has established precedents which seriously erode the Fourth Amendment. Examining cases in which people have lost property *without being convicted of any crime,* the *Monitor* seems sympathetic to law professor Samuel Walker who says this practice "violates the whole notion of due process" and Gene Guerrero of the ACLU who "wonders what Patrick Henry would have said if ordered to provide a urine sample."

One of the cases cited by the newspaper concerns Kevin Hogan, an Alaskan fishing skipper whose $140,000 boat got seized by the feds when a crewman was found to have 1.7 grams of Weed in his jacket. Hogan, who claims to have lost $30,000 by not having his boat during the halibut season, says, "I haven't been charged with anything and they've seized my boat. I don't think this could even happen in the Soviet Union."

The Bush Administration, still unmoved, continues to escalate the War.

Trashing The First Amendment

The latest casualty in the Bush War now appears to be the First Amendment protection of religious liberty. Ruling that members of the Native American Church—a group that lived here long before any white people—can legally be prosecuted for practicing their religion, the Supreme Court, in a 6-3 decision, has proclaimed that no religion has any Constitutional freedom if State governments enact a law against it. Writing for the majority, Justice Scalia said, "we cannot afford the luxury" of voiding laws just because they contradict the First Amendment. (This reverses over 100 years of Supreme Court rulings holding that the Fourteenth Amendment prevents State legislatures from the same invasions of individual liberty that the First Amendment forbade to Congress.)

The justification for the Scalia Doctrine: the NAC uses a psychoactive cactus, peyote, in their rites. Since the Roman Catholic Eucharist also claims to have psychoactive effects, an anti-Catholic government could use this precedent against them in the future, although that does not appear likely. As Justice Scalia bluntly stated in his opinion, this new ruling will most likely serve as a weapon against "those religious practices that are not widely engaged in."

Mr. Justice Brennan naturally dissented, as did Marshall and Blackmun. O'Conner concurred with the majority, but wrote a separate opinion dissenting from Scalia's wide-ranging renunciation of First Amendment rights, declaring the First Amendment "was enacted precisely to protect those whose religious practices are not shared by the majority."

Rev. Pat Robertson continues to agitate, on TV, for some kind of Crusade or Holy War against Buddhists and Hindus. The Court has perhaps given him and his followers the legal mandate they need to get the witch-trials on the road...

(Source: L.A. *Times,* 17 April 1990*)*

Taking Hostages

Following the war on Panama and the kidnapping of Manuel Noriega, the Supreme Court ruled, in February, that a similar kidnapping of a Mexican, Dr. Humberto Alvarez Machain, by DEA agents, does not violate the Fourth Amendment's "due process" clause. Civil libertarians see in this ruling an implication that the U.S. can violate its own laws any time it wishes, when dealing with foreigners. An angry Mexican writer, Luis F. Rubio, writes (L.A. *Times,* 4/25/90): "Is the U.S. government initiating a process against Mexico that will end like the Noriega case? Is it preparing the groundwork for an invasion of Mexico?...[this case] amounts to a return to the age of the cave man...There are many Mexicans—and, for that matter, many Latin Americans—who believe that the United States has only one purpose in mind: to exploit Latin America and, whenever convenient, to invade its nations."

Well, as somebody noted, truth is the first casualty in any war, and it now seems the Bill of Rights is the second.

▲   ▲   ▲

123

The War On The Medfly

or

How They Celebrated Earth Day in L.A.

You've probably heard about California's War against the Medfly, in which millions (yes, literally millions) of humans have had poison dumped on them from the skies in hopes that the pesky Medfly will get "exterminated" in the process. You see, the Medfly lays its eggs in fruit, and this ruins the fruit. In balancing the possible financial losses to Agri-business against the risk to the citizens' health from toxic spray, the State naturally sided with Agri-bucks.

"Abuse of power comes as no surprise," as Mencken noted.

This dose-the-people policy has led to a great deal of heated debate, and only two things seem certain:

1) All the medical authorities who say malathion *in small doses* can't hurt humans also coincidentally work for the State of California; and

2) All the medical authorities who deny this and say *any* dose of malathion hurts people coincidentally do *not* work for the State of California.

In all my years of bemused study of synchronicity, I have never seen such a run of strange coincidences. It almost looks as if the salaries of State employees might affect their judgments; but such a thought appears uncharitable. I will leave this string of coincidences to the analysis of Jungians, or Forteans.

Not being a professional toxicologist, I don't claim to know how much harm small doses of malathion can do to human beings. I just know—from observation—that when their own government keeps sending helicopters to dump poison on them, people begin to get a bit paranoid. When their city governments vote to ban the spraying, as over a dozen municipalities in Los Angeles County have, and the State ignores this and goes on spraying them, the people get more paranoid, and some become bloody damned furious.

Many Southern Californians by now even believe the Left Wing Nuts among us, who claim the chemical companies bribed the State to use up the poison because the E.P.A. plans to ban it soon. (18 other countries have already banned or severely restricted it.) But, of course, that kind of conspiratorial speculation seems unwholesome and morbid. Besides, nobody

124

has really *proven* malathion harms humans, in the doses currently used, just as nobody has really *proven* it doesn't harm us—not in a hard scientific sense of "proof."

Most crucially, none of the State "experts" so far has cited any studies of the effects of *repeated* dosing of humans with malathion. They have been citing all the studies that remotely support their case (including one repudiated by its author, Dr. Mark Lappe, who claims the State altered his statistics) but they have not found one study about repeated dosing. I almost suspect no such study exists, or they would have found it and publicized it by now. (The current campaign has gone on since August, 1989, and some communities have gotten dosed every two weeks.)

Lacking an existing study of repeated dosing, what is going on appears to me as a kind of *research*—the first toxicology experiment ever conducted on millions of human subjects. If no hard data on repeated dosing of humans with malathion exists now, it will at least exist after this experiment; perhaps that will console some who want real data before deciding on this issue. (It doesn't seem to console those getting sprayed regularly.).

Whatever the uncertainties now, we will definitely discover some of the results of such repeated dosing in the next few years (or in about 20 years—one breeding generation—for the long-range genetic results.) Meanwhile, we simply don't know what all this malathion will do to us, and the people doing it don't really know either. They just think they know—or think they can convince the rest of us that they know.

Somehow this reminds me of another country, 50 years ago.

Among his other obsessions, Adolph Hitler ardently loved animals and could not bear the terrible sufferings inflicted on helpless rodents by cold, rationalistic scientists. He therefore banned all animal research in Germany and allowed scientists to experiment only upon those humans Adolph considered "social undesirables"—Jews, homosexuals, Gypsies, labor unionists and "mental defectives" who did not believe the moon consists of solid ice (as Nazi dogma claimed). Dr. Joseph Mengele remains legendary for the experiments he conducted under the aegis of this Animal Rights policy.

Perhaps we in California have a governor who sincerely shares Hitler's reluctance to inflict unnecessary pain on rats and hamsters, but feels we do need hard data on the toxicity of malathion. Perhaps, like Hitler, he looked around for "undesirables" to conduct the experiments upon. Since Hitler's list of "undesirables" seems unacceptable to most Americans—

except the Skinheads—Governor Duke has decided to experiment upon the one group that *everybody* in the country seems to regard as ineluctably Undesirable: the citizens of Los Angeles. In short, just maybe the Duke has been spraying us with malathion because he feels soft-hearted, like Adolph did, about testing the stuff on rodents

I don't know for sure, but that seems to make more sense then the Duke's own explanations of this experiment. He might even announce it publicly, eventually, when ready to run for President on an Animal Rights ticket.

According to radio station KPFK, over 10,000 citizens have reported rashes, allergies, asthma-like and flu-like symptoms, nausea and eyestrain after the helicopters dumped malathion on them. The State explains this as "auto-suggestion" or "hysteria." Hundreds of others have called radio talk shows to report an increase in dead birds, sick dogs and cats, the disappearance of bees and other insect species from some townships, etc. The LA *Times* reported (4/19/90) that aphids have increased, leading to gardens dying, because the insects that normally control aphid population have disappeared. Ecologists mutter darkly of damage to the whole eco-system.

The State has hired a Public Relations firm to answer that kind of "hysteria." ("When the amateur liars fail, hire professional liars" —J.R. "Bob" Dobbs.)

Meanwhile, Dr. James Carey of UC-Davis, one of the State's scientific advisers, now asserts that the Medfly has become "endemic" to California and no amount of malathion can totally eliminate it. We should think in terms of biological controls, rather than chemical "extermination," he asserts. The majority of the State's bug-experts rejects Dr. Carey's conclusions, and the spraying continues.

They dosed the neighborhood of Mayor Bradley of Los Angeles on Earth Day...a nice irony, since Bradley appears the only Mayor in the County not to have joined the protest against malathion spraying.

Addendum I

When I wrote the above article, I thought of my comments on Animal Rights and Dr. Mengele as satire. Now, I do not feel so sure. According to the LA *Times* (4/27/90) the State has decided not spray an area of five square miles around Woodcrest, because this area contains an endangered species: Stephen's kangaroo rat. Naturally, anti-malathion activists regard this with less joy than Earth First people might. "I'm just appalled to think rats have more rights in the State's eyes than I do or my children do," said Garden Groves activist Mollie Haines.

Maybe we should seriously re-examine the arguments of those who claimed Mengele "faked" his alleged death. Could he possibly have changed identity again and now be serving as scientific advisor to California's pesticide warriors?

Addendum II

Prof. William Jordan of UC-Davis published an article "Medfly vs. Macho" in the Los Angeles *Times* for April 23, 1990 (Shakespeare's birthday, we can't resist mentioning) in which he suggests "the high command of pest control is hooked on the pesticide equivalent of saturation bombing." Describing the attempted "extermination" of the Medfly as "an artifact of the male mind—or, rather...of a particular kind of male mind," Prof. Jordan says the war on the Medfly seems entirely staffed by males of a particular type, which he describes as "husky men in their late 50s or early 60s...(with) sagging jowls...deep, coarse voices....deep creases of experience and, yes, of courage, toughness, endurance.... This is the portrait of a warrior—a dominant warrior. In the study of animal behavior this would be called an alpha male."

Jordan argues that wars of extermination result from alpha male mind-sets. He also suggests that the Medfly has become too established in California for "extermination" to work and that we need to resort to more subtle tactics of biological control — such as bringing in more insects that devour Medflies. Such scientific (and Taoist?) thinking seldom appeals to alpha males, he warns us sadly.

Prof. Jordan also points out that pesticide extermination campaigns destroy the natural controls that limit insect populations. In 1948, he says, American farmers used 15 million pounds of pesticides and lost 7% of their crops to insects; today, after 42 years of "wars of extermination," we have altered the natural controls and now use 125 million pounds of pesticides yearly and lose 15% of our crops.

Why does this remind me of the alpha types in charge of our War on Drugs?

▲   ▲   ▲

Robert Anton Wilson

Entering Cyberspace

On April 30, 1990, I entered Cyberspace.

I had been invited to share a presentation of the new "virtual reality" hardware and software at New York University, in association with Dr. Timothy Leary. I looked forward to it eagerly; after all, I have wanted a Trip into Cyberspace ever since I read William Gibson's novel *Neuromancer.*

Of course, I had heard that some people react negatively to "artificial reality" and experience dizziness or nausea. I wondered if that would happen to me. It seemed unlikely, I thought, considering the hours I've logged in "virtual" space-time worlds, but who knows? One alternative reality does not necessarily prepare you for another, far different alternative reality.

Well, I need not have worried. I enjoyed my entire Trip and found it exhilarating.

I got my chance to enter Cyberspace during a press conference before the evening lectures. With the hardware and software available at this presentation, you get a helmet that fits over your head and a glove with controls that permit you to "move" in any direction you wish. Once inside the helmet and glove, you leave Consensus Reality and navigate around in Alternative Reality.

The software gave me a bit of countryside and a bit of city. If I turned to look to the right, I saw the view in that direction. If I turned to the left, I saw the view there. Turning around, "just like in real life," I could see behind me.

Since humans rely largely on their eyes to collect information, my brain accepted this "reality" as—a few seconds before — it had accepted the consensus "reality" of the room in which my body sat. (Cyberspace suits, which will harmonize what you see in Virtual Reality with kinesthetic reinforcement, exist already in prototype.)

I headed for the city and enjoyed exploring its streets and alleys for a while. Each time I turned my head, the helmet showed me what I would see if in "real" space and turning my head. This made 3-D movies seem absurdly primitive, I thought. But then I got curious about a UFO hovering above the landscape.

This spheroid seemed like a possible space colony to me. Or might it contain extraterrestrial surprises...? I carefully did not ask Eric Gullichsen, designer of the software, to identify the gizmo for me. I wanted to explore.

Pointing the glove upward I began to fly. It took a while, but soon I found myself on the outside of the UFO/space colony/spheroid gizmo. Alas, I could not find a door.

I wandered around a bit and then gave up on the Mystery. I returned to ground-level and explored the city a bit more, jumping over a pyramid—an exciting experience.

Then, for me, the demonstration period had to end, and the members of the press present—those who wanted it—got their own chance to explore Cyberspace.

Later that evening Dr. Leary, Eric Gullichsen, another neuro-mancer named Myron Krueger and I gave another presentation to a larger audience. In order to let as many of the audience as possible have their own experiences, I gave up my chance for a second flight to Virtual Reality. It didn't matter. I still felt high from my first Trip.

Naturally, a lot of people asked about erotic (pornographic?) implications. Myron Krueger replied soberly that the designer of "MacPlaymate" has already started work on Cyberspace version...

Obviously, Virtual Reality will impact first on computer games and sweep the market. (Nintendo, which inspired the Cyberspace glove, has already captured 60% of the game market. It will either evolve into Cyberspace, or get replaced by it.) Then innovative film/video artists will produce the Virtual Reality equivalents of *2001, The Wizard of Oz, Behind the Green Door, Like a Prayer, King Lear, Lethal Weapon* and any kind of classics and/or junk you can imagine.

You can visit other planets, before the spaceships exist to take your body there. You can visit Oz, or Wonderland, or Dickens' London, or the Egypt of Cleopatra...

The educational implications of this leave one breathless. My Trip, for instance, occurred entirely in Euclidean space, but designing a Trip into Reimanian space would present no new problems for the software wizards. A first-year physics student who has entered Reimanian space will understand Relativity on a gut level much quicker and more deeply than has ever before seemed possible. You can imagine the implications for medical students, if you ever saw *Fantastic Voyage.*

Leary spent most of his time talking about the communication possibilities of Cyberspace. You will soon have the capacity to "visit with" your loved ones without traveling, he pointed out. Quantum jumping past the video-phone (which already seems obsolete before it can even hit the market), Cyber-space will allow you, at home, say, in Maui, to converse with Mom and Dad in their home in St. Paul, while all of you experience the visit as occurring in a marvelous restaurant in Paris.

Personally, I see the ultimate implications of Virtual Reality as Techno-Zen—a comment that probably needs some explanation.

The most important discovery of the modern neurosciences, I think, consists of the fact that every "reality" we perceive has emerged from an ocean of more or less random signals, which our brains have edited, organized and orchestrated into glosses, or sets, or grids, or (in Leary's wonderful term) reality-tunnels. Becoming conscious of the process by which we generate these reality-tunnels out of a potential chaos definitely liberates us from many forms of unconscious bigotry and unexamined assumptions. (This awareness of our role in creating our individual Virtual Reality may even cure neuroses, as Korzybski thought.)

Unfortunately, until the invention of this new Head Hardware, the methods of becoming aware of ourselves as co-creators of our "reality" have had major drawbacks. Some of these methods come from shamans or yogis and arouse the violent prejudice of Fundamentalist Materialists, who never cease attacking research in this area. The other method of awakening from conditioned perception relies on psychedelic drugs, and it seems not only impossible to explain this to most people, it has even become illegal to continue the research. "Drugs" and "mysticism" serve as potent thought-stoppers for most of the educated and uneducated fools in the world—in other words, for the majority.

Virtual Reality hardware and software, however, teaches the same lessons as yoga, Zen and LSD—the brain, guided by a deluge of photons and other energy-blips, creates a Virtual Reality which, in most cases, we believe literally; and, just like yoga and LSD, this new technology forcibly reminds us that any Virtual Reality, including Consensus Reality, contains elements, colors, structures, meanings, etc., put there by our brains.

In short, without drugs or yoga, this technology forces us to recognize that, as Nietzsche said, "We are all greater artists than we realize." It casts doubt on all perception, just as yoga and LSD do. And, once perceptions become recognized as a species of gamble, all inferences from perception become recognized as gambles, also; we enter the "detachment from fixed ideas" that both Buddhism and science have always sought.

131

And the wonderful thing about this technology lies in the fact that it doesn't come from a non-Christian culture, and not even the most dogmatic Fundamentalists (Protestant or Materialist) can seriously call it "Satanism" or "superstition." Yet, like yoga, it functions to de-brainwash or liberate, and nobody can avoid realizing that.

In short, as this technology invades computer games, entertainment, education, etc., the Zen detachment from conditioned perception and conditioned dogma will become available to millions, and not even the most chauvinistic "mental imperialists" in CSICOP can claim "it isn't science."

And the pace of events continues to accelerate...

"How long before we can have a holodeck, like they have on *Star Trek?*" one member of the audience asked.

"If somebody gave me the money," Myron Krueger answered, "I think I could build it starting tomorrow."

▲   ▲   ▲

Tomorrow's News

Futurescope I: Megatrends

According to *Megatrends 2000* by famed forecasters Naismith and Aburdene, the next decade will feature:

• A second artistic Renaissance, with arts even replacing sports as the dominant leisure activity;

• The rise of "Free Market Socialism" as Welfare States increasingly encourage private enterprise;

• The dominance of the new Pacific Rim culture, as the focus of world economy continues its shift from the Atlantic to the Pacific;

• More women in leadership positions: women in management have reached a "critical mass" and will soon graduate to the top levels;

• Biotechnology will provoke the greatest religious and philosophical debates since Darwin;

• From New Age to traditional churches, a "religious revival" will continue to accelerate, in many forms, worldwide.

Futurescope II: American Renaissance

Dr. Marvin Cetron and Owen Davies offer 74 other trajectories of coming events in their book *American Renaissance* (St. Martin's Press, 1989). Among their more interesting future scans:

• Increase in "knowledge industries" and information processing, with 44% of the labor force engaged in collecting, analyzing or retrieving information by 2000;

• Even greater population mobility, and Bucky Fuller-style modular housing that can be packed up and shipped each time a family moves;

• Personal robots in the home by 2000, and real Artificial Intelligence by 2001;

• Jets big enough to carry 1000 passengers;

• Cable TV will reach 87% of American homes by 1992;[1]

• Medical breakthroughs by 2000: artificial blood, more artificial organs, memory-recall drugs, "bloodless surgery" using lasers;

• Computer competence will reach 100% in U.S. urban centers by 2000;

• Increased decentralization in the information society: corporations by 2010 will have fewer than half the present number of management "levels" and one-third the number of "managers."

• A resurgence of liberalism in the 1990s (based on Cetron's graph of a 30-year conservative-liberal swing in American politics);

• Birth rates will continue to decline in advanced nations, and Feminism will continue to grow.

---

[1] As of 1994, it has reached only 60%, according to the FCC. However, the Information Superhighway will bring a quantum jump...

Metaphysical Harbingers

Despite the Reagan Supreme Court (see "War On Drugs," in this chapter), other trends suggest that religious diversity may increase in the future. According to *Religion Watch* (February, 1990) the Gallop poll organization has concluded that American population in the next decade will become "more Catholic" and "less Protestant," but it will also become "more non-Western, more Mormon and more unaffiliated".

Examining current trends, *Religion Watch* also reports that Catholic Bishops show a rapid movement away from liberal social activism and back toward conservatism. Charismatic and evangelical Protestants increasingly interpret the rapid changes in the Eastern bloc nations as evidence that "Armageddon" draws near. Also, booksellers report the words "New Age" no longer attracts many readers and "crystals and channeling are history"—but many New Age subjects remain popular. And ideas and themes from Hinduism increasingly appear in popular comic books, especially the "mainstream" Marvel and D.C. publications.

Further spook stuff: under *glasnost* an "occult" revival has started in Russia, with special interest in faith-healing; the two most popular characters on Soviet TV now are both faith-healers. However, while the formerly "godless Reds" turn New Age, in once-Christian England, the number of persons seeking non-religious funerals has quadrupled in the last few years and a book, *Funerals Without God,* has become a brisk seller. Back in the States, with an increase in the number of persons going public after having "out-of-body experiences" support groups have sprung up to help those who have emotional problems integrating the once-taboo perceptions that occur in this kind of Altered State. (University of Connecticut investigators report that those who've had the OOBE tend to become "more compassionate").

And, finally, while the GAIA hypothesis has continued to gain ground in scientific circles, more scientists (including James Lovelock, the GAIA pioneer) clearly reject New Age adaptations of the idea and now sharply differentiate the scientific GAIA theory from similar mystical theories. GAIA, the scientists say, has self-correcting (feedback) circuits but shows no signs of instant infallibility, "femininity" or compassion.

Will the Real Jesus Please Stand Up?

A newly-translated Gnostic gospel, titled *The Secret Book of Judas of Kerioth,* promises to blow more fuses than *Holy Blood, Holy Grail* and *The Last Temptation of Christ* put together. According to this seemingly authentic early-Cainite-Ophite text, translated from the Coptic by Mohammed al-Murtada and Francis Bendik, Jesus had an active bisexual love life, including relations with John, Lazarus and Mary Magdelene, served an LSD-like psychedelic at the Last Supper, faked his own crucifixion (in collaboration with Judas and Joseph of Arimathea) and died a natural death in India many years after the alleged Resurrection. Worse: the Old Testament god, as described by Jesus, appears as an evil demiurge who perverted the creation begun by the true Creator. This very interesting text, found in 1986 near the Nag Hammadi library, has an introduction and annotations by Dr. Maxwell Selander of Briggs-Melton Theological Seminary and sells for $10 from Abrasax Books, PO Box 1219, Corpus Christi TX 78403.

The Nag Hammadi Library (Harper and Row, 1978) contains excellent translations of the Gnostic scriptures hitherto unearthed, and presents more than a dozen alternative Christs to compete with the one in this Cainite text, or the one in the three Synoptic Gospels—or the weirdest one of all, in the Gospel of John. Pick-your-favorite-Jesus, a possibility since the rise of Protestantism, seems destined to grow as more Gnostic material becomes available to larger audiences.

Wilhelm Reich in Purgatory

As readers of my *New Inquisition* know, although Dr. Wilhelm Reich's books were burned in 1957 and he died in prison later that year, the "Reich Case" continues to haunt the scientific establishment, as various Damned Heretics continue to publish results confirming Dr. Reich's most controversial experiments.

An interesting current instance: Dr. James DeMeo now heads up an organization called Orgone Biophysical Research Laboratory Inc., devoted to using as much of Dr. Reich's technology as is not specifically forbidden by the 1957 FDA anathema. (That leaves quite a bit, actually, since the Feds only forbade experiments in orgonomic medicine.) In an interview with *Wildfire,* Vol. 4, No. 2, Dr. DeMeo tells a story that will profoundly shock those who think we live in a free scientific society: in 1975-77, he did his Master's thesis, at the University of Kansas, on Reich's "cloud-buster" (an orgone device to produce rain.) Most of the staff, De Meo says, expected his experiments to refute Reich and acted quite disturbed when the results actually confirmed Reich.

Although De Meo hoped to continue the research, doing further cloud-buster experiments for his Ph.D., fierce opposition blocked this, and funding from the National Science Foundation terminated. As usual, none of the opponents of the cloud-buster research claimed to have performed their own experiments refuting Dr. Reich. They just "knew" *a priori* that Reich's theories "are cuckoo." Ironically, De Meo finally got his Ph.D. from the University for a study of the historical effects of deserts on human behavior... which, among other things, offered a new (neo-Reichian) theory of why certain types of persons fear certain types of research..

I have corresponded a bit with Dr. De Meo and he sent me an article, "Response to Martin Gardner's Attack on Reich and Orgone Research in *The Skeptical Inquirer.*" You might find some interest in one paragraph from Dr. De Meo's paper:

"Several years ago I produced a detailed *Bibliography on Orgone Biophysics* which covered the period from 1934 to 1986. It contained over 400 separate citations from more than 100 different authors, most of whom possessed the M.D. or Ph.D. degree. Beside my own thesis and doctoral dissertation which were presented to and accepted by a group of respected scholars at the University of Kansas, I have listed in this *Bibliography* 17 other theses and dissertations which drew heavily on Reich's works, confirming various aspects of his bioelectrical formulations. There are 38 indexed citations in the *Bibliography* covering Reich's bion and biogenesis experiments, including Professor du Teils's confirming presentation on the bions to the French Academy of Sciences. The *Bibliography* also includes more than 80 indexed citations on the electroscopical, thermical and biological effects of the orgone energy accumulator. This includes 22 studies on plant-growth responses, and 8 on cancer retardation or wound-healing in laboratory mice. Another 12 citations discuss or evaluate the Reich bioenergetic blood test. More than 50 citations focus on cloud busting, with 20 papers discussing methods of direct visual observation of the atmospheric orgone. Of particular note is the recent German dissertation on "The Psycho-Physiological Effects of the Reich Orgone Accumulator," which was a double-blind, controlled study, confirming many details of Reich's original assertions on the parasympathetic stimulation of concentrated orgone energy on the body, and the weather-dependent pulsation of the orgone in the accumulator... I ask: can [Gardner] cite anyone, even a single person, who has duplicated any of Reich's experiments and obtained a negative result?"

Evidently not knowing the policy of CSICOP, Dr. De Meo submitted this (and detailed documentation) to their magazine, and seemed quite shocked that they absolutely refused to publish it. He appears to think that because CSICOP has the word "Scientific" in their title, they will actually follow normal scientific procedures of open debate and civilized courtesy. He evidently did not know that Prof. Marcello Truzzi resigned as their editor because CSICOP absolutely will not follow such scientific protocols.

Dr. De Meo continues to do as much Reichian research as the federal bureaucracy permits. (He claims good results at rain-making during the drought of 1988.) For further information, write: Orgone Biophysical Research Laboratory, PO Box 1395, El Cerrito, CA 94530.

Invisible Man?

Nikola Tesla, just about the only 20th Century scientist to arouse as much controversy as Dr. Reich, also has his ardent defenders. In a recent issue of *Santa Fe Spirit* (sent to us by Sound Photosynthesis of Mill Valley) appear two versions of an interesting photo. The first, from a 1921 newspaper, shows Einstein, Tesla and Steinmetz together. The second, from a current biography of Einstein, seems exactly identical to the first, except that Tesla appears to have disappeared or to have gotten air-brushed out...

Incidentally, I attended an engineering high school and an engineering college and emerged with the impression that Marconi invented radio and Steinmetz pioneered AC electrical systems. Only years after graduation did I discover that Tesla's accomplishments in those fields preceded both Marconi and Steinmetz and made their discoveries possible.

Some say Tesla has vanished from orthodox scientific history because his later prototype AC generators threatened to make energy so cheap all monopolies would collapse; others claim his opposition to atomic energy caused his consignment to the status of non-person. I don't know, but whatever the explanation, Nikola Tesla seems the Invisible Man in the history of modern technology.

High IQ and 'Arousability'

According to recent research by University of Sydney neuroscientist David Robinson, students who score highest on IQ consistently score in the middle range on cortical "arousability." Those with either very quick brain reactions, or very slow brain reactions score lower in IQ than those with "middling" reactions.

High-speed brain reactions traditionally correlate with extroversion and low-speed reactions with introversion, so the ambiverts seem likely to have the highest IQs in any crowd. The middling-speed ambiverts, *Brain-Mind Bulletin* speculates (April, 1990), probably have "ideal access to information."

(And I have a personal hunch that those high-speed extroverts make up the majority of the pro-pesticide types analyzed by Prof. Jordan in the article "The War on the Medfly" in this anthology, and probably will also appear disproportionately among the Warriors against drugs...)

Psi Tests Validated

In *Foundations of Physics* 19 (1499-1514) two Princeton scientists—Dean Radin and Roger Nelson—review and evaluate over 800 experiments in one form of "PSI" and conclude that the results cannot be explained away by any of the debunkers.

Radin and Nelson concentrated exclusively on RNG (random number generator) experiments in which subjects attempt to "mentally" influence the random numbers generated by a computer to move away from chance toward a prechosen direction. After scrutinizing 832 reported experiments, and the criticisms of the debunkers, Radin and Nelson conclude that "a consciousness-related anomaly in random physical systems" exists which the debunkers have not explained.

Examining five arguments against the data, Radin and Nelson find all five inadequate. The arguments and their rebuttals:

(1) *The effect does not seem consistent with existing scientific models.* Radin and Nelson call this "philosophical" and say it carries little weight against "repeatable experimental evidence."

(2) *The experiments contain serious defects.* Radin and Nelson find no experimental flaws to support this vague (but often-repeated) evasion of the data.

(3) *Fraud plays a role in such experiments.* Radin and Nelson find no evidence of the systematic fraud necessary to account for 832 successful experiments.

(4) *Skeptics have failed to find similar results.* Radin and Nelson, after hard study, could find no published experiments by proclaimed skeptics.

(5) *No theoretical explanation for the data exists.* Radin and Nelson argue that this objection does not refute "experimental observations"; e.g., no theoretical explanation existed for the Michaelson-Morley experiment, and later experiments which duplicated it, until Einstein.

Radin and Nelson also examine the possibility of what some call "the file drawer effect," which holds that experimenters who obtain negative results in this field (as in others) simply do not publish their results. Radin and Nelson conclude that it would require 90 x 832 (or 74,880) unpublished negative studies to bring the data back in line with chance. No anecdotal or other evidence indicates that such a mass of unpublished data exists, and to reject actual experiments on the basis of such purely hypothetical and unproven "possibly lost" data would permit the rejection of virtually all established scientific models.

Healthy Cities

"Healthy city initiatives"—attempts to cope with ecological problems on the local level—have begun in over 300 towns in Europe, Canada, Australia and the United States. "The city is the smallest unit of government...and where the most creative solutions to problems are likely occur" says Beverly T. Flynn in the May-June *Futurist*..

Redistributing the Wealth

The House Ways and Means Committee has determined that, as most of you may have suspected, the rich got richer and the poor got poorer during the Reagan years. Citing the Congressional Budget Report, the Committee determined that the tax rate for the poorest 20 per cent of American taxpayers increased 16.1 per cent during the 1980s, while their real income only rose 3.2 per cent. At the other end of the spectrum, the richest 20 per cent of the population enjoyed a stunning 31.7 per cent increase in real income, but their tax bite did not increase at all — it *dropped* by 5.5 per cent. Does this qualify as the greatest "redistribution of wealth" ever actually achieved in human history? It certainly seems that in practice (as distinguished from theory) no socialist regime has ever successfully redistributed income downward with such magnitude as Reagan redistributed it upward.

(Source: Los Angeles *Times*, February 6, 1990*)*

▲   ▲   ▲

Read At Your Own Risk

by Arlen Wilson

The Rights of the Born

When you regard the bewildering variety of adults, "equality" is not easy to see. But when you look at new-borns, the "created equal" phrase in our dear old Declaration—i.e., equal in needs and equal in rights—really does become "self-evident."

Certain energies within the United Nations have for years been trying to get a "Children's Bill of Rights" formulated and recognized. Needless to say, there is a great deal of resistance to this proposal, since it would necessarily cross over class, economic, race, religion and gender lines. Such a Bill, or even the concept of such a Bill, profoundly threatens innumerable entrenched and time-honored taboos and traditions.

As the child grows, there will be plenty of time for differentiation in regard to varying temperaments, talents, physical capacities and the like. But human life needs to get off to as good a start as we can give it, and we can no longer afford the disparities that exist.

Broadly speaking, all human children have identical rights, wherever and to whomever they are born: rights to such things as love, shelter, learning, etc. Viewed from this perspective, there are no "superior" or "inferior" races or genders.

The National Commission on Children recently reported to the federal government that the largest poverty group in America is composed of children. They articulated the principle that in order to learn, "children must be healthy, fed, rested and secure." (L.A. *Times,* 4/27/90)

Imagine for a minute a world where such rights of all children were taken seriously. The implications of expediting merely those four adjectives—"healthy, fed, rested and secure"— for the young of the modern world would be wilder and more revolutionary than anything ever dreamed of by Karl Marx, or for that matter, by Thomas Jefferson.

Religious Notes

I personally could never relate very much to Father/Son religions, having no experience of being either myself. Now a Mother/Daughter religion might hold my interest a little longer––probably not much longer, though, because then I'd have to worry about Big Sister coming along to interpret Mama to ordinary me. (No thanks.)

Whether you pray to Big Mom or Big Dad you're still stuck with a Single Parent-in-the-sky theology. This creates its own problems too formidable and boring to go into here. And yet I must admit I do pray...a lot. I just try to keep gender out of it.

A friend writes from Madrid that exorcism is coming back into style in Spain, mostly in Granada and Andalusia (the South, wouldn't you know?). It's the usual combination of scam and religious hysteria. Males—some of them priests, some of them free-lancers—offer to get the "demons" out of young girls or adult single women. These always seem to be the categories most afflicted.

A recent exorcism involved a spread-eagled woman having a crucifix rammed up into her. The woman died. My correspondent did not go into the legal consequences of this particular act of criminal lunacy. One can only hope to God (neuter) that there *was* some legal action.

I've reconsidered my original formulation that the most suspect form of all human communication is "God told me to tell you..." Even worse is, "God told me to *do* this to you." For examples, look to the horrors going on in the Middle East any day of the week.

The Middle East is the homeland and source of our three "wonderful" He-god religions: Judaism, Christianity and Islam. The Torah, the Bible and the Koran are *wonderful* guides to better living. What would people ever do without them? Probably live better.

Holy land, holy books, holy mess...Give me a break.

The earth is holy; living, breathing human flesh is holy; the safety of children is holy. Everything else, however amazing, colorful, necessary, useful, ingenious, inspiring, challenging, valuable, intellectually stimulating, etc., is secular. So there you have one woman's heresy.

I have different moods toward matters of religion and religious believers. I felt free to express this particular one here. Actually, I do know better. Evacuating and cordoning off the Middle East as a toxic dump of contagious religious fall-out will

143

not do the trick. Atrocities against the unarmed and against the earth have resonances all over the world. The basic disorder is endemic, though it may be more virulent in some places than others.

Violence is rationalized by countless ideologies. However, it goes deeper than any belief system. What we've got here, friends, is a Species Problem and we better start thinking about it that way.

Strangely enough, just about the only people willing to even try to address this species-wide-darker-side to the wonder of being human are the theologians — hardly my favorite breed. Let's get some better heads to work on it.

▲   ▲   ▲

Book Review:

The Grant Swinger Papers
by Daniel S. Greenberg

*(1990; Science and Government Report, Inc.,
P.O. Box 6226, Washington, DC 20015. $8.95.)*

Reviewed by Arlen Wilson

A tabletop particle accelerator?

This might sound like an unlikely project for tax-based financing, but to Dr. Grant Swinger, Director of the Center for the Absorption of Federal Funds, it's only a research proposal away. After the Utah state legislature granted five million dollars for cold fusion research on the basis of *one press conference*— no peer review, no testimony, no boring research reports or dull articles in scientific journals—anything at all seems possible to the euphoric Dr. Swinger.

Justly or not, he immediately claimed the Utah caper as the epitome of Grant Swingerism, a philosophy of grantsmanship he's been promulgating for the last twenty-five years via his publicist, Daniel S. Greenberg. "This is a triumph," he proclaimed. "We've worked for years to get the Congress, the press and the public to this stage." And the metaphysical beauty of the grant for cold fusion was that "if there's anything to it, no one can find it!" (Not that *Trajectories* is not delighted when promising new technologies are explored, but this case did give us pause.)

Grant Swinger's Center for the Absorption of Federal Funds is not interested in findings, only probings—expensive and prolonged probings. "We do not operate in the closure mode," he states politely but firmly. The longer and more inconclusive the study, the better for his intrepid investigators.

One of the projects for which the Center expects funding is the setting up of a Pan American Chair. The establishment of such a chair would have nothing to do with Latin American studies, but would pay to set aside a permanent seat on Pan American for his traveling scholars. Grant application experts often get to do studies of exotic sites for which we ordinary mortals would have to pay tourist season prices. For those academics who travel in the winter, the Center puts out *A Skier's Guide to Scientific Conferences.*

The Center provides many services for its member institutions in the scientific and academic world. For a fee, for instance, they will provide twenty-five flawless footnotes. All the university student has to do is create a paper making use of them in the given order. For floundering colleges they have a Rent-A-Dean service, and more.

The Center also has a few industrial clients on the side. From the fast food industry they obtained a lucrative grant for genetically engineering a 200 pound chicken. Project Mega-Chicken was a scientific success, but the creature turned out to have some "disgusting habits" which Dr. Swinger prefers not to go into, as well as a foul (fowl?) temper which almost cost the life of an animal technician. Funding was terminated.

Nothing deters Grant Swinger, however. Possibilities are endless. In fact, one of his favorite expressions is, "While you're up, get me a grant."

As to current environmental concerns he perceives a "goldmine in the greenhouse." He says he is also "very optimistic about poverty." Asked if by this he meant its elimination, he replied, "No, I mean it's going to make a comeback as a growth field for research." He points out that most of the work has already been done in this area. Notwithstanding, insights that go as far back as the Sixties to the effect that "unheated homes are bad for old people, malnutrition is harmful to kids and unemployment is hard on family life" can generate new grants and thus be recycled into the funding process. There's always good money in poverty for those with degrees who have the right connections. The fact that these studies will tell us what we know already is all to the good. The Grant Swinger Center for the Absorption of Federal Funds would obviously not be interested in rocking the gravy boat.

This book of interviews with the quintessential manipulator of government largesse is replete with other tips for would-be fundees. As for Grant Swinger, Ph.D., the great man himself, it's too bad that Peter Sellers didn't live long enough to play the part.

Anyone who has ever had funding hassles, or anyone who just enjoys a bit of voyeurism regarding the unholy marriage of science, government and greed in our society would do well to read the reports in this short, concise volume, many of which were first published in *Science* magazine.

▲   ▲   ▲

1994 Update

"Nothing would surprise me anymore."

–Mikhail Gorbachev

A while after Mr. Gorbachev uttered the above sentiment, a conspiracy of hard-line Communists seized the major government buildings in Moscow, took him and his family hostages, and attempted a *coup d'etat*. This conspiracy, like most conspiracies in the real world, proved inept: the army refused to obey the usurpers' orders and the citizenry failed to support them. After they had all gotten placed under arrest, Gorby and family returned in triumph to Moscow—for a few weeks. Then the people threw him out, too, and elected a chap named Yeltsin, whom most of us outside Russia had never heard of until then...

I don't know if any of this surprised Gorby, but I doubt it did. Like Al Gore, he seems to have a fairly clear comprehension of the chaotic changes through which this planet must pass before it arrives at a new, temporarily stable level of techno-eco-(nomical-and-logical)-social organization.

Anyway, Mr. G. had more than the "15 minutes of fame" allotted to everybody by Andy Warhol, and during his few years at the center of world attention, he liberalized the communist monolith to the point where it could finally become non-communist; he ended the Cold War—perhaps the greatest achievement of any politician of the past half-century; and he had the honor of having his face on every tab of the best blotter Acid in Amsterdam during the summer of 1989.

Not a bad record, I would say.

As the Soviet Union broke up into several new countries, all of them more or less market-oriented, the Right Wing in this country, confused as always by every Chaotic Change, hunted more and more frantically for a new Devil to hate. For a while, they seemed likely to confederate around the idea of simply reviving the original down-home Devil (Nick Scratch, *aka* Shaitan, Satan, Old Horny, etc.); but that idea doesn't seem likely to fly as the 20th Century slowly fades into the 21st.

Now they have (for a while) located a new Devil-figure—one who they can really diabolize, because so many of the resentful and embittered members of other out-groups share their paranoia on this matter. Best yet, all the mediocrities in the lower ranks of the media share it also, as one could predict from Nietzsche's writings on envy and resentment. I refer, of course, to the new Fear-and-Rage Cult that Schulze, White and Brown have called "the Madonna-haters." As these scholars write ("A Sacred Monster in Her Prime: Audience Construction of Madonna as Low-Other," by Laurie Shultze, Anne Barton White and Jane D. Brown, in *The Madonna Connection,* ed. by Cathy Switchtenberg, Westview Press, 1993):

> Feminists, fundamentalist groups, Planned Parenthood and the Veterans of Foreign Wars, among others, have publicly denounced Madonna's [*oeuvre*]. She has been accused of being anti–Christian and anti-family...a bimbo, a tart, and a man-eater...In sum, Madonna is often positioned as the low-Other in the domain of esthetic culture.

The "low-Other," a category that sociologists originated to describe the despised out-groups of a society (African-Americans, gays, science-fiction writers ,etc.) also includes the post-Modernists and Futurists, the two groups to which I belong which also happen to have the greatest affinity with Madonna's work. Inevitably then, I feel a strong kinship with her, and see in her videos, films, etc., many of the same satiric (and "chaotic") techniques of Deconstruction that I myself use to awaken people to the fact that all past reality-signals, gender-signals, status-signals, etc., have collapsed and become absurd in the acceleration our evolution. Not coincidentally, the same people who wish my gender-bending in *Schrödinger's Cat* had never escaped into the bookstores would also like to burn Madonna's best videos. Both of us represent the "low-Other" to the custodians of mainstream "culture."

I write this salute to a fellow artist in utter seriousness, but with a mournful conviction that 99 readers out 100 will think I can't really mean it. Can I possibly see a true similarity between my Immortal Writings and the "crazy" Punk art of *that bimbo?*

If I followed the post-modernist technique entirely, I would end with a suggestion that maybe, just maybe, I have intended this as a joke. However, I do have some reactionary, "modernist" tendencies, so I will tell you frankly: Yes, I admire no other living artist more than Madonna Louise Veronica Ciccone.

▲   ▲   ▲

chaPTEr Eight

Fire You

by D. Scott Apel

When Supreme Court Justice Oliver Wendell Holmes opined that "Freedom of speech does not imply the right to shout 'f—' in a crowded theater," the "f"-word he had in mind was "fire."

A different "f"-word is in the news these days, often in connection with rap group 2 Live Crew, who have been arrested on more than one occasion for performing outrageous and audacious stag party songs from their brilliant comedy album, "As Nasty As They Wanna Be." (I'd recommend The Crew's album, incidentally, but only for the most open-minded among our male readers. Not because it's chock full of obscenity, but because it takes a very female-subservient view of sex. And there's really no way to defend this except to point out that the macho-stud stance is *so* outrageous that it's difficult to view it as anything other than exaggeration for comic effect and a lampooning of angry adolescent male sex attitudes in general. That so few people have even noticed this point makes me wonder what's happened to a sense of humor in this country. But that's another story...)

Regular readers of *Trajectories* may have noticed Robert Anton Wilson's frequent pieces about the erosion of Constitutional rights in recent years, primary among them First Amendment freedom of speech rights. But apparently these rights removals are selectively applied. For instance, if 2 Live Crew can be arrested for using profanity in public theaters, it's high time we arrested Robert De Niro, Al Pacino, Paul Newman, and dozens of other actors who made the 1980's the "f"-word decade in films.

As evidence, I've chosen five films from the past 15 years or so, tallied their obscenities, and calculated their curse-words-per-minute "Cuss Quotient." Every one of these films is readily available on video and highly recommended viewing—unless the language offends you, in which case you are hereby given "the word."

* ***Raging Bull*** (1980; MGM/UA; rated R; 127 mins.)

Director Martin Scorsese's story of boxing champ Jake La Motta (Robert De Niro) was the most acclaimed American film of the '80s, according to an *American Film* magazine critics' poll.

The film's realism is intimately tied to its lower-class language; to sanitize the speech would compromise its artistic integrity.

The Count: "F"-word: 125 times. Excremental "s"-word: 9. Lord's Name In Vain: 8. Naughty body parts: 21.

Total curse words: 178. Cuss Quotient: 1.4.

* ***Midnight Run*** (1989; MCA; R; 125 mins.)

Robert De Niro stars in this four-star action comedy as a bounty hunter transporting an embezzler cross-country while pursed by the FBI, the Mob and a rival bounty hunter. De Niro—one of the most respected dramatic artists of our time—is brilliant as the unconsciously obscene hunter; a man who makes "Have a nice day" sound like an expletive.

The Count: "F"-word: 123. The dread Oedipal "mf"-word: 3. Excrement: 25. SOB: 20. Lord's Name: 24. Body parts: 8.

Total: 227. Cuss Quotient: 1.8

* ***Scarface*** (1983; MCA; R; 170 mins.)

The epic saga of the bloody rise and bloodier fall of a Cuban refugee who becomes a drug kingpin. The talent that Oscar-winning writer Oliver Stone (*Platoon, JFK*) has forced to be foul-mouthed reads like an Oscar nomination list itself: Al Pacino, Michelle Pfeiffer, Robert Loggia and F. Murray Abraham.

The Count: "F"-word: 208. MF: 3. Excrement: 17. Body parts: 23.

Total: 265 (excluding Spanish). CQ: 1.6.

* ***Slap Shot*** (1977; MCA; R; 123 mins.)

Paul Newman plays the harried coach of a failing hockey team in this wild and violent comedy that accurately captures locker room jock talk—and which was written by a woman!

The Count: "F"-word: 73. Excrement: 21. Lord's Name: 33. Body parts: 21. Manure (chicken, bull, horse): 17.

Total: 223. CQ: 1.8.

* ***Richard Pryor Live In Concert*** (1979; Vestron; R. 78 mins.)

The first of Pryor's four hilarious and uncensored concert films. This is post-heart attack Rich, but prior to Pryor flambé, and packed with poetic profanity.

The Count: "F"-word: 79. MF: 45. Excrement: 111. Lord's Name: 19. Body parts: 75. Total: 397. CQ: 5.1.

The winner and still champ: Richard Pryor, although his use of the six-letter "N"-word for African-Americans 36 times is probably the one word among them all that we might consider morally offensive.

Some people I've approached with this idea claim I'm confusing my contexts; that it's OK to use "fuck" as a hostile expletive, for instance, as most of these movies do, but not OK to use "fuck" to refer to sex, as 2 Live Crew does.

I'm confused? Isn't their objection a little like saying it's OK to use "Jesus Christ" as an invective, but not in a religious context? Fornicate that feces!

What's the point? Nothing that should come as any surprise to regular readers of RAW's material: It's only words, not sticks and stones. Only morons waste their moral outrage on profanity people have to pay to hear—and are willing to. The choice not to listen is theirs. But the right to expression is everyone's.

And if you don't agree with me...you're fired.

▲   ▲   ▲

Jury Nullification:
Freedom's Last Chance

An old idea has resurfaced that may have major potential to slow or even reverse the terrifying erosion of the Bill of Rights under the Reagan-Bush Team and their right-wing Supreme Court. I refer to the revival of the ancient Saxon doctrine of *Jury Nullification* which has now become a projected Constitutional amendment under consideration in 22 states.

Since Mr. Justice Brennan, the last plumb-line defender of civil liberties, has retired, and the Supreme Court seems fated to move even further toward the authoritarian right-wing, only Jury Nullification can preserve what still remains in this perishing Republic of Anglo-American libertarianism.

Jury Nullification rests upon an old Common Law principle (which Lysander Spooner in his scholarly "Essay on Trial by Jury," [1852] proved to underlie the Jury clause of Magna Carta) —*viz. that the only way to prevent the government from imposing unjust or nefarious laws is to grant juries the right to negate such laws*. This right, as Spooner demonstrated, explains the tradition that a jury should consist of twelve citizens selected *at random* and thereby representing (as far as scientifically possible) the full range of common sense and common morality of the population in general (including the recalcitrants and cranks among us, upon whom liberty has always depended in bad times.).

In a once-popular formulation, the doctrine of Jury Nullification holds that "a jury may judge the law as well as the facts in the case." Since Magna Carta this has been repeatedly upheld by courts in both England and America, only occasionally denied, inevitably upheld by higher courts when denied by lower, and currently remains the law of both countries, although judges have no legal obligation to inform juries that they possess this right.

In fact, in one infamous decision, in the 1890s, the U.S. Supreme Court upheld the right of jury nullification but simultaneously ruled that the judge not only doesn't have to tell the jury they have this right but can prevent the defense attorney from telling them. In other words, American juries have the right to nullify the law, but the judge, if so inclined, can do everything in her (or his) power to prevent them from knowing it.

In only one state out of the 50—Maryland—does the State Constitution oblige the judge to inform the jury that they have the right to acquit where the facts prove the defendant technically guilty but the sensibility of the jury holds that he or she did no real wrong. In the other 49 states, the right exists nebulously, like a ghost, haunting old parchments; judges do not talk about it, and juries, not knowing that they hold in their hands the final checkmate against tyranny, do not exercise the authority they possess.

As Lord Denman wrote (in O'Connel v. Rex, 1884): "Every jury in the land is tampered with and falsely instructed by the judge when it is told that it must accept as the law that which has been given to them, or that they must bring in a certain verdict, or that they can decide only the facts of the case." Outside Maryland, every jury in America is still tempered with and falsely instructed in that manner.

The Fully Informed Jury Amendment can change all this, since it would require judges to inform juries of their right to judge the law as well as the facts and to refuse to enforce any law they find repugnant, tyrannical, nefarious or just plain idiotic.

Under the current government, we can expect abortion to become illegal again, and some women will die in back alleys the way they did before Roe v. Wade. But an informed jury can nullify an anti-abortion law by refusing to convict doctors or patients or the counselors who send the patients to the doctors; they can nullify the law "in the teeth of the facts" of the case; and even one informed juror can hang the jury and cause a mistrial.

Similarly, the present idiotic "war" on drugs will continue indefinitely, at a cost of billions, with further erosion of the Constitution, and with no tangible good results credible to anyone with more than a half inch of forehead. But an informed jury can refuse to enforce the laws in this case, and even one informed juror can again cause a mistrial. Certainly, the anti-pot law, the silliest of all our drug laws, could not survive, in a nation with a least 70 million pot-heads, if juries knew they had the right of nullification.

In the landmark William Penn case in England in the 1670s, the State proved beyond doubt that Penn "was guilty"; i.e., he did consciously and deliberately violate the law by preaching in a public street a religion not that of the Anglican Church. The jury refused to convict, finding religious persecutions repugnant. The judge, in a fury, confined them to the Tower of

155

London until they would agree to convict. After those twelve ordinary unheroic Englishmen had served enough time in the Tower, public opinion forced the judge to reverse himself and admit the jury had the right to decide the law as well as the facts. And that, children, is how religious liberty came to birth in the modern world after 200 years of bloody religious wars: 12 simple men who felt sick and tired of religious bigotry and refused to enforce an intolerant law.

Similarly, in the John Peter Zenger case (New York, 1734), the State proved conclusively that Zenger violated the law by printing anti-government articles in his newspaper, the New York *Weekly Journal.* The jury simply refused to convict him and nullified the law. That was the beginning of freedom of the press in this country, even before the Revolution and the First Amendment.

As in Penn's and Zenger's day, Anglo-American juries today still have the right to cry "Halt!" to any government that tramples upon human liberty; and even if the FIJ Amendment does not pass all 50 states in the near future, the very fact that it exists and is receiving publicity means that some jurors at least will know their rights when they enter the jury box.

Groups in 22 states, as I said, already have formed to advance the FIJ Amendment. For further information, write to: FIJA, P.O. Box 59, Helmville, Montana 58843.

"The jury has the power to bring in a verdict in the teeth of both the law and the facts."

> — *Oliver Wendell Holmes,*
> *Horning v. District of Columbia, 138 (1920)*

"Since natural law was thought to be accessible to the ordinary man, the theory invited each juror to inquire for himself whether a particular rule of law was consonant with principles of higher law. This view is reflected in John Adams' statement that it would be an 'absurdity' for jurors to be required to accept the judge's view of the law 'against their own opinion, judgment and conscience'."

> *—Unsigned article,*
> Yale Law Journal, *74, 172 (1964)*

"I consider trial by jury as the only anchor ever yet imagined by man, by which a government can be held to the principles of its own constitution."

> *—Thomas Jefferson,*
> *letter to Thomas Paine, 1789*

"If a juror accepts as the law that which the judge states then that juror has accepted the exercise of absolute authority of a government employee and has surrendered a power and a right that once was the citizen's safeguard of liberty."

> *—Bancroft,*
> History of the Constitution

"if the jury feels the law is unjust, we recognize the undisputed power of the jury to acquit, even if its verdict is contrary to the law as given by a judge, and contrary to the evidence."

— *4th Circuit Court of Appeals,*
U.S. v. Moylan, 1969

"For more than six hundred years—that is, since Magna Carta, in 1215—there has been no clearer principle in English and American constitutional law, than that, in criminal cases, it is not only the right and duty of juries to judge what are the facts, what is the law, and what was the moral intent of the accused, but that it is also their right, and their paramount duty, to judge of the justice of the law, and to hold all laws invalid, that are, in their opinion, unjust or oppressive, and all persons guiltless in violating or resisting the execution of such laws."

—*Lysander Spooner,*
"Essay on Trial by Jury"

"When a jury acquits a defendant even though he or she clearly appears to be guilty, the acquittal conveys significant information about community attitudes and provides a guideline for future prosecutorial discretion... Because of the high acquittal rate in prohibition cases in the 1920s and early 1930s, prohibition laws could not be enforced. The repeal of these laws is traceable to the refusal of juries to convict those accused of alcohol traffic."

—*Alan Sheflin and Jon Van Dyke,*
Law and Contemporary Problems 43, No. 4 (1980)

"No man's life,
liberty
or property
are safe
while the legislature
is in session."

— H.L. Mencken

H.E.A.D. Hardware News

Time for an update on H.E.A.D. hardware—machines contributing to **H**edonic **E**ngineering **A**nd **D**evelopment, or the Art and Science of using the human brain for fun and profit.

Brain machines fall into several groups, but all use the "frequency following response"—the brain's tendency to mimic a frequency impressed upon it. Electrical machines use low currents, similar to those of the brain itself; light machines use light; light-and-sound machines use both light and sound, etc. In each case, the frequencies move the brain into those wave patterns characteristic of deep meditation (low alpha to theta or even delta waves.)

Anecdotal and clinical evidence suggests many psychological and even psychosomatic benefits in this technology, but few controlled double-blind studies have appeared until recently. The double-blind studies thus far published, insofar as I have seen them, all tend to confirm the anecdotal-clinical impression that these machines aid relaxation, reduce tension, improve mental functioning and probably boost the immune system. We need a lot more research before these benefits appear documented beyond further doubt, and we do not know yet if any negative side-effects result from any of these machines.

We begin with some objective reports:

Alpha-Stim: Two Validations

A reader has sent us a study published in the *American Journal of Electromedicine* (March, 1987) in which the Alpha-Stim electrical brainwave machine improved the motor skills of a group trying to master a computer game while a control group playing the same game without the Alpha-Stim showed significantly less improvement. (The graphic depiction of results looks as if the Alpha Stim group improved almost twice as fast as the control group.) The study, by Richard Madden, Ph.D., and Daniel Kirsch, Ph.D., employed a classic double-blind placebo-controlled methodology, and the Alpha-Stim group continued to score well above the control group in repeated trials.

In a footnote, Madden and Kirsh mention another study, by T.H. Gibson and D.E. O'Hair, in which the Alpha Stim proved significantly more effective than controls in reducing anxiety and muscular tension.

Mind Tuners and AIDS

For quite a while, I have pondered the possible use of these new brain machines in the treatment of AIDS. It seems probable that these machines produce neuropeptides that boost the immune system, and thus will ameliorate all immune disorders, including AIDS. This remained only theoretical in my mind, because no clinical subjects in mind-machine research volunteered to have their brains and bodies chopped up so scientists could see directly whether the neuropeptide stimulation actually occurs, and evidence of such an effect thus remains indirect and inferential. *(Note: For more on the case for a theoretical link between mind machines, neuropeptides and increased immune system efficiency, see "Mind-Body Problem Solved?" in Chapter 1. —Ed.)*

Now comes a report that the IM-1 brain machine (a light-and-sound device) has shown some promising results with some AIDS patients. This research, by the not-for-profit Penwell Foundation, does not appear "pure," since the director, William Harris, M.D., also gives his patients high doses of Vitamin C; and results at this point have not included double-blind placebo controls and nobody has replicated them. Nonetheless, without raising false hopes that a "cure for AIDS" lurks in mind machines, this research seems worthy of mention...even if it only encourages a few other physicians to try this approach. When Dr. Harris publishes some hard data, I will inform our readers.

Personality Changes

Basic personality change has not appeared in the literature of brain machines previously (as far as I know), but *Megabrain Report,* Vol. I, No. 1, has some striking comments on this. Dr. Robert Becker, reporting on his observations of Dr. Meg Patterson's work treating addiction with an electrical machine in England, observes that "personality alteration" of a beneficial sort appeared in many of her subjects. Dr. Kirsch (Dean of the Graduate School of Electromedical Sciences at City University of Los Angeles) adds that addicts treated with the Alpha-Stim have shown "a big personality change—their levels of self-sufficiency, dominance, assertiveness and ego strength, for example, had more than doubled, in some cases more than tripled." Dr. Kirsh also mentions a study in which patients treated for back pain with a TENS unit also showed an unexpected decrease in depression.

*   *   *

A few comments, of a more subjective nature, about the H.E.A.D. hardware I have used recently:

The Inner Quest

Among the newer brain tuners, I have found the Inner Quest-II (also abbreviated IQ-II by its manufacturer) especially rewarding and almost inexhaustibly fascinating. The IQ-II employs both light and sound, but no direct electrical stimulation of the brain, and contains a tape cassette compartment allowing you to combine its programs with your favorite music, or with self-help hypno-tapes. Since the IQ-II comes with 16 standard programs and a keyboard allowing you to create your own programs, the possible combinations, although finite, appear large enough to keep you busy for many years before you have sampled all possible variations.

Program 6, for instance, gives you 30 minutes of deep alpha and theta (12 hertz to 5 hertz); I find it produces deep relaxation while I'm "on" the machine and extra energy for a few hours thereafter—especially when combined with Bach in the cassette. Program 15, running 40 minutes long, ranges from 30 hertz (beta) to 9 hertz (low alpha) and seems quite stimulating with Romantic music, especially Ravel's *Bolero.* Program 14 covers 25 hertz to 5 hertz, with a left/right balancing program for both brain hemispheres, and I have found it potentiates hypno-tapes—especially the Healing Sleep tape from Acoustic Brain Research. In fact, all of the "psycho-immunology" tapes from ABR seem to work better (for me) combined with the Inner Quest. Other hypnotapes also seem somewhat potentiated by IQ-II—but none quite as much as the ABR tapes.

Program 16 gives you an hour in low theta and delta and always puts me to sleep. I find nothing great about this, personally, but it might help some insomniacs escape the trap of barbiturate abuse and/or addiction.

I feel it will take another two or three years (at least!) before I have adequately explored the potentials of this machine. Meanwhile, "evidence remains anecdotal and subjective"—which means I haven't seen any double-blind studies yet. Nonetheless, I suspect this will prove one of the most effective brain tuners, when tested rigorously.

The IQ-II is available from Psych-Research Inc., 10002 West Markham, Suite 200, Little Rock, AR 72205.

162

Mind Gym

Acoustic Brain Research, whose tapes for the treatment of drug abuse problems scored well in one double-blind test has a new and quite astounding series of tapes available called "Mind Gym."

ABR tapes must rank as the most portable and convenient of the new mind tools on the market. You can take them anywhere, and as long as there's a stereo or Walkman with earphones available when you get there, and you can use them at once (a wonderful pick-me-up for the tired lecturer struggling with jet-lag...). The tapes combine sounds in the alpha-theta range with various verbal conditioning techniques based on Ericksonian hypnosis and Neurolinguistic Programming, and—subjectively—I find them as useful as any of the more complex mind machines, and more useful than most.

The Mind Gym tapes, unlike ABR's psycho-immunology tapes, do not seem to combine well with the IQ-II or any other machine; they work best alone, because they require alert concentration. One tape carries you through an exercise of visualizing a ping-pong ball bouncing back and forth between your right brain hemisphere and the left; another has you visualize an arc of numbers in the air, the odd numbers flowing one way and the even numbers flowing the reverse way; etc. Some tapes have much more complicated visualizing exercises, intended to stimulate specific brain areas. All have the usual subliminal and liminal alpha-theta rhythms behind the words, and I have found the effects include increased mental alertness, but nothing else notable while using the tapes—however, much more striking results appear in the hour or two *after* usage. (Which seems to indicate increased neuropeptide activity, I suspect.)

Having only my own impressions of these tapes at present, and no published scientific studies, I can't swear I know what's going on here, but I feel that after a Mind Gym tape I have a "braced" or "wide awake" feeling, increased energy and greater *clarity and depth* of perception/thought/feeling than with any other mind-altering technique I've tried, with less "spooky" side-effects such as dreamlike states or "out of body" experiences. (In Eastern terminology, the Mind Gym state resembles Zen's vivid alertness rather than Hindu bliss-out and fog.) I will definitely explore Mind Gym further and report more in due time.

For information, write Acoustic Brain Research, 100 Europa Drive, Suite 430, Chapel Hill, NC 27514.

163

Hazards of Electrical Brain Machines?

Readers may remember my "debate" with Dr. E.W. Kellogg III concerning possible hazards of electrical brain machines *(Note: See "Brain Machine Debate" in Chapter 4 of this volume— Ed.).* Since then Dr. Kellogg has sent me more data about the documented hazards of electrical radiation associated with currents and frequencies very similar, in some respects, to those of electrical brain tuners, and I have undergone an "agonizing reappraisal" of my position.

In this connection, some interesting debate appears in the *Megabrain Report* cited above (Vol. I, No. 1). Dr. Robert Becker, generally considered the leading authority on both health-enhancing and health-damaging effects of electricity and its associated radiations, calculates the risk factor of electrical brain machines thusly: "When Meg Paterson used (electric brain stimulation) it was for a serious medical condition that was potentially life-threatening, namely addiction to hard drugs. On a risk/benefit ratio basis I have absolutely no problem with that... But when you're saying 'I'm going to put this on your head and you'll do your homework better,' I part company. There my risk/benefit ratio is skewed heavily toward the risk."

Dr. Becker, however, goes on to say that the frequencies used in electrical brain machines "are those that one normally encounters in the brain" and the risk thus seems not as great as in some machine that might pour 60 cycle or 1000 cycle waves into the brain. Still, he feels we need more studies of the "power density" of various electrical brain machines before pronouncing them "non-harmful."

Dr. Robert Beck disagrees with Dr. Becker: "I have tremendous respect for Dr. Becker. I consider him Number 1 on the Nobel Prize list forever—he's been nominated several times, and I think he deserves it." Nonetheless, Dr. Beck claims that all Dr. Becker's evidence of harmful effects of electrical fields relate to devices that do not resemble brain machines very much. The best-documented electrical risk, he says, involves the clustering of leukemia cases around electrical power lines carrying 60 hertz. (Brain machines generally run from around 20 hertz down to 4 hertz.)

Dr. Daniel Kirsch sides with Dr. Beck and evaluates the risk/benefit ratio thusly: "With all (therapeutic) drugs, there are side effects. Yet, with electromedicine we haven't seen anything *close* to the kind of side effects associated with most drugs."

As of now, no data documents ill effects of the machines themselves, and I do not feel sure enough of the inferences between data on similar radiation levels found elsewhere and the possible dangers of the machines. Thus, I do not feel justified in issuing a general warning against such machines, as Dr. Kellogg does.

But I do feel increasingly dubious about the electrical brain machines; the data from related fields does disturb me, and—to play fair with all of you—I must now declare that I have personally stopped all self-research with electrical brain machines. I don't feel sure of how to calculate the risk factor, and the debate between Becker, Beck and Kirsh confused me more than it enlightened me, so I prefer to experiment only with light and sound machines or with the ABR tapes.

That should keep me busy, and entertained, for quite a few years, I suspect.

▲　　　　▲　　　　▲

Tomorrow's News

Atomic Circuits

While nanotechnology (the construction of molecular-sized computers) has received international media coverage, a more radical but less publicized breakthrough has occurred at IBM's Almaden Research Center in San Jose, CA. Scientists there have used a scanning tunneling microscope to maneuver individual atoms for the first time ever. While it has no immediate applications (except perhaps to print a couple of thousand encyclopedias on the head of a pin) the new technique will allow the creation of atomic-scale electrical circuits, leading to incredibly dense data storage devices—and eventually a whole new generation of mini-mini-mini computers.

The Almaden technicians used the new technique to move chains of xenon atoms and spell out "IBM" on the atomic level.

(Source: Nature, 5 April, 1990*)*

World Game News

The World Game Institute, founded by Buckminster Fuller, has experienced dramatic advances since last we reported on it (*Note: See "Gabel and the World Game" in Chapter 5 —Ed.*).

The World Game uses 100 players, each representing 1% of the world's population. Computer data provides real problems and players try to solve them, working alone or as teams and getting quick feedback on how each individual move impacts the other 99% of the planet.

The Rockefeller Foundation gave WGI a grant to develop World Game seminars for UN officials, and Hitachi gave WGI a grant to develop a playground-style model of the Fuller Big Map, which will allow students to explore global resource issues in an active, experimental way. A Teacher's Manual comes with the playground Map, showing 50 problems for students to solve, and integrating the Game with all their regular classes, from history to geography.

Meanwhile the staff of WGI has increased from 15 to 35, and the number of World Game seminars in 1989 totaled twice as many as in 1988. Their biggest recent Game Workshop took place at the International Conference Center in Peace Park, Hiroshima—ground zero of the atomic bomb of 1945.

(Source: World Game Report, Spring 1990*)*

America on the Skids

A bipartisan commission of prominent American businessmen, educators and labor leaders has urged that the U.S. "quickly" invest tens of billions of dollars in public schools and on-the-job training in order to compete successfully with Western Europe and Japan. The Conference on the Skills of the American Workforce said bluntly that workers in other industrial nations have better education than American workers, handle a far broader range of responsibilities and produce higher quality goods, because American businesses rely on "an outdated system in which a small educated...elite" directs the activities of a mass of uneducated workers possessing only "minimal skills."

The study also showed that 90% of American employers did not consider low skill levels a problem and that the vast majority showed more concern about an applicant's "social behavior," or conformity to norms.

William E. Brock, former labor secretary under Reagan, said for the Commission that "by silently accepting America's descent into a low-skill, low-wage economy, we are on the brink of sentencing our children...to a lower standard of living."

(Source: Los Angeles *Times,* 19 June, 1990*)*

Two more recent studies by the Commerce Department warn that the U.S. has lost its technological cutting edge. The first report concludes that Japan will lead the U.S. in electronics in the early 1990s, and the second, more gravely, predicted that Japan will lead the U.S. "in most emerging technologies" by 2000.

(Source: Los Angeles *Times,* July 18, 1990*)*

Editorial Comment

Can't help noting that the nations listed as having better educated workers than the U.S.— West Germany, Ireland, Denmark, Sweden, Japan and Singapore—also have multi-party political systems, offering a wide spectrum from right to left. Could our system of only two political parties, both right-wing, survive if we invested in creating an educated working class?)

Murder, She Wrote

According to a recent study by the National Center for Health Statistics, the homicide rate for young men in the U.S. measures from 4 to 73 times higher than that of other industrial nations. 21.9 out of every 100,000 American males between 15 and 24 died by murder in 1987, as compared to a world-wide low of 0.3 per 100,000 in Austria and a second-place 5 per 100,000 in Scotland—second place, but still 16.9 per 100,000 less than the U.S. rate.

Said Lois Fingerhut, co-author of the study: "I knew intuitively that our rates were high, but I never dreamed they would be so staggering..."

The number of homicide deaths among African Americans ranks 85.6 per 100,000 or 63.7 per 100,000 higher than our already bloody national average.

(Source: Santa Monica *Outlook,* 27 June, 1990*)*

Pop Quiz

Does anybody see any form of causal or other connection between this study and the data above about our low-education, low-wage, low-skill proletariat?

Meditation and Longevity

According to *Religion Watch* (May 1990), a recent Harvard University study has found that meditation can prolong life. The findings, originally published in the *Journal of Personality and Social Psychology,* indicated that Transcendental Mediation worked better than two other techniques in extending life span and also in lowering blood pressure and improving measurable aspects of mental functioning.

Smart Houses

Design News (24 April, 1990) predicts that automated "smart houses" will develop rapidly in the 1990s. Predicting a $2 billion home automation market by 2000, the engineering journal says our increasing number of elderly citizens will eagerly buy cybernetic systems that provide greater security against crime or medical emergency, and high-income families will also want the latest in "smart" home furnishings and appliances.

168

Neural Nets in Hardware

Intel Corporation, working together with California Scientific Software, has created an "electronic brain" more like the human brain than any silicon creation to date. Known as the N64 "neural network chip," this component provides an analog model of the brain, unlike the digital models provided by other computers and computer parts. N64 also achieves 5 *billion* interconnections per second; the closest digital competitor achieves only 100 million (10 million remains the norm) and its recognition speed reaches 100,000 characters per second (as compared to hundreds of characters per second in conventional chips.)

Mark Holler, designer of the N64, says the component precisely models neural processes in humans.

(Source: Electronic Engineering Times, 14 May, 1990)

Evil Spirit Geography

Charismatic Christians have identified various "evil spirits" with specific locations. New York City, they say, has the evil spirit of "greed" haunting it, while Los Angeles has "pornography," Annapolis has "bondage" and Washington, of course, has "power."

(Source: Charisma and Christian Life, April 1990)

Clergy Credibility

According to the Princeton Religion Research Center, the number of Americans who rate the clergy as "high" in ethical behavior dropped from 67% in 1985 to 55% in 1989; and those who rated the clergy's ethics as "very high" dropped from 22% to 12% between 1987 and 1989.

More people (62%) trust pharmacists than trust the clergy, but the clergy scores better than car salesmen (6%.)

(Source: *Religion Watch*, June 1990)

In a related story, the U.S. Embassy in New Delhi, India, after an audit by Price Waterhouse, said officials of the Roman Catholic Church have engaged in massive fraud. Bishops, priests and nuns working for Catholic Relief Services of Baltimore, the audit showed, stole millions of dollars in funds donated by American Catholics to feed the starving and used the money to run profitable businesses instead.

(Source: Santa Monica Outlook, 25 May, 1990)

169

More Support for Dr. Pauling

Two-time Nobel laureate Linus Pauling has received more statistical support for his views on the therapeutic value of Vitamin C.

A study at the Medical College of Georgia found that, of 67 Georgia and South Carolina residents, the seven with the lowest levels of Vitamin C had the highest blood pressure—and the seven with the highest Vitamin C levels had the lowest blood pressure. A similar study of 228 elderly Chinese Americans in Boston, performed by Tufts University scientists, also found high C correlated with low blood pressure.

(Source: Santa Monica *Outlook,* 30 May, 1990*)*

(Note: For more on Dr. Pauling and Vitamin C, see our interview in Chapter 1. —Ed.)

Computer Radiation

Ever since 1982, statistical studies have shown *some* degree of linkage between frequent computer use and a variety of illnesses, including cancer, miscarriages, birth defects and less serious conditions, including eyestrain. In recent developments:

• Suffolk County, NY, passed a law requiring employers to pay for eye examinations for computer workers, but a judge overturned the law on the grounds that *county* governments have no authority to make laws for the workplace;

• New York City passed a law to provide that pregnant women would get transferred from computing to another department until delivery, but departing Mayor Koch vetoed the law on the grounds that such matters should be decided by collective bargaining and not by law;

• A similar law to protect pregnant computer workers has passed its first reading in the Massachusetts legislature.

• The Swedish government publishes guidelines on radiation levels of various computers, which the Swedish public studies carefully. Manufacturers have learned that only shielded, low radiation monitors will sell in Sweden.

• With increasing discussion of this problem appearing in scientific journals, IBM has produced a new computer that shields the user from VLF (very low frequency radiation) but not ELF (extremely low frequency radiation); the Safe Computing Company has a model that emits no detectable radiation at all; Hewlett Packard offers a "refit" option that lowers radiation; and Apple remains "extremely and surprisingly silent" on the issue.

(Source: Electric World, May/June 1990*)*

And The Band Played On

The staggering burden which the "War on Drugs" has placed on the court system *(Note: See "War On Drugs" in Chapter 7 —Ed.)* has continued to worsen, according to a report by the State Judicial Council of California. Noting that drug cases now make up 60 to 65% of overall criminal case loads, and "drug-related" cases make up an additional 20%, the Council concluded that the War "threatens to clog the judicial system" and expressed "serious alarm" at the growing backlog of civil cases indefinitely postponed. (San Diego courts ceased to hear civil cases at all for one month recently, to catch up on drug cases.)

William E. Davis, state administrative director of the courts, commented that the system has not yet broken down only because many defendants plea-bargain or plead guilty to avoid the heavier penalties that usually follow a full trial. "I hate to say it," Davis told the press, "but *if even 1% or so started going to trial, instead of pleading, we couldn't sustain it.*"

Judges contacted by the Council in 24 courts concluded that "prison alone is not the answer" to the problem.

(Source: L.A. Times, 23 May, 1990)

12 Steps and Sweatlodges

According to Robert Allen Warrior (who has interesting initials) the Alcoholics Anonymous 12-Step program, combined with traditional Native American traditions, has become "the key to recovery for many Indian alcoholics." Native Americans, who have had a chronic alcoholism problem ever since their conquest by Whites, seem to find "the AA model is the Indian model," according to one Lakota leader, who adds "If the god you choose to use keeps you sober, it's the right god. There's not a lot of dogma to it."

The Native American AA movement includes the usual 12 step program together with such Indian traditions as the sweat lodge. In one Indian community, formerly ravaged by massive alcoholism, 98 per cent have now attained sobriety.

(Source: Christianity and Crisis, 19 March, 1990)

The Coffee Menace

A recent study shows that men who drink five or more cups of coffee a day have two to three times the rate of coronary heart disease as men who do not drink coffee at all.

171

In another study, subjects of both sexes showed no ill effects from their first cup of coffee in the morning. Given a second cup within two hours, however, the subjects showed elevated diastolic blood pressure and increased heart rate.

(Source: Brain/Mind Bulletin, June 1990)

Einstein's Relative

Physicist Evan Harris Walker, Ph.D., (author of *The Compleat Quantum Anthropologist*) has recently unearthed evidence that Einstein's first wife, Mileva Maric, herself a physicist, played a crucial role in the development of Relativity. According to the *International Magazine of Research and Development* (June 1990), Walker's evidence includes early papers on relativity by Mileva Maric and a letter from Albert to Mileva calling Relativity "our theory."

Liars Lying About Liars?

According to *Fate* magazine (August 1990), a little journal called *Saucer Smear* recently charged that CSICOP "skeptics" Philip Klass and Zan Overall employed "vicious efforts" to stop publication of a UFO book, *The Gulf Breeze Sightings,* by one Ed Walters, by "supplying the publisher with unproven negative claims." In the next issue, *Saucer Smear* printed a letter by Mr. Klass flatly denying that he and Overall had sent such unproven claims to the publisher.

Unfortunately for Klass, *Saucer Smear* also received and printed a letter from Mr. Overall bluntly admitting they had sent the negative material to the publisher, and attempting to justify the act.

Fate comments simply, "Guys, get your story straight before you write such letters."

Meanwhile, Florida newspapers have uncovered rather convincing evidence that Walters tried to recruit a friend to help him fake UFO photos for his book...a model of a fake UFO was found in Walters' previous home...and five soldiers working for Army Intelligence in Germany went AWOL, were found in Walters' home town, Gulf Breeze, Florida, were taken into custody by the CIA and then were mysteriously released without any charges pressed against them for going AWOL. The soldiers denied reports that they belonged to an "End of the World" cult and said they just came to Gulf Breeze to visit a friend who lived near Walters.

(Sources: Radio and TV news shows, 3-6 August, 1990)

Calling Dr. Feelgood

Elvis Presley no longer holds his position as the most famous 20th Century celebrity destroyed by a doctor with a overly obliging personality and a busy prescription pad.

Among the drugs and compounds given to Adolph Hitler from 1937 on by physician Dr. Theodore Morell: methadrine (statistically linked to paranoia, megalomania and delusional thinking); Ultraseptyl (now known to cause nerve damage); Sympatol (a heart stimulant); Vitamins A, B-12, D-3, C, D, E, K and P; Optalidon (containing addictive barbiturates); cocaine (linked to paranoia and all the other aberrations mentioned under methadrine); amino acids; enzymes; Dr. Koster's Anti-Gas Pills (containing strychnine and belladonna, a hallucinogen); a variety of hormones from young bulls; Dolphamine (named after Adolph himself, but now called Methadone: the only drug considered more addicting than heroin); and morphine (another addictive drug).

Although never quite a "dull-normal" human, Hitler only conceived his most original and innovative ideas (fighting two wars in the East and West simultaneously, the "no retreat" defense which wiped out most of his army, the Werewolf brigades, the attempted genocide of the Jews, etc.) while Dr. Morell was stuffing him full of all those weird and/or incompatible compounds.

(Source: "High Hitler," by Irv Yarg, *High Times,* May, 1982*)*

Lizard Wine and Longevity

An undated story from the *Wall Street Journal* (sent in by a New York reader) says the people in Bama, a province in Southwest China bordering Vietnam, live longer than any other group on Earth. Although the Bamans indulge in chain smoking, over-eating and heavy booze-drinking, they remain healthy into their 80s, 90s and often past 100. When asked, they attribute their longevity to a local wine made of lizards, three kinds of poisonous snake, dog penises and secret herbs.

A 102-year-old woman, married to a 95-year-old man, offered also this practical advice: "If you're near the big river, drink from the big river. If you're near the little river, drink from the little river." (Sort of summarizes Taoism, doesn't it?)

Chinese officials told the *Journal* that old birth records and census data prove the Bamans outlive anybody else.

Yeah, It's True—Turn On the Air Conditioner

The widespread belief that violent crime increases in hot weather has been validated by University of Missouri psychologist Craig Anderson. Reviewing a body of statistical data dating from the 1920s to the present, Anderson concludes that hot countries have a higher violent crime rate than cooler lands and general aggression (unsocial behavior ranging from mild hostility to such extremes as wife battering, assault, riot and murder) all peak on the hottest days of the year.

(Source: Psychological Bulletin, 74-96)

Orgone Experiment in Germany

A Ph.D. dissertation on the Reich Orgone Accumulator, by Stefan Muesinich and Rainer Gebauer, University of Marburg, confirms several of Dr. Reich's claims for this device. The authors used a randomized double-blind methodology so that neither the volunteer subjects nor the persons recording data knew who was sitting in a Reich accumulator and who was sitting in a "control" box that looked similar but had lacked the orgonomic construction. Subjects in the accumulator consistently showed a higher temperature, and generally reported a variety of pleasant subjective sensations, compared to those in the "control" box. Most interestingly, just as Reich claimed, one subject found the accumulator unpleasant and always felt happier in the box that did nothing.

You can order a copy of this dissertation, in German, from Natural Energy Works, P.O. Box 864, El Cerrito CA 949530.

Research on the orgone accumulator remains illegal in this country.

Conspiracy/Covert Action Update

According to the reputable Philadelphia *Inquirer* (28 January, 1990) a ritualistic secret society has ruled South Africa "for more than four decades." This Afrikaner "shadow government" (as the *Inquirer* calls it), quite like the secret societies imagined in paranoid fantasies, has controlled every South African government since 1948, the newspaper alleges. Called the *Broederbond,* this esoteric clique invented, imposed and perfected apartheid; every South African head of state and virtually every cabinet minister has been a member. The *Broederbond*, the *Inquirer* also states, has decided that apartheid can not work any longer and masterminded President de Klerk's recent efforts to negotiate with Blacks for the sharing

174

of political power. "It is impossible to promote Afrikaner interests without promoting everybody's interests," says Prof. J.P de Lange, chairman of the secret society, which critics once compared to the Ku Klux Klan.

Meanwhile, P2, the "shadow government" of Italy back in the '70s and early '80s, came back into the news recently, when the Italian government began a new investigation of covert CIA influence on P2, prompted by evidence that the CIA financed terrorist bombings committed by P2 and set up to look as if they had been left-wing in origin.

(Source: Santa Monica *Outlook,* 24 July, 1990*)*

(The late Penny Lernoux argued that P2 always served as a CIA front in her book, *In Banks We Trust.* Stephen Knight, in *The Brotherhood,* argued that P2 actually worked for the KGB. David Yallop's *In God's Name* presents the case that P2 took money from both the CIA and KGB and double-crossed both. Whoever P2 "worked for," Italian magistrates have charged the ringleaders with numerous acts of terrorism, laundering Mafia drug money through the Vatican Bank, and having an odd symbiosis with Mafia and CIA cocaine smuggling in Latin America.)

The Christic Institute, which won the notorious Karen Silkwood case against Kerr-McCann, continues its efforts to prove the existence of a similar "shadow government" in the U.S. Under the RICO act, Christic has filed suit against George Bush, Oliver North, General Secord, John Hull and several others, charging them with clandestine activities involving drug smuggling, gun dealing, terrorism, perjury and conspiracy. You can hear about the Christic suit's slow progress on Pacifica Radio or National Public Radio, but so far as we know, not a word about this explosive case has appeared in any major newspapers or on TV news shows.

▲   ▲   ▲

Weird Times

The latest *Fortean Times* has finally arrived, and I still find it the most mind-boggling journal in the English-speaking world. In a single issue (FT #53, in this case) you might feel amused, puzzled or frightened by such items as:

• Cases of several people in various parts of England hit (and sometimes seriously injured) by mysterious flying food seemingly thrown from automobiles. Typical assaults include:
— Elderly people in Middlesex hit frequently by eggs in the street
— Kerry Mofan of Yorkshire blinded in one eye by another flying egg
— Alan Jones of Leytonstone badly injured by a flying cabbage
— Leslie Merry of Leytonstone actually killed when his ribs were broken by a viciously hurled flying turnip
— A woman in the same town hit in the eye by a potato; and
— Several people in Australia hit by pumpkins.
The "paranormal" seems ruled out, as witnesses saw the food hurled from cars in many cases, but nobody has yet explained the motives of the assailants or why this phenomenon seems confined to England and Australia.

• Several cases of people cured of major problems by what might be called "Three Stooges" therapy: being hit on the head. This includes two mutes who regained speech when hit on the head (one of them got hit by a falling picture of the Virgin Mary); twelve cases (yes, *twelve*) of blind people who regained sight after similar blows on the head; three deaf people who regained hearing after getting banged on the skull; and four cases of baldness cured by similar Three Stooges misadventures.

• A report of a lamb born in Kenya with markings that seemed to spell the word "Allah" in Arabic, and, nine months later, a report of a fruit on a mango tree in India with markings that looked like the whole sentence "There is no God but Allah" (*La Ilaha Illallah*).

• Reports of mysterious kangaroos in Leeds, Buckinghamshire, Argyllshire (Scotland) and Devon.

• Reports of a "tiger" in Middlesex, England, a "panther" in Essex, a "large jet-black cat-like" critter in Devon, a "puma-like" thing in Cornwall, and another "puma" in Derbyshire. Also, a mysterious giant Hound near the Welsh border, in the vicinity once frequented by the legendary Black Dog of Hergest (which inspired Conan Doyle's *Hound of the Baskervilles*.)

• Eight thoughtful, original and analytical articles on the "crop circle" mystery which has puzzled English researchers since 1980.

• A well-documented "poltergeist" in Aspley, Nottingham, which terrified one family out of its house and now terrorizes the new tenants. The phenomenon includes loud "heart beats," strange lights, organ and guitar music, smashed windows, locked doors opening, etc., and has been witnessed by social workers, police and a priest (who had his holy water thrown back at him when attempting an exorcism.)

FT scrupulously identifies sources, tells you frankly if a printed source has a history of sensationalism or inaccuracy, and conducts on-site investigations when possible.

Subscription are available at $6 per year from *Fortean Times,* 20 Paul Street, Frome, Somerset , BA11 1DX England.

▲   ▲   ▲

Sex, Satanism and Sodomized Dogs in Southern California

Ten little Indians going out to dine...
—Old Ballad

The Manhattan Beach Satanism/porno/child abuse case has at last come to a climax, or at least a temporary anticlimax. After all the hysteria and hoopla about devil worship, a sodomized dog, other tortured animals, a "kiddie porn" industry in the schools, and assorted rites of Voodoo and Black Magic; after the closure of schools and the repeated vandalization of a church; after the ruin of dozens of careers and severe damage to hundreds of lives; the final tallies, as far as we can determine, run about as follows:

• Number of Manhattan Beach schools accused by rumor of having Satanic teachers during the original 1983 panic: 9.

• Number of churches similarly accused: 1.

• Total number of institutions accused: (9 + 1) = 10.

Additional charges originally circulated:

• "An AWOL Marine sodomized the dog of one of the molested children!"

• "Teachers at the nine schools belonged to a child pornography ring!"

• "Teachers also belonged to a Satanic cult!"

• "The cult existed not only in Manhattan Beach and nearby towns but throughout the United States!"

• "Animal mutilations and bloody sacrifices occurred in all local schools and at one local Protestant church, St. Cross Episcopal in Hermosa Beach!!"

• "Hundreds of children had suffered molestation or had unwillingly participated in Satanic rituals!!"

• "Heavy Metal Rock caused it all; if you play certain records backwards, you can hear voices saying '*Satan is my Master!!!*'"

Additional interesting information:
• Number of teachers accused of child molestation and/or Satanic rituals: No exact figure can be found now, but somewhere in the neighborhood of one hundred.

• Mental status of original complaining witness: Previously judged paranoid schizophrenic by psychiatrists; at the time she made the charges, receiving Welfare on grounds of continued paranoid schizophrenia..

• Number of Manhattan Beach institutions at which the District Attorney finally decided enough evidence existed to indict suspects: one out of the 9 schools (the McMartin Pre-School), or 11.1 %. Including the church, one out of the 10 institutions, or 10.0 %.

• Number of schools at which evidence to indict was deemed insufficient by District Attorney: 8 out of 9 (88.9%).

• Number of institutions at which evidence was deemed insufficient to indict: 9 out of 10 (90.0%)

• Fate of the 8 schools at which prosecutors found insufficient evidence to indict: Due to public hostility, all 8 closed down and never re-opened.

• Fate of the McMartin school: Sold to pay legal expenses of defendants.

• Disposition of the alleged "Satanic" St. Cross Episcopal church: No evidence to indict found by D.A.; however, under harassment and death threats, the pastor closed the church and moved to another part of the country.

• Evidence of Satanic rituals considered by the D.A. strong enough to bring into court: None (0.0%).

• Evidence of a "child pornography ring" strong enough to bring into court: None. (0.0%).

And then there were seven...

• Number of original defendants indicted for child molestation: 7, out of the nearly 100 originally accused by rumor (approximately 7.0%).

• Approximate ages of said defendants: An elderly woman, her middle-aged daughter, her 20ish grand-daughter and grand-son, three youngish female teachers.

• Genders of these defendants: 6 female (85.7%), one male (Ray Buckey; 14.3%).

• Number of offenses alleged by the State against 7 defendants: 208 counts of child molestations, 0 counts of Satanism, 0 counts of pornography.

• Disposition of Satanism/animal mutilation rumors: After initial 1983 investigation, regarded as an embarrassment by police and D.A., who not only would not bring this matter into court but prefer not to discuss it anymore; said Satanist cult still widely believed in by some people who call radio talk shows regularly to protest alleged police "cover-up."

• Disposition of original 7 defendants: Charges of molestation dropped for lack of evidence: 5 cases (71.4%); charges actually brought to trial: 2 cases (28.5%).

• These percentages as calculated against all those originally accused by rumor:

— Nearly 95 cases never arrested = approximately 95% ;

— Five cases arrested but not brought to court for lack of evidence = approximately 5% ;

— Two cases brought to trial = approximately 2% of all teachers originally accused. (Totals equal 102% because exact figure on all accused in 1983 not available.)

And then there were two...

• Of 208 original charges against two remaining suspects, number of charges finally considered strong enough to bring into court: 53 (20.6%).

• Charges against these two remaining defendants dropped for lack of evidence: 155 (89.4%)

• Fate of original prosecutor, Glen Stevens: He became convinced of the innocence of both defendants and resigned; now sells real estate.

• Opinion of Ira Reiner before he was elected D.A. and took over prosecution of the two defendants: Told newspapers the case against all defendants was "incredibly weak."

• Time the jury deliberated in first trial: 9 weeks.

• Reasons jury gave for not believing child witnesses: Films of interrogation appeared to jury to show children being coached or coaxed into saying what the investigators wanted to hear. Some children had lapses of memory while testifying.

• Result of first trial: Defendant Peggy McMartin Buckey, acquitted on all charges (100%) ; Defendant Ray Buckey, acquitted on 40 charges (75.4%); jury deadlocked on 13 charges (24.6%)

• Number of defendants then remaining still legally accused out of approximately 100 originally accused by rumor: One, or approximately 1%. (Ray Buckey.)

• Percentage of all accused teachers not brought to court for lack of evidence or not believed guilty by jury: 99%

And then there was one...

• Disposition of remaining 13 charges against Buckey: 5 dropped by D.A. Reiner (38.4%); 8 brought into court in Ray Buckey's second trial. (62.6% of remaining charges, or 3.8% of all original charges against him, or 0.0038% of all charges against all teachers.)

• Medical examiners who testified to finding physical evidence of molestation in alleged victims: 1 (25% of all medical examiners testifying.)

• Medical examiners who testified to finding no physical evidence of molestation: 3 (75% of all medical examiners testifying.).

• Last official act of second jury before declaring deadlock: Re-reading all medical testimony.

• Time the jury deliberated in second trial before reaching deadlock: 15 days.

• Reasons given by jury for not believing child witnesses: Films also convinced them children had been coaxed or coached into making charges. One child repudiated former charges while on witness stand and announced she could not remember what happened.

• Result of Buckey's second trial: Mistrial declared.

• Poll of jurors on the 8 remaining charges about which they deadlocked:

— Majority wanted acquittal on 6 charges, but could not convince minority;

— Even split on 7th charge; majority wanted conviction on the one remaining charge of the original 208 charges against him (0.47%, somewhat less than one-half of 1%), but could not convince minority that Buckey was guilty "beyond a reasonable doubt."

And then there were none...
• Result for Ray Buckey: He has, due to high bail, served more time in prison (five years) than anybody actually convicted of child molestation in California in this generation, although he has not been convicted of any crime.
• Result for Peggy Buckey, mother of Ray: although eventually acquitted of all charges, she served two years in prison awaiting trial.
• Results for others:
— One of the original suspects died of a deliberate or accidental drug overdose;
— One accuser died of alcoholism;
— One defense investigator committed suicide.
• Alleged hope (according to political pundits) of District Attorney Ira Reiner in fighting this "incredibly weak" and increasingly diminishing case for so long, with less and less charges (from 208 to 53 to 8) against fewer and fewer defendants (from nearly 100 to seven to two to one lone man): Mr. Reiner hoped to become State Attorney General.
• Result of Mr. Reiner's alleged hope: He did not win the nomination for Attorney General. He has declined to bring Ray Buckey to trial a third time.
• Cost to the taxpayers:
— According to L.A. *Times,* more than $14,000,000 for the trials;
— According to Michael Jackson (KABC radio), more than $20,000,000;
—Cost of keeping Ray Buckey in prison five years, and Peggy Buckey in prison two years: not known to this author.

The Sequel. . .

• One hour after the judge declared a mistrial in the second Buckey case, radio talk-show host Carol Hemingway (KGIL, Los Angeles) placed Mr. Buckey on trial again, beginning proceedings by declaring "I believe the children." Two agents of the prosecution appeared on this show; nobody from the defense appeared. Ms. Hemingway, after 28 minutes (by my watch) of this one-sided testimony, repeated her original verdict: "I believe the children."

• Ambiguity of Ms. Hemingway's verdict: She never specified if she believed only the children's charges against Buckey, or their charges against the seven original defendants, or their charges against virtually all Manhattan Beach teachers during the original 1983 panic.

• Audience reaction to Ms. Hemingway's extra-legal "trial:" After hearing the case for the prosecution and not getting confused (like the juries in the two trials) by the case for the defense, all callers but one lone heretic agreed with Ms. Hemingway's "pro-child" verdict and pronounced Buckey guilty.

• Ms. Hemingway's response to the one lone heretic who claimed the children had been manipulated by adult hysteria: Ms. Hemingway described him as "sick, sick, *sick!*"

• Graffiti reported on McMartin Pre-School:

RAY MUST DIE

• Movie that opened in Manhattan Beach the day of declared mistrial of Ray Buckey: *Presumed Innocent,* starring Harrison Ford.

• Source of title of said movie: An ancient Anglo-Saxon legal principle unknown to Ms. Hemingway and most inhabitants of Manhattan Beach.

• Statement of said ancient Anglo-Saxon legal principle: *An accused is presumed innocent until proven guilty beyond a reasonable doubt.*

• Reasons adduced by local residents for not according Ray Buckey this traditional presumption of innocence even after 24 jurors, pouring over the evidence for 11 weeks and one day, failed to find enough evidence to convict him of anything:

    — "There's no smoke without fire."
    — "It can't *all* have been hysteria."
    — "The police never arrest an innocent man."
    — "I believe the children."

• Fate of Peggy, sister of Ray Buckey: Fired from her job with Orange County; regained it after prolonged legal battle.

• Fate of Peggy, mother of Ray Buckey: Sued the State for malicious prosecution, on grounds that officials knew original complaining witness:

　　— (a) suffered mental illness, and

　　— (b) had filed false crime reports before.

• Results of this suit: Judge ruled against Mrs. Buckey; case under appeal.

• Fate of five others arrested but never brought to trial:

　　— All lost their jobs and reputations.

　　— All have filed suit against the State, charging malicious prosecution.

　　— All have lost in original trials;

　　— All cases under appeal.

• Reaction of one (unaccused) teacher who called Michael Jackson talk show (KABC): As coach of a girl's basketball team, he announced he intended in the future to have a female teacher present at all training sessions.

• Lapse of logic of said teacher: He forgot that in the original indictment, Ray Buckey was alleged to have performed molestations while two or more female teachers were present and assisting in said molestations.

• Summary for those confused by excess detail:

　　— Years spent by the State trying to convict at least some teachers of some crime: 7.

　　— Money spent in this endeavor: Between $14 million and $20 million.

　　— Teachers actually convicted: None (0.0%.)

• Location of the dog-sodomizing Marine:

　　— Never seen by anyone but the paranoid schizophrenic who started all this.

　　— Never found by police.

　　— Never heard of again.

• Disposition of allegedly sodomized dog: Unknown.

Sources: Santa Monica *Outlook,* 29 July, 1990 and 7 August, 1990; L.A. *Times* , 28 and 29 July, 1990; *Carol Hemingway Show,* KGIL, 27 July, 1990, 2 to 4 PM; *Michael Jackson Show,* KABC, 28 July, 1990, 10-11 am.

1994 Update

After I wrote "Sex, Satanism and Sodomized Dogs," the new witch-hysteria continued to escalate all over the country, and in a few foreign countries as well. It finally seemed to reach the point where those of us that the "experts" could not induce to "remember" Satanic molestations and cannibalistic rituals, UFO abductions, or at least run-of-the-mill incest seemed an increasingly small part of the population.

Many "experts" explained, lamely, that we few unmolested people simply suffer from a collective amnesia brought on by horrors too awful for the mind to recall. This total forgetting of alleged years of hellish terror even has a "scientific" (or "pseudo-scientific?") name now: "robust repression."

Curiously, in the case of the best-documented atrocity of the 20th century—the Holocaust—not one recorded victim has suffered from "robust repression." The survivors *all* remember very well every horror they saw, and none of them ever needs hypnosis or psychological suggestion to help them "remember" (much to the annoyance and inconvenience of Holocaust revisionists). People only seem to suffer this mysterious "robust repression" when confronted by Satanists, UFOnauts, or inconvenient fathers (blokes that their mothers want to dump after first hitting them hard in the divorce court).

Odd, wouldn't you say?

As noted elsewhere in these pages, sociologists Jeffrey Victor of Jamestown Community College has recorded 33 "rumor panics" similar to the McMartin case in the past decade.. The FBI's Behavioral Science Unit has continued to dig and dig and dig in the alleged sites of the "mass graves" of these Satanic groups and found not one skeleton.

Not even a shin-bone.

Not even the intercostal clavical that Cary Grant pursued so frantically all through *Bringing Up Baby*.

This total lack of real evidence has led to some re-examination of the new witch-hunt. The False Memory Syndrome Foundation, with over 3,700 members, both psychologists and laypersons, has gotten publicity in most of the media, producing many cases where the accuser later recanted. The FMSF has also produced reams of evidence from clinical tests showing that people under hypnosis will "remember" anything the hypnotist wants them to remember.

The New Yorker for May 17 and May 24, 1993, presented, in detail, the case of an accused Satanic child molester who, under persistent questioning, gradually admitted he "remembered" all the atrocities alleged against him, including defecating on his daughter after raping her. Then a psychologist demonstrated that this poor weak-minded guy would also "remember" *anything*, however absurd or impossible, that the psychologist invented and told him his accusers had charged against him.[1] Similar exposes of the "persistence of false memory" have received wide publicity in the media—including Ann Landers' column and the *Donohue* show on TV.

True Believers, however, still believe truly. *MS.* magazine declared its Faith in Satanic Child Abuse cults a decade ago and no Radical Feminist will disagree with MS., the Holy Scripture of their dogma. A Ms. Linda Napolitano still appears at UFO conventions telling how UFOnauts sexually assaulted her and two CIA agents tried to drown her after she revealed the horrible details. (Apparently, the CIA doesn't know how to drown somebody, although they have a damned impressive record of assassinating heavily-guarded leaders of unpopular nations...)

And a chap named David Huggins goes around selling paintings he has made of several female UFOnauts who have sexually molested him. If you want to see a voluptuous *Playboy*-like version of the "monsters" in bad sci-fi, some of Mr. Huggins's paintings appear in the May 15, 1993, issue of a cynical journal called *Saucer Smear*. The editor, a wonderfully witty fellow named Jim Moseley, has met Huggins and says he thinks Huggins really believes his own yarns.

---

[1] A mildly retarded fellow named Whitmore confessed to a murder in New York, back in the early 1960s, and later evidence proved him totally innocent. This led to the Supreme Court ruling that a suspect must have an opportunity to obtain legal counsel before the police work him over, a rule later made more stringent in the more famous Miranda case. In both the Whitmore case and the above "Satanism" case, no evidence of police brutality or torture, etc., ever appeared. Nor did anybody hypnotize these persons. Some low-self-esteem types will evidently confess to anything if the police insist on their guilt often enough and loud enough. See my *Cosmic Trigger II* for an Irish case in which a whole family confessed to a crime they had not committed.

Why not? Thousands, or tens of thousands, of horny men in the Medieval Age believed female demons had siphoned off their seed in the night...

Robert Anton Wilson

Piss Wars

Dear Mr. Wilson:

I thought your readers might be interested in the following letter, which I have sent to Sen. Wayne Fowler and others in Congress who represent me:

Dear Senator Fowler:

The Department of Transportation has issued regulations demanding the implementation of random urine testing throughout the pipeline industry. I find the institution of this program, mandated by the federal government, to be an insult to my integrity. I have been in the pipeline industry for five years, advancing to my present position as a controller for the nation's largest refined petroleum pipeline. I take pride in my work. I would not report to work if I felt I was in any way not fit for the demands of the job. I resent the implication that the government would believe otherwise.

Article IV of the Constitution says, "The right of the people to be secure in their persons, houses, papers and effects against unreasonable searches and seizures shall not be violated; and no warrant shall issue, but upon probable cause, supported by oath of affirmation, and particularly describing the place to be searched and the person or thing to be seized."

189

The list of horror stories of humiliating experiences while providing a urine sample, and of tales of shattered lives after "false positive" test results, is endless. A joint CDC/NIDA study in 1985, as reported in the Journal of the American Medical Association (26 April, 1985) led to this conclusion: "Error rates for thirteen laboratories on samples containing barbiturates, amphetamines, methadone, cocaine, codeine and morphine ranged from 11% to 94%, 19% to 100%, 0% to 33%, 0% to 100%, 0% to 100% and 5% to 100% respectively. Similarly, error rates on samples not containing these drugs (false positives) ranged from 0% to 6%, 0% to 37%, 0% to 66%, 0% to 6%, 0% to 7%, and 0% to 10%, respectively."

There is something very Un-American and very scary about this whole drug-hysteria witch-hunt. It reeks of McCarthy Era loyalty oaths, Nazi SS troops, King George's redcoats. I urge you to sponsor legislation to stop this Gestapo-like invasion of privacy and violation of due process.

David Ross
Norcross, GA

An Addendum by RAW
According to Byrd Laboratories, Austin, TX, the following have all led to "false positives" in urine tests: Dristan, Vick's Formula 44, Actifed, Alka -Seltzer, St. Joseph's Cold Tablets, Robitussin, Contac, Sucrets, Tylenol and even poppy seeds on bagels (which have led to false "opium" readings.)

▲   ▲   ▲

190

SAVE YOUR BREATH

Don't budget deficit me you old men
    with eyeglasses and no lips who say we can't
    afford to house the houseless or to heal the
    sick.
Don't fiscal responsibility me you devourers
    of the fat of the land may it clog your
    devious up-for-election arteries.
Don't balance of trade me you horny-handed
    peddlers of shoddy shares in fingers-crossed
    bonanzas based on non-existent enterprise.
Don't national security me you who make
    deals behind our backs under
    cover of law-proof dark.
Don't family-values me you who force
    apart man woman and child in the interest
    of an ever grosser national product.
Don't state of the union me you unctuous
    apologists for quotidian horror may you choke
    on your aw-shucks-just-plain-old-me
    charisma.
Don't pay your speechwriters one more cent
    on my account, or your column writers
    or The News Tonighters.
Epoxy in my ears before I hear
    another word.

                    —Arlen Wilson

Humor Department

"Will you pay $23 to be

<u>brainwashed</u>

by the **CIA**?....

Both LEARY and WILSON

have been **funded** by the **CIA**
since at least the late sixties...

Mr. Wilson <u>does</u> have a sense of humor,

but REMEMBER

his <u>smirking antics</u> are

at YOUR expense. "

—Anonymous leaflet handed out at the April 30, 1990, demonstration of Virtual Reality hardware at New York University

Mr. Wilson responds: **HAR! HAR! HAR!**

"Wilson describes himself as a

'GUERRILLA ONTOLOGIST,'

signifying his intention

to ATTACK language and knowledge

in the way

TERRORISTS

ATTACK their targets:

to JUMP OUT FROM THE SHADOWS

for an UNPROVOKED ATtacK,

then SLINK BACK

and HIDE behind

a HEARTY BELLY LAUGH."

—Robert Sheaffer,
The Skeptical Inquirer, Spring 1990

Mr. Wilson responds:
HAR! HAR! HAR! HAR! HAR!

**FOR SECURITY PURPOSES,
THIS FNORD
INTENTIONALLY LEFT BLANK**

CHApTER NInE

- ☞ California's Suppressed
  Drug Report

- ☞ High Weirdness:
  A UFO Update

- ☞ 1994 Update

- ☞ Tomorrow's News

- ☞ Book Review:
  The Rebirth of Nature:
  The Greening of Science and God
  by Rupert Sheldrake
  Reviewed by Arlen Wilson

- ☞ "To The Persian Gulf:
  Thanks"
  A Poem by Arlen Wilson

California's Suppressed Drug Report

Introduction

In 1969, the California legislature created a scientific research advisory panel to study "the drug problem," and each year since then the panel of experts has written a report, which the State has published. Optimists may believe that some legislators actually read these scientific reports and maybe even thought about them.

Until 1990.

The research panel submitted their report, as usual, to Attorney General John Van de Camp, who looked at it and decided that it should not be published. The scientists had come to conclusions that differ in some respects from Official State Dogma. Van de Camp, acting to protect the public from mental confusion, insisted on removing a key section of the report, where the scientific conclusions most strikingly contradicted the Revealed Dogma.

To some extent, we sympathize with Mr. Van de Camp. People look at scientific magazines when they want facts. When they look at government reports, they expect the usual B.S. If people found scientific reasoning in a government report, it might shake their whole concept of "reality" and set them adrift in epistemological angst. It might even seem like a "psychedelic experience" to some.

Nonetheless, scientific reports should not be buried alive if we are ever to have "the free market place of ideas" which Justice Holmes thought the first amendment authorizes. We were glad to learn that Dr. Frederick H. Meyers, one of the authors of the report, has made copies of the censored portions available to anyone who writes to him requesting a copy. We wrote, got a copy by very quick return mail and are happy to share the highlights with our readers.

What follows is quoted directly from the report.

For legal reasons, we must warn you that the Attorney General has determined that this material may be hazardous to your Dogma.

Highlights: Executive Summary

In this annual report, the Panel presumes to suggest that the Legislature act to redirect this State away from the present destructive pathways of drug control.

Our "War on Drugs" for the past fifty years has been based on the principle of prohibition and has been manifestly unsuccessful in that we are now using more and a greater variety of drugs, legal and illegal. As with the "noble experiment" of the 18th Amendment, prohibition as opposed to regulation has not controlled drug use and a societal over-reaction has burdened us with ineffectual, inhumane and expensive treatment, education and enforcement efforts. These efforts at reducing the social cost of drug use fail to distinguish between drug effects and associated criminal activity and fail to recognize that different drugs pose different problems and that we do not have one massive drug problem...

Legislation aiming at regulation and decriminalization (not "legalization") should be formulated as novel efforts that could quickly be modified if unsuccessful. The Panel suggests that this legislation be formulated following four principles. First, separately consider the different drugs involved and not consider that there is one massive drug problem; second, distinguish between the effects of drugs and the associated criminal activity; third, design the legislation being aware that these are initial efforts subject to change with experience; and fourth, think of drugs as including alcohol and nicotine and not as being separate substances.

Immediate Needs

The traditional activities by enforcement and regulatory agencies, however expanded by the long standing war on drugs, whether directed at the individual drug user or small or large purveyor, have not been able to alter the course of the problems, of the extent of use, of individual damage or of the associated criminal activity. Even in the judgment of the enforcement agencies, this traditional approach has accomplished little except possibly to increase prices and encourage experimentation with alternate drugs. In spite of the sanctions imposed upon drug users, we have over the past 22 years seen massive epidemics involving high-dose intravenous methamphetamine, heroin, marijuana, hallucinogens, sniffed cocaine, synthetic narcotics, PCP and now smoking free-base or crack-cocaine.

It appears incontrovertible that whatever policies we have been following over the past generations must not be continued unexamined and unmodified since our actions to date have favored the development of massive individual and societal problems.

Not only should the leaders of this State act now, but they must act differently. They must adopt actions unlike those we have tested and found wanting over past generations.

The responsibility for initiating change appears to us to be passing at this moment from the intellectual and scholarly community to the Legislature. There is more than an undercurrent of published discussion favoring radical change and questioning what, for convenience, we will call the "prohibition policy." Technical journals and leading intellectual periodicals across the political spectrum have published carefully reasoned discussions establishing that our present policies are worse than useless. "Legalization" (not our term) has even been supported by conservative leaders such as William F. Buckley and Milton Freedman.

Differentiate Different Drugs

There is no basis for progress in talking about *the* drug problem and looking for *one* magic solution to the massive problem as it is perceived by the public. The approach must be based upon a separate consideration of each of the several drugs involved.

We must then not be naively permissive in our attitude toward alcohol and other depressants that disinhibit and cause inappropriate reactions. And we should not react emotionally against less harmful drugs in such a way that their regulation generates more problems than would their ungoverned use.

In our judgment, a first step in rationalizing our approach would be to further isolate marijuana from other illegal drugs...

With a drug like marijuana, which enjoys popular approval in the face of legal prohibition, the associated criminal activity is regarded as nominal. And in the face of a refusal by a significant fraction of the population to support the laws against marijuana, it will be impossible to control the market in marijuana. Indeed, although the huge illegal market for imported marijuana may add significantly to our negative balance of payments, that market is not associated with drive-by killings or other devastating criminal activity.

199

Suggested Legislation

• *Remove penalties for possession of needles and syringes.*

The AIDS virus has spread through the drug-using community to an extent that varies with the sanitary practices of the local population. The prevalence of infection is much higher, for example, in New York City than in San Francisco.

There are two suggested methods of controlling the spread of this relatively new virus. The first, demonstrably ineffective, is to adopt a moralizing attitude, continue our current practices and simply add the individual tragedy and economic burden to the community of more AIDS patients...

The other method of controlling the spread of AIDS virus would be to encourage sanitary practices at the time of injection by making it possible for each heroin user to use his own "outfit," that is, syringe and needle, rather than accept the risk of using one contaminated with another addict's blood.

• *Allow cultivation of marijuana for individual use.*

We resist the use of the word "legalization" in relation to any drug, including marijuana. On the other hand, an objective consideration of marijuana shows that it is responsible for less damage to the individual and society than are alcohol and cigarettes. the other social drugs mentioned above. A further consideration in forming a reaction to the wide use of marijuana is that it is a source of conflict between generations and of disrespect for the law.

The Panel therefore suggests that the law be changed to permit cultivation for personal use. Such cultivation would be permitted only on property serving as the residence of the individual, that is, it would not authorize the cultivation of fifty plants on a National forest and it would not permit the possession outside the home of more than the present one ounce, nor would it sanction the provision to others in or out of the residence whether by sale or in the form of "parties."

• *Prohibit legal drug use in special State establishments.*

Overall, prohibition is not feasible but restricted use of alcohol in inappropriate places is justifiable and would be an essential step in projecting the attitudinal change desired.

The Panel applauds the establishment of tobacco free areas in State institutions. As a condition of their funding the Legislature should now insist that certain agencies within the State system not sell or provide alcoholic beverages within the confines of their campus or building. This should be immediately applied to any medical center campus or hospital.

200

*   *   *

Well, there you have it. We have cut a bit for space reasons, but these are the major portions the Attorney General did not want California voters to see, for fear they might be confused if they learned that scientific experts often disagree with government policy. We trust that our readers, unlike the voters of California, have enough maturity to think and to judge for themselves.

▲   ▲   ▲

High Weirdness:

A UFO Update

"It is the *third aspect* of the UFO phenomenon which deserves full attention...The third aspect is the social belief system which has been generated by...the expectation of space visitors. This belief...is *generating new religious, cultural and political concepts* of which social science has taken little notice."
— Dr. Jacques Vallee, *The Invisible College*

About four years ago, more or less, a remarkable document started circulating through computer networks. Written by John Lear—heir to the Lear jet fortune—this statement, purportedly based on first-hand knowledge of government secrets, alleged that:

(a) the U.S. government has engaged in communication with extraterrestrials since 1947;

(b) the CIA has maintained a disinformation cover to conceal what is going on;

(c) the ETs maintain a base, or bases, in one or more underground locations in the Southwest;

(d) these Aliens have broken their side of the agreement and have engaged in various nefarious activities, including conducting strange experiments on our cattle, abducting humans, and engaging in sexual, genetic (and other) tampering with the human abductees—all of which, because of their superior technology, cannot successfully be opposed; and, finally;

(d) neither the CIA nor any other branch of government knows what to do about the problem and are frantically trying to hide the evidence of their involvement.

This Lear document contained virtually no evidence to support its paranoid-sounding claims. Lear simply asserts that friends in the Intelligence community had revealed all this to him. If one decided to "believe" this yarn, that belief could only rest upon the feeling that Lear's style did not contain any of the usual stigmata of paranoid writings—"raving and ranting," hyperbole, grandiosity, etc.—and also that it seems hard to imagine why a man of such straight Establishment background would invent such a yarn and allow himself to look like a nut-

202

case. (Lear has not tried to cash on in his story.) If one dogmatically disbelieved it, on the other hand, that could only rest upon the neophobic principle that anything new and shocking to our traditional beliefs *must* belong in the realm of hoax or lunacy.

I decided to neither believe nor disbelieve. I just filed John Lear in my "I don't know what the hell to think about it" category, along with rains of frogs, "spontaneous human combustion," crop circles and the Loch Ness Monster—but I certainly inclined more to disbelief than belief. On a scale of 0 to 10, where 0 represents total rejection and 10 total belief, I put the Lear story about 0.001.

In the next couple of years, similar documents began to circulate, both through computer nets and ordinary mail. William L. Moore emerged as one of the main sources, and, like Lear, claimed he had been given the "inside story" by Intelligence agents. Another source, William Cooper, alleged that he himself was a former Naval Intelligence officer and had actually seen documents relating to the Aliens in our midst. (Cooper's mailings usually include his service discharge, or a good forgery of same, showing that he did serve a very minor function in Naval Intelligence.)

These stories basically agreed with Lear's original scenario, but Cooper added many unique and blood-curdling details, including the claims that the CIA originally got into the cocaine trade to get money for the ET project without leaving a paper trail, that George Bush's oil business was always a front for running cocaine, and that John F. Kennedy had been assassinated by the CIA for trying to oppose the Alien take-over of our country. Much of this stuff seemed far wilder than Lear's claims and I classified Cooper, on my 0-to-10 scale, somewhere around 0.00000000000000000001.

William Moore claimed one of his sources was a government agent who used the code name "Falcon." Since this whole scenario seemed more and more dubious to me, I was rather astounded when "Falcon" appeared on a syndicated TV documentary hosted by Mike Farrell of *M.A.S.H.* and called *UFO Cover-Up : Live!* which has been shown on several channels in the last two years.

On this show, "Falcon" sat in a dark room, speaking through a voice distorter, and basically backed up all the claims of Lear and Moore, although he did touch upon the more classically "paranoid" embellishments of Cooper.

203

The producer of the show and an allegedly "independent" journalist both swore that, although they could not authenticate "Falcon's" story, they had verified that he was indeed attached to one of our Intelligence agencies.

That's peculiar, to say the least of it. Why would one of "our" Intelligence agencies try to peddle the line that our government has engaged in a very monstrous conspiracy against all of us?

A Strange Loop

A Strange Loop appears in logic or computer circuitry when an integral part of a system contradicts or undermines the whole system. I have always found these Strange Loops fascinating, even before Hofstadter gave them that name, back when we still called them "paradoxes" and thought they existed only on the linguistic (or symbolic) level.

We now know that Strange Loops can exist in hardware as well as software; and Paul Watzlavick and Gregory Bateson, among others, have demonstrated that many forms of "mental illness," or seeming "mental illness" derive from sociological-cultural Strange Loops. Watzlavick has also demonstrated, in his *How Real Is Real?*, that modern Intelligence Agencies, involved in both the collection of information and the creation of disinformation (to deceive rivals) create Strange Loops that, like Heller's famous Catch-22, seem beyond all rational solution.

The Strange Loops have now invaded the Alien Invasion meme.

According to *Fate* (April, 1991), William Moore, one of the major sources of this CIA/Alien Conspiracy story, last year confessed that he had unknowingly served as a funnel for disinformation. That is, he announced that he now believes "Falcon" and his other sources deliberately deceived him on some points, *but he does not know which points.*

Wait. It gets spookier.

Moore now acknowledges that he had twelve informants, all of whom he believes hold positions in our Intelligence community. He has given them all bird-names to protect them, so "Falcon" now belongs to an aviary including "Hawk," "Partridge," "Heron," "Sparrow," etc., and even, God save us, "Chickadee."

Moore says that these sources wish the American people to believe the stories they told him, but that *they also wish to hide the full truth, which they haven't yet told him.*

Try thinking about that, without prejudice or anxiety, and see where it gets you. It seems, as I said above, that the Intelligence people—or a renegade faction therein?—wishes to make us paranoid about our own government. What possible purpose could this serve? It would only make sense if "our enemies" did it...

Well, disinformation systems often function merely like a stage magician's misdirections. They focus our attention on A, so we won't notice what has transpired at B. Are these UFO-CIA conspiracy yarns supposed to distract us from other, even more hideous conspiracies? That's an unwholesome line of thought...

Always remember this: a "good" disinformation system contains a high element of truth mixed with its clever lies; otherwise, it would not deceive enough people for a long enough time to serve its function. This reasoning seems to lead us back to where Moore wants us to go: we end up thinking part of his yarn contains fact, but we can't decide *which* part.

A Video Review

Bill Cooper Exposes Top Secrets (available from Shining Star Productions, 7820 East Evans # 900, Scottsdale AZ 85260; no price listed on my review copy) presents Mr. Cooper in a rambling two-hour medley of wild accusations and very unconvincing documentation.

Mr. Cooper shows dozens and dozens of slides of UFO photos. Some of these have long ago been proven to be fakes, at least to my satisfaction, but Cooper either doesn't know or doesn't care about that. Others could be space-ships, weather balloons, ordinary aircraft giving off heavy glare in high sunlight, or whatever you care to imagine. Cooper also shows government documents with "revealing" sentences in them; if you stop the video, as I did, and read the surrounding text, you will often find that he has taken these sentences out of context and reversed their meaning.

Cooper's highlight, however, is a blotchy 19th or 20th generation copy of a copy of a copy of the notorious Zapruder film. Cooper insists that if you look close, you can see the secret service agent in the front of the limo turn around and shoot John F. Kennedy as they pass the Grassy Knoll. He shows this clip about five times and keeps insisting that you can see the gun if you try. If you are suggestible, or just interested in the subjectivity of perception (as I am) you can indeed see the "gun" finally. I did, with great effort. But I can also see the sniper in

205

the bushes in the famous Garrison photo, and things even more remarkable than that. I have no faith in the infallibility of perception, yours or mine.

David Lifton, one of the most scientific and scholarly of the Kennedy assassination critics, points out that you can clearly see that the secret service man has no gun at all (at least not in his hand) in any first-class reproduction of the Zapruder film. Cooper's demonstration only works with very blurry old copies of the film, and only with audiences willing to try really hard to see the damned gun.

You begin to gather that I do not much trust Bill Cooper. Nonetheless, I find this video a fascinating part of the new UFO demonology for a variety of reasons:

1.) Cooper drags in two very interesting quotes that don't fit his thesis at all, but in fact *undermine* the thesis. I don't believe he is stupid, and this "blunder" arouses my curiosity. Both quotes—one from philosopher John Dewey and the other from the satirical Iron Mountain Report (which Cooper treats as literal, rather than parodic)—point out that *one way to stop war on this planet is to fake an Alien invasion, forcing all Earth people to unite against the interplanetary threat.* Is this some kind of Broad Hint? Does the "evil" CIA and its allies (Naval and Military Intelligence) have some benevolent long range Peace Plan of this sort? Does that explain this disinformation system?

2.) Cooper's "slant" seems directed to a right-wing, somewhat Fundamentalist market, but he says many, many things that can only shock and probably infuriate that kind of audience. Could this serve as a "blooper" maneuver, intended to confuse us about what political agenda he actually wishes to promote?

3.) The video ends with an image that entirely fails in its declared purpose: The famous photo of the Chinese protester standing in front of the tanks headed for Tianamin Square. Cooper gives a moving speech about how one person can resist entrenched tyranny, but the image carries a defeatist message to anybody who remembers that the tanks were not stopped and the protesters in the Square were all killed or imprisoned. The soundtrack says that we can throw off the tyranny of the Alien/CIA/cocaine cartel; but the photo calls up thoughts of heroic folly ending in failure. Is Cooper telling us to fight back, or telling us that if we dare fight back we will be destroyed?

I don't draw any definite conclusions, but I offer you the hypothesis that Cooper, knowingly or unknowingly, serves as part of the disinformation system that has also led William Moore around by the nose.

The Latest on Whitley Strieber

Meanwhile, the most famous victim of Alien abduction and/or the biggest liar on the planet—i.e., Whitley Strieber—has disappeared from the lecture circuit, as many have noted with concern.

The explanation appeared in a letter to one Richard Capozzola (reprinted in *Saucer Smear,* Vol. 38, No. 2), in which Strieber complained that all he had accomplished by revealing his Close Encounter of the Weirdest Kind was to make himself "a public laughingstock [and] a despised outsider to both the UFO and scientific communities." Whitley doesn't mention all the money he made, but on the other hand I wouldn't want to change places with him; he ends his letter with a pathetic sentence saying he still finds himself "facing the visitors alone in the middle of the night with hardly a clue."

According to his publishers, Strieber has passed three separate lie detector tests. I tend to believe that. Whenever I have seen him on TV, he always leaves me with the uneasy feeling that (a) he has had some terrifying experiences and (b) he honestly does not know how to explain them.

Gulf Breeze Mysteries

The town of Gulf Breeze, on the northwest of Florida, facing the Gulf of Mexico, has probably had more UFO sightings than just about anywhere; even the Mayor and the editor of the local newspaper have seen strange lights in the sky, and hundreds of other citizens have reported anomalies of one sort or another.

As you may have heard, a local named Ed Walters produced some photos of UFOs which looked exactly the way spaceships ought to look. I mean, these things were definitely not "swamp gas" or lights reflecting off the wings of migratory birds, or anything that banal. On the basis of these photos, Ed got a contract from William Morrow publishers and wrote a book.

At this point, *Saucer Smear* (quoted above) enters our story again. Published by a witty chap named Jim Moseley, *Saucer Smear* takes a skeptical attitude toward everybody on all sides of the UFO debate and has the honor of once being called "a boil on the ass of Ufology" by John Keel. Moseley charged that two members of the Committee for Scientific Investigation of Claims of the Paranormal (CSICOP) had tried to prevent publication of

Ed Walters' book by sending unproven negative material about Ed to the publisher, William Morrow.

The two accused were Phil Klass and Zan Overall. They responded in *Saucer Smear,* Vol. 37, No. 2—but, alas, they hadn't bothered to get their stories in line with each other.

Phil Klass flatly denied that he and Overall had fed such negative material to Morrow, but Zan Overall admitted that they had, and defended the action, invoking Free Speech and other noble ideals to justify their attempt to stifle Ed Walters' free speech.

This does not appear to qualify as a Strange Loop. More simply, one of these guys just flatly lied. Either Klass lied in saying they didn't send such material to Morrow, or Overall lied in saying they did.

It seems once again that CSICOP people, like the priests of other Orthodoxies, have no compunction about using sleazy tactics in their war for the True Faith. (Unless, of course, CSICOP itself functions as part of the CIA disinformation system...in which case, the purpose of Klass and Overall in making idiots of themselves was to get all of us *more* interested in Gulf Breeze.)

Meanwhile, a model of the "spaceship" in Ed Walters' photos was found in his former house and at least two neighbors gave evidence that they had helped Ed fake his photos. Of course, this does not end the Gulf Breeze enigma: there are still hundreds of witnesses who saw weird things in the sky, even if they didn't photograph toy spaceships as Ed evidently did.

And then things got really weird.

Around July 9, 1990, six soldiers disappeared from a classified Intelligence unit in Germany and then showed up mysteriously in Gulf Breeze. Initial reports claimed they were members of an Apocalyptic sect called "The End of the World." Later reports contradicted this, and it now appears that no such sect ever existed.

The soldiers were picked up at the home of one Anna Foster, a psychic who once worked at a book store in Gulf Breeze called the New Age Shop.

As reported in Saucer Smear, Vol. 37, No. 7, *agents of the FBI, the CIA and even the NSA* soon descended on Gulf Breeze, as if somebody in high places thought something important was involved in this minor case of six AWOLs. The Gulf Breeze police, meanwhile, questioned the soldiers at length about their interest in and knowledge of Bill Cooper *and his claims that George Bush runs the cocaine business and Aliens run the CIA.*

Strange, what? Ordinarily the police would only ask about facts relevant to whether the soldiers were or weren't AWOL...

Then somebody unknown from somewhere unidentified sent a seemingly ordinary UFO photo—the kind you see in any book on the subject, containing nothing that looked new or special— together with a very weird letter to the Gulf Breeze *Sentinel* and several other news sources, threatening to reveal "*everything*" if the six soldiers were not released.

The usual nut or hoaxter who intrudes on all such events?

Six days later, *all charges against the six soldiers were dropped*—a rare event in the history of the U.S. Army, which does not regard AWOLs lightly. The soldiers refused to give interviews.

Thereafter a Great Darkness fell upon the face on the media and no further news about the whole mystery has come forth.

A Grasp at Sanity

Dr. Jacques Vallee, quoted at the beginning of this piece, has, in several brilliant and offbeat books, offered a variety of tentative models that might explain the UFO mystery. One of Dr. Vallee's models, in his *Messengers of Deception* (And/Or Press, 1977) holds that the UFO phenomenon has been manufactured and manipulated by an Intelligence agency as an experiment, to see to what extent their current technology-and- psychology allows them to manipulate *both the ideas and the behavior* of masses of people.

I don't "believe" this model—but right now I don't have a better idea.

"I am no longer young enough to know the answer to everything."

—Oscar Wilde

▲   ▲   ▲

1994 Update

People in Gulf Breeze still continue to report UFOs regularly, according to Jim Moseley, who lives in nearby Key West.

Nobody in the major media or in the underground UFO journals has yet satisfactorily explained why the hell the six soldiers went AWOL from Germany and headed straight for Gulf Breeze.

I conclude that some unsolved mysteries of 1991 remain unsolved in 1994—but may get themselves solved in '95 or '96—or sometime before the Heat Death of the Universe.

And, then again, some mysteries may *never* get solved.

I, personally, still regard the birth of language as a totally unsolved mystery, and I often wonder why more social scientists don't appear to realize just how mind-boggling that mystery seems when you sit down and really think about it for a long time. When you add the birth of religion, the enigma of human history grows even darker and deeper.

As far as I can make out, at some point—call it "Year X"— our ancestors had no more language or religion than a pack of hogs, and at some other point—"Year Y"—they had hundreds of complexly inflected languages and complexly incredible religions —and arts and sciences and philosophies for good measure. And nobody knows just what happened in between X and Y. Or even if it happened in one quantum jump or in several slow increments. (Either theory has severe problems, if you really think about it...)

Does that not give one ferociously to wonder, and wave one's arms about, as the French say?

As for UFOs, I still like to peruse the saucerian literature now and then, but I find the whole subject much less puzzling and exciting than those neuro-psychological missing links (language, religion, "culture") which transformed us from ordinary mammals to highly unusual, perhaps unique mammals.

And, besides, most people do not realize how normal—how drearily normal—a UFO seems to me, after decades of studying perception psychology. I see dozens of UFOs every week, and even more UNFOs—Unidentified *Non-Flying* Objects. The world presents countless objects I cannot positively identify, and most of them zoom by so fast that I will never get a chance to check them out again and pronounce even a tentative identification.

210

People who find unidentified objects so puzzling as to rank in the realm of the "unearthly" (extra-terrestrial and/or supernatural) merely indicate to me that they have an uncritical habit of identifying most "ordinary" objects just a bit uncritically. Or, to paraphrase Josiah Warren, they just have a tendency to "understand new things too quickly."

The best cure for that habit of uncritical identification consists of:

STEP ONE: Avoid the "is of identity" in writing. When you have mastered that, go on to the next step (on which I have not yet succeeded, myself):

STEP TWO: Avoid the "is of identity" in your speaking. And then, of course:

STEP THREE: Avoid the "is of identity" in your thinking.

I think the last stage of this process qualifies as "Enlightenment," at least in some schools of Buddhism.

▲   ▲   ▲

Tomorrow's News

GENI Out of the Bottle

Bucky Fuller's Global Energy Network *(Note: See "The Global Energy Grid" and "GENI Update" in Chapter 6 —Ed.)* continues to move forward on many fronts. In recent developments:

• The conference on a Mid-East grid, scheduled for Kuwait in February, 1990, had to be canceled due to a Neolithic gang rumble over oil. (You may have heard of that...) But the American Society of Mechanical Engineers stepped in to sponsor a larger conference on the global grid in Manitoba, Winnipeg, Canada later in 1990.

• In a remarkable editorial, the prestigious *Florida Business Review* (10 Oct., 1990) stated bluntly that a global grid could have prevented the conflicts leading to the Gulf War and urged that the grid be adopted soon as the best way to stop pollution and decrease the chance of future wars.

• The grid has been endorsed by VIce Preesident Al Gore, by Sergeny Velikhov (Vice-President of the Soviet Academy of Sciences) and by David Cline (Alaskan director, Audubon Society.)

"I'm Mad As Hell..."

Speak Out Software has a package that will enable you to really express yourself whenever you feel like Howard ("I'm mad as hell") Beale in the classic film *Network.* The Speak Out bundle gives you a mailing list of 3000 top public officials in the U.S. and elsewhere, including not only addresses but phone numbers, and also provides sample letters for those unskilled at polemic. The firm's president, Ken Roseman, says he hopes this package will reverse our nation's long-term trend toward political despair and apathy.

(Source: The Futurist, March-April 1991)

Go Directly To Jail

The United States imprisons black males at four times the rate of the Union of South Africa, according to a recent study by the Sentencing Project, a nonprofit research organization.

The same study found that the United States now leads the world in total number of citizens imprisoned in proportion to total population. This development occurred since 1980, when the U.S. trailed South Africa and the USSR in number of prisoners in proportion to total population. The U.S. rate of imprisonment has increased 50% in the Reagan-Bush years—mostly due to the "war on drugs," the study said—while the prison population of South Africa only increased 11% and that of the Soviet Union dropped dramatically.

"If we continue to pursue the policies of the 1980s," the study said, "we can expect black males may truly become the 'endangered species' that many have predicted."

(Source: L.A. *Times,* January 5, 1991*)*

In related stories from our newspaper files:

• The number of people executed in the U.S. since 1900 and subsequently proven to be innocent: 23.

(Source: L.A. *Times,* Oct. 18, 1990*)*

• Fastest growing branch of the Federal government: the bureau of prisons.

(Source: Santa Monica *Outlook,* Oct .17, 1990*)*

• The only "advanced" industrial nations that have not banned capital punishment: the U.S., U.S.S.R and South Africa.

(Source: Syracuse *Herald-American,* July 8, 1990*)*

• Actual increase in U.S. crime rate as against increase in persons imprisoned: Crime rate up 1.8 per cent in past decade, imprisonment up 50 per cent in same decade.

(Source: Syracuse *Herald-American,* July 8, 1990*)*

Computer "Mind-Reading"

Dr. Erich Sutter of Smith-Kettlewell Eye Research Institute in San Francisco has designed a system called Brain Response Interface (BRI) which allows a computer to scan your brain waves and virtually "read your mind." The Sutter system divides the monitor screen into boxes and each box represents a letter, punctuation mark, word or icon. Instead of pressing a key, the user focuses on one of the boxes and the interface interprets the brain waves to determine which box the user has selected.

Intended to help the handicapped, BRI moves us closer to the day when "people are going to be controlling computers using thoughts," according to Tom Clifford of CyberTechnics. Clifford predicts that will occur in "10 or 15 years."

(Source: PC/Computing, Nov., 1989*)*

Cyberpunk Lives! The Merry Pranksters Return!

A new computer virus has appeared which invades the internal memory of consoles, freezes the keyboard and flashes the message: "Your PC is now stoned. Legalize marijuana."

213

In a similar vein, a group called the Alice B. Toklas Society has sent out press releases announcing that it has successfully infiltrated pizza parlors in the Washington, D.C., area and spiked government pizzas with marijuana. The ABTS warns that it will continue similar tactics until "no one, no matter how innocent of drug use, will ever be safe from drug testing."

(Source: The Realist, March-April 1991)

In The Wind

Although the Bush Administration continues its allegiance to oil and nukes, wind power has made advances in California. Accounting for only one per cent of California's electricity (8% of San Francisco Bay Area's electricity) a wind turbine plant in Livermore nonetheless produces as much energy as any nuclear plant in the state, and two other wind turbines now exist near Bakersfield and San Diego.

(Source: L.A. Times, December 24, 1990)

EgoSoft: Psycho-active Software

According to a press release we have received, Dutch publisher Luc Sala has launched EgoSoft, a center in Amsterdam for the exploration of psycho-active media. Major areas of interest include isolation tanks, electronic drugs, mind machines, brain machine live concerts, total environment applications, psycho-active audio, psycho-active video, psycho-analytical software, cyberspace research, Virtual Reality and professional New Age software.

For further info: EgoSoft, Niewe Kerkstraat, 1018 DZ Amsterdam, Nederland.

MindsEye Plus Passes Test

We have received another controlled study of a light-and-sound brain machine, in which the basic claims made for these machines again appear vindicated. Dr. Bruce Harrah Conforth of Indiana University used the MindsEye Plus machine and a similar machine which produced only "pink noise." The pink noise stimulation produced only the normal alpha waves seen when the subjects relaxed and closed their eyes, but the same subjects showed significantly greater relaxation, more theta waves, reduction in heart rate, lower blood pressure and demonstrable right brain/left brain synchronization when using the MindsEye Plus.

214

The Browning of America

Before we all got mesmerized by Saddam Hussein as the latest incarnation of Lucifer, four different publications ran feature articles on the growing (if often grudging) evolution of the U.S. from a white-dominated culture to a multi-cultural society of many sub-cultures. *Time* (April 9, 1990) stressed that the "browning of America" now appears *inevitable* and White Supremacists seem doomed to fighting a losing battle. The New York *Times* (June 16, 1990) examined the trends, came to the same general conclusion and tried to document that the economic *self-interest* of white people will force them to adjust to new realities. The *Village Voice* (April 24, 1990) argued that giving each ethnic group its fair share was just plain *justice*— and long over-due.

New Options (June 25, 1990)—a magazine variously described as "post-Liberal," "New Age" and/or "Green"—took a different tack and argued that the coming multi-cultural America will "expand our mental horizons" and vastly enrich our psychological diet (just as multi-culturalism in the restaurant field has enriched our physical diet.)

One expert quoted in *New Options,* Molefi Kete Asante of Temple University's Department of African-American studies, says: "You can't force people to be Northern Europeans. But that is what we have done since the beginning of this country. Even Eastern Europeans have been psychologically forced to be Northern Europeans." When this Nordic nexus has to share power with other cultures and their reality-tunnels, *New Options* argues, America will blossom into new creativity, as painting, poetry and architecture did at the beginning of this century when they began incorporating Asian and African techniques.

Satan Claus?

The Truth Tabernacle Church in Burlington, N.C. recently had a mock trial of Santa Claus, whom they dub "Satan Claus." They found him guilty of being a pagan god disguised as a Christian saint, of "child abuse" (for encouraging people to buy booze), of perjury in claiming to be St. Nicholas, and of seven other counts. Then they took an 8-foot dummy in a Santa (or Satan) Claus suit out to the nearest tree and hanged him.

Mr. Claus was also removed from the official list of Roman Catholic saints in 1969.

(Source: Fortean Times, No. 56,Winter 1990-91*)*

215

Exo-Anthropology

James Funaro, the anthropologist who first proposed regarding our homeless population, not as "bums," but as a new sub-culture—"the urban nomads"—has now branched out into exo-anthropology, the study of how different intelligent species might react to each other. In collaboration with other social scientists and a few science-fiction writers, Funaro has created "Bateson," a game and/or set of experiments named after one of the great anthropologists of our century, Dr. Gregory Bateson. In "Bateson," two teams each spend two days creating a non-human culture of the sort encountered in the best science-fiction, and then the two cultures meet. All interactions are observed by a third team of social scientists and Funaro hopes that some lessons will emerge that can prove useful when and if our space probes encounter an intelligence that does not think in our categories.

In a recent paper, Funaro has criticized NASA for thinking of "human" in terms of American norms. Americans, he argues, may serve well as explorers but would score below the Japanese at maintaining space colonies once they're settled. Americans, he charges, are "individualistic, competitive, unused to sharing and poor at group dynamics" compared to the Japanese and many other human cultures.

(Source: West, Aug. 19, 1990)

▲   ▲   ▲

216

Book Review

The Rebirth of Nature:
The Greening of Science and God
by Rupert Sheldrake
(Bantam, 1991)
Reviewed by Arlen Wilson

The old yarn that Big Daddy in the Sky made a sort of terrarium down here and put his special pets into it with "dominion" over everything else has gone by the board in all but a few remote corners. But what should or could replace it?

While we were still living with the fallout from this old world-view, orphaned by the warfare between science and religion and doubtless still missing Big Dad, along came Lady GAIA back in the late Seventies to make us feel warm and wanted again— albeit with the stings of guilt inevitably induced by mothers both Jewish and Goyische.

We seem to like religion as soap opera, or soap opera as religion. Well, why not? We're all born into one form or another of the family drama. Spinoza said that if triangles had a god he would be triangular. It's no surprise that the religions and cosmologies we generate to some extent reflect our human relationships and concerns, particularly our sexual and repro-ductive preoccupations. I've even heard some women refer to the Big Bang as a typically macho conception.

When scientist James Lovelock first formulated the GAIA hypothesis back in the late Seventies, he chose the name of an ancient Greek goddess to personify Earth, in the sense of the total biosphere, as a single, conscious, intelligent being. All living creatures are enmeshed in an incredibly complex network of interrelationships but all are parts of Her, the all-encom-passing and aware presence.

The great NASA photographs of our beautiful blue planet, as well as subsequent satellite films, have helped to confirm the image of Earth as an ever-changing and very much alive single organism. It is well known by now that many astronauts and not a few cosmonauts had "mystical" experiences when first perceiving the loveliness and unity of our planet from space, a poignant contrast to what they "knew" of its conflicts and political divisions.

Now Dr. Rupert Sheldrake, a Cambridge cell biologist, has written a brilliant book—his third brilliant book, actually—which goes far and away beyond Lovelock or any other scientist that I'm aware of in creating a new paradigm for the next millennium. He explores Mother Nature, the biosphere, as an actual living, learning being, and no mere figure of speech useful in nursery tales. He dares to suggest that her very "laws" may not be eternally fixed but evolving and might better be thought of as patterns, habits, "morphic resonances." She lives, learns, explores, experiments, remembers. Human intelligence is a part, but only one part, of the larger intelligence involved in this process. Her "mind" may even be like ours—partly conscious and partly unconscious.

To a still very largely mechanistic scientific community, this is the very stuff of heresy. Sheldrake's first book, back in the 80's, *A New Science of Life,* disturbed a reviewer in the prestigious scientific journal *Nature* to the extent that the gentleman said that while he did not believe in book burning, *if* he did, Sheldrake's work would be a prime candidate. News of this review naturally got around and has helped sales ever since, not only of that work but of his next one, The *Presence of the Past*. Possibly *The Rebirth of Nature* will outsell them both.

The advent over three hundred years ago of the modern scientific worldview, dependent on severe detachment and close cause-and-effect analysis, has brought many undeniable benefits as well as increasingly acute problems in our relations with each other and with the rest of the natural world.

Sheldrake laments that modern science and technology has meant that the earlier feminine, maternal conception of nature gave place to viewing the surrounding world as essentially passive and dead—mere neutral "raw material," or at best, "natural resources"—there for man to ravage and exploit at will. The idea switched from accepting what was offered with gratitude to taking by force whatever was wanted. The sexual analogy here is inevitable.

Speaking as a woman, I would amend Sheldrake's formulation only to say that on some dim level of the dominant techno-male's psyche, the earth never stopped being alive and female, but rather, she became degraded from respected mother to helpless rape victim. You can't rape an inanimate object. There's no kick in that, but there's a lot of kick in the idea of conquest and subjugation when there's something conscious there to be overcome, humiliated and hurt. (But perhaps this is only my own feminine paranoia?)

218

At any rate, it becomes increasingly clear that nature is not as passive a victim as once believed, and that beyond a certain point, in hurting her we hurt ourselves. When we split ourselves off from nature we also split off from vital parts of our own inner and outer being. Just as in human relationships, in our interactions with nature there are certain boundaries which cannot be crossed without destroying the relationship itself. Some ten years after his first presentation of the GAIA hypothesis, Lovelock wrote in 1988, "GAIA as I see her is no doting mother tolerant of misdemeanors, nor is she some delicate damsel in danger from brutal mankind. She is stern and tough, always keeping the world warm and comfortable for those who obey the rules, but ruthless in the destruction of those who transgress."

But to Sheldrake, She—GAIA, Mother Nature, or whatever you wish to call her—is a much more fascinating and complex being than this. If we are to become more intimately and fruitfully and tactfully involved with her, a new kind of scientific approach is indicated which will require involvement of our whole selves. Such things as careful observation, mathematical rigor, and laboratory protocol are not necessarily excluded, but neither are such things as affinities, imaginative empathy, intuition and other qualities which have usually been assigned only to the subjective, aesthetic and religious dimensions of life.

Naturally, all this is a bit much for the old guard, and *The Rebirth of Nature* has already been assailed by one critic as "too New Age." The book is considerably more demanding, however, not to say rewarding, than the usual mush that goes under that label. Sheldrake's colorful and at times humorous recapitulation of the last three hundred years of science which have brought us where we are is alone worth the price of the book.

Labels are always inadequate and often misleading, but I must admit I've been trying to think of one for this person, Rupert Sheldrake, who reveals much of himself in this book. Several have occurred and been dismissed. It would be easy to kid around about things like upper-class British shamanism, intellectual neo-paganism, crypto-Christian nature mysticism, and a lot of other cute possibilities.

But I like him too much for such cheap shots. Perhaps we need to come up with a new term to describe Dr. Rupert Sheldrake: perhaps something like *philobiologist*—lover and student of that which lives.

▲   ▲   ▲

To The Persian Gulf:
Thanks

Thank you for reminding me I live in a world
    no longer home
To any of the seventy thousand
    counted by the Red Cross/Crescent.
Dead babies, with such
    parents, playmates, siblings, elders
As were incidental to a thing called victory.

    Both sides
    Were claiming victory today. I had forgotten that I
        live here
    In this multiracial residential club that howls with
        glee
    As members kill its members.

I must have joined. There is
No protocol for resignation. So cheers and here's to
    heroism
All around.

Surrounded as I am in this small corner by the
Kindness and intelligence of deviants I almost had
    forgotten
How it is, but thanks to this reminder
    you can bet
        I won't forget again.

—Arlen Wilson

chapter TEN

☛ Special Book Review Section

☛ Tomorrow's News

☛ Alvin and Heidi Toffler
    in Praise of our Kinder,
    Gentler War Machine

☛ Weaponry and Livingry

☛ Weirdness Updates

☛ 1994 Update

One Foot In The Future:
A Woman's Spiritual Journey
by Nina Graboi

(Aerial Press, P.O. Box 1360, Santa Cruz, CA 95061
(408) 425-8619; $18.95)

Reviewed by Arlen Wilson

"I was very tired...I am an experienced traveler but there are certain planets where the landing is especially rough, no matter how often you go through it; and this, obviously, was one of them."

The landing took place in genteel upper middle class Vienna in 1918, where Nina Graboi grew up as a privileged little girl, lovingly cared for by "native attendants".

Whatever one may think of the transmigration of souls, there can be no doubt that Nina Graboi has had an amazing variety of incarnations during this one lifetime. At present a cohort and friend of *avant garde* scientists and veterans of the psychedelic mind-exploration movement, Nina stubbornly resists labels like "intellectual." Still, her deep and abiding interest in human progress toward a higher consciousness always seems to take her to where the action is.

As frightened young girl she had to flee across Europe from the Nazis, ended up in a concentration camp in North Africa, escaped via Casablanca in an encounter reminiscent of the famous old flick by that name and in exactly the same time-frame. She was helped along the way by so many unexpected acts of kindness from people of all backgrounds, that she declares, "I could never hate the human race. Not even the Germans."

In the course of adjusting to the world of "overqualified" refugees she worked as a housemaid, factory employee, garment worker; whatever was necessary to survive. In the U.S. as a young wife she helped her husband set up a business which eventually thrived. Within a few years she found herself the pampered and chic Jewish wife and mother in a twelve room mansion outside New York, with servants, a nanny for the children; the whole schtick. During these years she became something of a socialite, entertained considerably and involved

223

herself with local theater. Glamour and success were part of her life.

Few would have predicted that during the next decade, the Sixties, the lady would leave all this—house, husband, grown children—to become a sort of official mother hen to a bunch of "dirty" hippies; live in one room; be involved with Timothy Leary in conducting the LSD Center in Manhattan; be part of the now-historic group around his commune at Millbrook; and make a precarious living in arts and crafts and running a little shop in legendary Woodstock, while enduring the drastic economic ups and downs of a middle-aged woman getting by alone in the world (albeit with many friends). For one brief period, she even became a welfare recipient before she could get on her feet again, though getting back on her feet was something Nina has always been able to do.

What brought about her flight from the American Dream? Some casual and life-shattering encounter with mind-altering drugs, perhaps? Such things were not unheard of in those days. As it happened, this was not her story at all.

Back in the bland Eisenhower years, in the midst of her prosperity, Nina had started on a long, lonely spiritual quest, keyed off by a book on reincarnation—but by no means limited to that subject. She read philosophy, occidental and oriental mysticism, theology and studied various so-called occult systems. In those times the books and people needed to explore these areas were not easy to come by. No one had yet heard of Leary or hippies, or turning on, or any of the rest of it.

What first attracted Nina Graboi to that whole scene was a report in a national magazine concerning a project called the Good Friday experiment at Harvard University. Divinity students were administered doses of psilocybin (a psychotropic mushroom extract). The mystical religious experiences "brought on" by the drug were indistinguishable from those induced by meditation or other means. Nina was tired, she says, of reading about the exalted, unitive religious experiences of others and wanted to have them for herself. Her longing for such states was strong. She had had only tantalizing glimpses of them now and then but knew she must change and restructure her life toward their pursuit.

She and her husband had long since drifted apart mentally. Her children were ready to leave home for college. As she was preparing to leave for her new and unknown life she wrote to her son and daughter:

"Whether you will hate me or love me in the years to come seems beside the point right now. You will extract whatever is most conducive to your growth from this experience, that much I know. The older generation is at best manure for the growth of the young, I was the rich black soil in which you grew, my children. It doesn't matter if that soil is now a stink in your nostrils—it fed you well!"

Emerging as she did from a world where money, propriety and prestige were the dominant values, Nina admits, "I fell in love with the hippies!" Whatever their faults and naivetés, she felt that they were trying to become that new humanity—without hatred, competitiveness and war—which Nina had been secretly dreaming of over the years. She was even then an "elder," and tried the best she could to shepherd them and protect them from their own unworldliness. At one point she successfully "chaperoned" a whole busload of chanting, pot-smoking, casually copulating hippies through the dangerous territory of the sheriff-laden southern states to a haven in Florida. Her own lifestyle remained considerably more conservative than her protégés'. But she nourished their spiritual aspirations. Her shop in Woodstock was "a thinly disguised shrine" where devotees of the new consciousness would gather.

During the Sixties and beyond, her life became enriched by getting to know many amazing people, including the major *dramatis personae* of the period: Leary, Alpert (aka Ram Dass), and many other eminent drop-outs, psychologists and gurus. Her book contains many fascinating, never-before-published vignettes and glimpses of these people.

As to Nina and drugs: When she first read about the divinity student experiment at Harvard she thought she someday might be ready to try drugs herself for that purpose, but felt she had much more study to do and work on herself. In fact, it was four years later, long after she had cast her lot with the counterculture, that she even allowed herself her first taste of marijuana. Actually, she reckons her preparation time to have been the twelve years since she had first started her spiritual quest and studies. Perhaps it was the long period of preparation or perhaps it was unusually powerful herb, but what happened to Nina Graboi as a result of that first toke on Alan Watts' houseboat will surely live in the more colorful annals of the period. So it was not drugs which brought her to the spiritual dimension but rather the other way around.

Even after that first experience Nina continued to be very cautious and aware about the use of mind-altering substances which she considers sacred and not to be trifled with. She feels that used rightly, reverently, they may be part of a person's spiritual life, though perhaps they are not as important as she once thought they were. But such substances should only be used in the right set and setting. No one could be more appalled than she at the proliferation of bad, addictive street drugs, totally unlike the psychedelics—drugs like heroin, cocaine, crack, killer amphetamines, etc. There are worlds of difference between families of substances we lump together under the one term "drugs," and people should learn these crucial distinctions.

Nina continues to enjoy life from her little hideaway on the California coast. She has hopes that all that was good about the Sixties will come back in the Nineties, though in a more mature and sophisticated form. When asked to make specific predictions, Nina shakes her head. Her eyes twinkle, surely as brightly at 72 as they did at 17, and she says, " No predictions. I like surprises!"

Her book is a delight. You'll enjoy it.

T.A.Z.:
The Temporary Autonomous Zone, Ontological Anarchism, Poetic Terrorism
by Hakim Bey

(Autonomedia, P.O. Box 568, Williamsburgh Station, Brooklyn, NY 11211)

An epiphany about this book and its publishers: I cannot find a price listed anywhere on the cover, or inside the book either. (However, other books by the same publisher, listed in advertisements at the back, do have prices.) Above the publisher's address, instead of the usual copyright, stand the stark words: "May be freely pirated and quoted—the author & publisher, however, would like to be informed." Obviously, these gents really mean it when they talk about rejecting bourgeoisie values.

TAZ, like Gaul, divides into three parts: "Chaos: The Broadsheets of Ontological Anarchism," "Communiqués of the Association for Ontological Anarchy," and "The Temporary Autonomous Zone." The first two parts consist of short pieces which burst like fireworks, seemingly in no particular order, as if the author wanted to throw all his most "outrageous" ideas at you as fast as he could get them on paper. The effect resembles some of the ranting poems of Ginsberg, the prophecies of Blake (or Phil Dick), the demonic sermonettes that periodically interrupt the novels of Burroughs, the first surrealist manifestoes by Breton, the late Nietzsche. Traces of a coherent thesis (relating anarchism to fractal mathematics) emerge out of the noise now and then, only to get drowned out in further flights of demented poetry and Dionysian revelry.

For instance, a brilliant exposition of Chaos in modern math and ancient mythology appears as scattered fragments; intercut with it one finds suggestions urging that we break the chains of bourgeoisie society by shitting on the floor of Citibank, or erecting official-looking plaques at every place we've experienced a profound spiritual insight or a great orgasm. Art criticism alternates with sociology, revolutionary neo-Freudianism, new insights into Stirner and Nietzsche; then Mr. Bey spends a two pages suggesting "poetic terrorist" graffiti that would class-up the garbage that usually decorates New York's subways—e.g.,

GAY ZIONISM/SODOM FOR THE SODOMITES or THE CHAINS OF LAW HAVE BEEN BROKEN. (A real quote from a real Sufi saint, but Mr. Bey doesn't bother to inform his readers of that.)

What we have here, I think, deserves the label Mr. Bey gives it—ontological anarchy. This prose does not sit on a shelf like a dead owl, in the fashion of the allegedly "serious" political thinking in this unfortunate country; it dances and sings and does epistemological acrobatics before our eyes; it imitates the mystical Chaos it invokes; its roots go far back, past the Ginsberg-Burroughs-surrealist axis I mentioned above, to Hermeticism, Sufi humor, Zen riddles. It does not try to explain itself to you, but to drive you to a point beyond linear thinking, where, in sheer self-defense, you set out to explain this roller-coaster ride for yourself.

The third part of the book, "The Temporary Autonomous Zone," although elusive in its own way, contains dense reasoning, and while refusing to define (i.e., limit) its central idea, it has all the linear, "left brain" structure our teachers told us a political argument should have. I regard this long essay, frankly, as the most important contribution to anarchist and/or libertarian thinking in this generation, and perhaps the most important since the heyday of Emma Goldman and Benjamin R. Tucker. One warning, however: It tilts so far into anarchy that most modern libertarians will recoil from it "as the devil would from holy water."

Without defining that which Hakim prefers the reader to intuit, I will hint that a "temporary autonomous zone" or TAZ exists wherever people have an hour, a week, a year, a decade or longer totally free of government and all other forms of coercion. Following the traditional anarchist position that "every revolution leads to a new tyranny" (now a commonplace among European radicals), the TAZ anti-ideology says simply: spend as much of your precious time as possible in temporary autonomous zones. If you work at it—in the Sufi sense of Work—you may soon have two months of every year free of every form of oppression; then, maybe, six or seven or eight months...

Thoroughly familiar with General Semantics (and, it seems, every other branch of social science) Hakim takes a novel slant on the problem of the Map and the Territory. Once the capitalist class had accurate maps of the whole world, his thesis holds, no place could remain safe from exploitation, regimentation and "the European Project" (the plan to make every square inch of the planet and every person thereon a rationally controlled source of profit for the planet's "owners": the primal form of the New World Order). The map, then, had *become* the territory, in a sense. Freedom remained a possibility only in the unmapped zones—those wild, fugitive places temporarily outside the Control System.

Pirate "Utopias," outlaw islands "governed" only by voluntary association—first described by Defoe and more recently brought back to our attention by Burroughs in *Cities of the Red Night*—represent temporary autonomous zones of surprising longevity. So do various backwoods "miscegenated" communes of Black-white-Indian-assorted refugees from the Control System. (Bey has some colorful data on the Eugenics movement as a rationale for destroying these last bastions of freedom.) But any stoned-out dinner party safe from the cops represents another temporary autonomous zone, albeit brief. Hakim Bey's new Zen koan for individualists posed by this long essay: How can you regulate your life to move from one T.A.Z. to another and never spend more than an hour or so passing through Enemy-Occupied Territory?

Of course, this point marks the place where Bey's political radicalism joins his mystical antinomianism: any moment when you feel truly alive and shaken to the core by the wonder and mystery of existence, you have found a Temporary Autonomous Zone. (Going back to one of the "chaotic" early essays, you should erect a bronze plaque to mark the spot of this Illumination.)

In sum: Anarchists who fail to read this book have lost track of the cutting edge of their own philosophy. Any disciple of Freud or Nietzsche or Wilhelm Reich who doesn't read it, has missed a chance to see their own beliefs in a new and Apocalyptic light. And any Sufi who ignores this Vision deserves twenty years imprisonment in a "respectable" white collar job with no access to any implements of suicide.

In Pursuit of VALIS:
Selections from the Exegesis
by Philip K. Dick
Edited by Lawrence Sutin
(Underwood-Miller Inc., Novato, CA; 1991)

The Eagle's Quest:
A Physicist's Search for Truth in the Heart of the Shamanic World
by Fred Alan Wolf
(Summit Books/Simon & Shuster, NY; 1991)

Food of the Gods:
The Search for the Original Tree of Knowledge
by Terence McKenna
(Bantam Books, NY; 1992)

Every year—sometimes every month—I receive a pile of manuscripts from publishers who want me to write jacket blurbs. Most of the books hardly seem worth elbow-room in Hell, and I would rather bury them than praise them.

This summer has represented a wonderful change in all that. I received, along with the usual garbage, three books that I not only felt happy to endorse but enjoyed so much that I want to review them at greater length than a jacket blurb allows, so I can encourage all of you to rush out and buy them as soon as they appear in the bookstores.

In Pursuit of VALIS tells the private, involuntary shamanic journey of a great science-fiction writer. *The Eagle's Quest* recounts the similar, but more traditional search of a quantum physicist who willingly entered the shaman's domain to learn how that other world relates to normal space-time. *Food of the Gods,* finally, presents a Grand Unified Theory of human social evolution in terms of the drugs people have used from the dawn

230

of humanity to the present, how shamanic drugs shaped and enriched some cultures and how other drugs have ruined other cultures. Taken together, this trio makes the most stimulating smorgasbord of scientific/philosophical ideas I've enjoyed in a decade or more.

To discuss the books separately before I start making a shotgun *menage a trois* out of them:

"Suddenly, the entire universe
blew up in his face." —*PKD*

Between the early 1950s and February/March, 1974, Philip K. Dick wrote the damnedest, weirdest, most philosophically mind-boggling novels ever to escape from the neo-surrealist underground into commercial science-fiction; after February, 1974, Phil began living in the world he had created. His fiction literally came alive around him. The philosophical masterwork he referred to as "the Exegesis" consisted of over 8000 pages of notes, in which he (writing chiefly for himself: but with one sly eye on Posterity...) tried to understand what the hell had happened to him. The Exegesis appears to have taken up more of his time than the few wonderful novels he wrote between the Apocalypse of 1974 and his tragically premature death in 1982.

A man who once wrote 17 novels in 5 years, Phil Dick became so involved in the Exegesis that he only wrote three novels in his last decade, and all of them revolve around the themes of the Exegesis; indeed, the best-known of them, *VALIS*, contains a few quotes, and many paraphrases, from the Exegesis, attributed—typically—to a lunatic (a lunatic who we only recognize as Phil Dick himself at the end.)

It's high time that Dick scholars and sci-fi fans in general got a peek at the fabulous Exegesis, and Lawrence Sutin, as editor, offers that here—a peek, or about 250 pages of the original 8000. Here we watch Phil struggle with such questions as: Did Soviet parapsychologists target him for some fiendish experiment in hypnosis-by-telepathy? Or did the ghost of his dead friend, Bishop James Pike, return to co-exist with him in one body?*

Phil seemed to have entered what he called "orthogonal time," at right angles to normal time. That is, he experienced both Rome 50 A.D. and Southern California 1974 A.D. "at the same time." Did this merely indicate Bishop Pike dumping his historical/religious erudition into Phil's brain? Or had a Gnostic named Thomas re-incarnated into Phil's body? Or did the

231

experience demand even more radical theories—Zebra, for instance?

("Zebra," in Phil's vocabulary, represented an unknown Intelligence far above humanity's, which usually remains invisible by blending into the environment—like certain insects. If you suddenly notice Zebra, people will probably say you're "seeing things.")

Could Phil consider Zebra extra-terrestrial, or did he have to admit it was "God?" Could he fit it into his VALIS model—a **V**ast **A**ctive **L**iving **I**ntelligence **S**ystem, governing Earth at behest of super-intellects from the Sirius system—or did the whole Zebra/VALIS experience merely prove he, Phil Dick, had gone loony? Perhaps the entire Gnostic/surrealist journey resulted from a delayed reaction to the psychedelics he did in the '60s? Or maybe the megavitamins he took in the '70s mutated his brain even more than the psychedelics?

Nietzsche says somewhere that "the mystics have never been honest enough." He couldn't make that claim seem valid if he tried to apply it to Phil Dick. Phil courageously and unflinchingly considers every possible alternative, and remains honestly zetetic all the way. He had somehow achieved a level of consciousness far above normal, but he never decided whether to consider it Gnosis or merely an unusually benign psychosis. In his last novels, *VALIS* sits on the fence like an agnostic owl, *The Divine Invasion* accepts the most Gnostic/Platonist models very literally and *The Transmigration of Timothy Archer* settles on plain, old-fashioned humanist skepticism. But the Exegesis shows that Phil never stopped questioning and wondering until he died.

Death and Other Nonsense

Around the time Phil Dick had his early struggles with "God" and/or Zebra and/or VALIS (and/or a Bishop's ghost and/or Soviet parapsychologists...), physicist Fred Alan Wolf began investigating shamanism with the notions that quantum mechanics might illuminate what shamans do, or shamanism might illuminate the unsolved enigmas of the quantum wonderland, or at least the two might interact in some synergetically interesting way.

Fred went to Peru to study the native shamans and join them in ceremonies using the local psychedelic, ayahuasca. He traveled to other worlds and non-ordinary realities which, in Phil Dick's metaphor, seem orthogonal to our normal space-time continuum. Fred had further experiences with Buddhists in Asia and Cabalists in Paris, and returned again to Peru and the shamanic initiation process. Like all others who have undertaken this quest, Fred soon had his own experiences of synchronicity and similar Jungian weirdnesses.

In *The Eagle's Quest*, Dr. Wolf writes with the same scientific precision as in his previous books but also with a flaming poetic intensity new in his prose; he also uses *avant garde* literary techniques, totally abandoning linear narrative to take us into those non-linear modes of consciousness explored by artists like Joyce, Borges and Burroughs.

One of Fred's most interesting theories about the shamanic/ quantum interface, I think, concerns the importance of near-death or symbolic death or "out of body experience" in the shamanic initiation: "Shamans enter the death world to alter their perceptions in this world...By becoming aware of processes that were not chiefly concerned with my bodily survival, I was able to see other realities." In quantum terms, as Dr. Wolf explains at length, the "observer effect"—the principle that we cannot meaningfully separate the phenomenon from the observer—here explains that the normal bio-survival ego cannot perceive as much as the transformed (or exploded) mind that has entered the dying process.

I find this especially significant because, quite independently of Dr. Wolf, and without tramping into the jungles to meet the shamans, I came to similar conclusions, while studying the role of "secret societies" in European history. Every such occult lodge, from the Freemasons and Elks to the Golden Dawn and Wiccans, has some central ritual which either attempts to recreate the shamanic death/rebirth process or else shows clearly in its dramatic structure that it derives originally from such an initiative process and has merely become empty "play acting" because the meaning has gotten lost over the centuries. (Masons may at this point consider the Widow's Son and the meaning of High Twelve and Low Twelve...)

An even more important point, I think, concerns the role of "nonsense" in shamanism. "Shamans use any device to alter a patient's belief about reality," Dr. Wolf writes. To adopt one of his examples, a cock crows, an airplane passes overhead, a woman in labor gives birth; and the shaman says, "The child would not have come out now if the cock had not crowed before the airplane roared." The Dumb Schmuck—you or me or Carlos Castaneda—blinks, and wonders if he has just heard Wisdom

233

transcending his own meager intellect, or has been the victim of a deadpan joke.

(Zen variation: "What is the Buddha?" asks the Dumb Schmuck. "Last night I lost three coins under my bed," replies the Zen Master.)

In Dr. Wolf's terminology, such meta-logic creates a quantum "observer effect." In quantum mechanics, if you take a measurement during a process, the end of the process will change. In Fred's quantum anthropology, if you change the frame of reference, the world as a whole changes its meaning and becomes less predictable (less Newtonian/deterministic, more Heisenbergian/indeterminate.)

Phil Dick, who had fully entered the shamanic universe without knowing that he had landed there, always retained the conviction of a deep, cosmic and yet very personal connection between his Zebra encounters of February-March 1974 and Richard Nixon's resignation in August that year. Phil did not see the link in terms of "mere" synchronicity in the Jungian metaphor. Rather, in orthogonal time, he saw that Thomas the Gnostic in Rome 50 A.D. and Phil Dick in California 1974 A.D. functioned as parts of a network that inevitably causes the fall of Caesar, and of Caesar's "Black Iron Prison."

(The "Black Iron Prison," or "BIP," represented for Phil the amnesia or hypnosis that prevents most people from ever catching a glimpse of Zebra. Psychologists call it conditioned perception, neurolinguistic habit, or the defined gloss.)

As one of the few non-Christian Scientists who have actually read every page of *Science and Health With Key to the Scriptures,* I once spent a lot of time brooding over why Mrs. Eddy makes so much sense on one page and then seemingly degenerates into total gibberish on the next page. I got my first clue about this mystery when reading Aleister Crowley, who does the same thing but with tons more of literary flair, humor and panache than Mrs. Eddy. "Nonsense frees us from conditioned thinking," I decided, "but only if we're not quite sure it's nonsense." Then, of course, I discovered that the Zen Masters and Sufis knew all about that long, long before me...

So do the shamans, Dr. Wolf points out at length. Their "nonsense" serves the function that psychologists call "re-framing"—getting us out of our conditioned reality-tunnel (the Black Iron Prison) to a framework in which we can suddenly see Zebra move.

(You can learn more about "nonsense," and its role in therapeutic hypnosis, in Dr. E.L. Rossi's *Psychobiology of Mind-*

Body Healing. See Chapter 1 for a review of this groundbreaking book.)

Curiously, or with cosmic inevitability, Phil, the science-fiction writer, who did not so much enter the shamanic world as he got pulled in from the other side, arrives at some insights similar to those of Fred Wolf, the scientist who entered that world with his eyes open and nine hypotheses to test in the crucible of his own Chapel Perilous. Among their joint conclusions:

The universe consists essentially of information (Phil Dick) or of a Bohmian "implicate order" more like information than anything else (Fred Wolf.) Out of this enfolded (archetypal) information, temporary "realities" unfold spatiotemporally, but which "realities" we encounter/perceive depends on our state of consciousness. Normal consciousness, or the Black Iron Prison, consists of a kind of delusion in which one conditioned "reality"-tunnel appears to us as the only possible "reality." The terror of seeming insanity (Dick) or the confrontation with death (Wolf) jar us out of that one "reality"-tunnel and opens us to multiple universes.

Or we can make the quantum leap—escape the Black Iron Prison—simply by contemplating the right kind of deeply meaningful nonsense long enough. Christian Science practitioners heal all sorts of seemingly hopeless cases because they have studied the more "irrational" passages in Mary Baker Eddy until their minds flipped over into an alternative shamanic reality where they can transcend the Newtonian determinism of ordinary medicine.

The Dominator Ego

"Descending from the asphalt to the concrete" (Joyce, *Finnegans Wake*), let us recall that we live in a culture based on warfare, abstract "rationality," contempt for all other cultures, and what Riane Eisler calls the Dominator model (class/caste rituals) as distinguished from the Partnership model. (For a summary of Eisler's theories see our review of *The Chalice and the Blade* in Chapter 4.) The most widely used and legally acceptable drugs of this culture include sugar, caffeine, alcohol and tranquilizers. The sugar and caffeine keep us "wired" enough to survive in the cut-throat competitiveness, or "consensual paranoia" (T. Leary), of this culture; the booze and tranks provide us with occasional numbing in which we almost achieve a temporary counterfeit of relaxation.

235

Terence McKenna, with a background in this culture and some training in anthropology and botany, went to the Amazon in the early 1970s and, like Dr. Wolf, sampled the ayahuasca of the local shamans. Ever since, he has been producing articles, books and lectures trying to define and explain the difference between our sugary/Dominator culture and the psychedelic/ shamanic culture of the Indians whom our society has sought to exterminate for 500 years. Out of these years of groping and questioning, he has produced, finally, a masterpiece.

Some of the ideas in *Food of the Gods* seem dubious to me; some will certainty be challenged, and many will eventually get revised (by McKenna or his intellectual heirs). These details do not matter. What McKenna has produced will shake all the social sciences like no book of our century. He has brought together dozens of sciences to give us a completely new view of our relationship to the natural world in general and our relationship to those plants that give us a buzz in particular.

Every society allows some drugs and violently prohibits others: I learned that when I first started studying the literature of psychoactive drugs in the late 1950s. Ever since, dozens of theories have appeared, trying to explain how and why these social drug traditions function. McKenna's seems the best and most complete model yet published, and gives me for the first time a real sense that perhaps now we begin to understand how a society's drug preferences shape the institutions of that society and how these institutions in turn determine which new drugs will win acceptance and which will provoke violent and "irrational" hysteria.

A sociological truism: *All "irrational" customs serve some social function.* Corollary: The most "irrational" morals and/or mores serve functions so deeply embedded in the mythic unconscious that it requires something like a full synthesis of psychoanalysis and ethnomethodology to dig them out and verbalize them clearly enough to examine them. *This applies, e.g., to capital punishment, and it applies even more to "the war on (some) drugs,"* which continues to baffle and infuriate Rationalists because it does not and cannot attain its declared purposes and merely makes the Mafia richer.

The "war on (some) drugs," in McKenna's analysis, perpetuates the Western-style Dominator ego and the capitalist form of Dominator society. In other words, to keep our "consensual paranoia" alive, we need lots of sugar and coffee and we need, just as desperately, to keep shamanic-style drugs out of reach of our general population. This explains the

236

paradox noted by Judge Robert Sweet: the government talks a lot about the very real dangers of crack cocaine, but spends 85% of its anti-drug budget harassing and imprisoning—guess who?—pot smokers. Ignorance? Hypocrisy? Not at all. Cocaine does not really threaten a "wired" sugar-and-adrenaline-driven system, but marijuana teaches people to relax and even to laugh at the absurdities of the Dominator class-rituals. It poses the threat of a real cultural revolution.

In *VALIS,* the "lunatic" Horselover Fat writes, "We did not fall because of a moral error; we fell because of an intellectual error: that of taking the phenomenal world as real." Phil Dick accidentally walked into the parallel worlds of quantum theory; Fred Wolf and Terence McKenna deliberately walked into the parallel worlds of psychedelic shamanism. The reports that all three have brought back can have a liberating and revolutionary impact on every reader of their voyages. If you believe in George Bush's "reality"—the New World Order and all that blood-soaked mythos—the Empire has you trapped in its Black Iron Prison, c. 50 A.D. and Caesar still rules. If you want to know how to organize a jail break, these three books will give you all the dynamite you need.

* *Curiously, Bishop Pike became convinced, some time before his death, that he had achieved communication with his dead son. Then Phil Dick's mystic experiences began with seeming communications from Pike. More recently, two other writers (Ray Nelson and Scott Apel) have alleged possible communications from Phil. Whatever we call this, it seems contagious.—RAW*

Pissing Away
the American Dream
edited by David Ross

(Digit Press, P.O. Box 920066, Norcross, Georgia 30092.
Price: 8 Federal Reserve notes)

David Ross *(Note: See "Piss Wars" in Chapter 8 —Ed.)*
continues his struggle against government-mandated urine
testing, and I regard him as one of the bravest men in the
country today. Ross does not have the economic freedom of a
self-employed writer or artist, and he doesn't work for the
ACLU. He has a job with a pipeline company, and he has
already gotten a few hints that his crusade for the Constitution
may cost him dearly. Yet his fervent commitment to libertarian
ideals will not permit him to shut up and look the other way as
this country turns more and more toward a Police State.

He even tells us that he personally doesn't use any *verboten*
chemicals, and considering the risks he runs and the attention
he attracts, I tend to believe that. If he ever came within 100
yards of the Devil Weed, I imagine, he'd have gotten busted by
now.

In this book Ross gives us a small group of essays and news
clippings that should convince anybody with an IQ above the
average annual temperature of Helsinki that the "war on drugs"
has become the greatest threat to civil liberties since the
founding of our Republic.

• The Fourth Amendment prohibits searches of our
"persons" as well as our houses "without probable cause," but
urine testing occurs not only without probable cause but totally
at random.

• Since urine testing can incriminate the person whose piss
has been searched, this also violates the Fifth Amendment
prohibition of forced self-incrimination.

• Since protesting this totalitarian practice can get a worker
"in trouble" with his/her boss, this has a chilling effect on First
Amendment guarantees of free speech.

• Urine testing functions as part of a concerted effort to
destroy traditional American freedoms, in which the Bush Team
justifies all manner of fascist-style tactics by invoking the "Drug
Terror." Police may now fly over your property to spy without a

238

warrant, stop your car without a warrant at a random road-block, obtain a warrant on the basis of an anonymous informant, or even raid your house with a defective warrant if they claim they believed they had a legal warrant. In short, we have all the abuses of the Inquisition and Star Chamber, which the Constitution totally forbids.

• The Constitutional demand for "probable cause" before searches and seizures specifically intended to prevent precisely the abuses implicit in any random (or allegedly random) spying on the citizenry.

• The spirit behind Piss Wars gets uglier every day. "Drugs are a menace, and if it was left up to me, I'd have public hangings in front of the courthouse out here." —Garfield Hammonds, DEA chief in Atlanta.

• In January, 1989, the cops blasted into a Minneapolis home with "flash-bang" grenades, setting the house on fire and killing its two elderly Black residents. *The police found no drugs but the chief explained, "This is war."*

• In Newark, CA, in 1990, a Korean family suffered a terrible beating by police, who also smashed all their furniture and dishes, without finding drugs. *The same explanation came from the narcotics bureau: "This is war."*

But, as Oliver Steinberg writes in one of the essays in this book, "It is inaccurate to speak of a War on Drugs...You don't lock drugs up in jail—you lock up people. You can't kill drugs—you kill people. *Our government is not waging a war on drugs—it is waging a war on the people."* (italics added)

I can't recommend this book too highly. Everybody who can afford it should buy a few extra copies and re-circulate them where they might do some good. Ross doesn't even ask real money (I guess he has figured out that no real money circulates in this country anymore.) He'll let you have as many copies as you want for 8 Federal Reserve Notes each, or a check in that amount.

Oh, yes—Ross also publishes a little newsletter called *Urine Nation News*. It keeps you up to date on the latest legal cases, new evidence on the unreliability of urine tests, recent crimes against the Constitution, etc. He'll let you have it free, if you send him one postage stamp per issue.

P.S. Since I wrote the above, the Supreme Court has ruled that police may stop a train or bus, walk through it and ask to look in anybody's luggage. Citizens still retain the right to say "no," and the police theoretically may not search them then. Since blacks, Hispanics and many other minorities (including political radicals) firmly believe that saying "no" to a police officer generally results in having a baton bounced off your head 30 or 40 times, we will all find it interesting to see who, besides ACLU attorneys with hidden wires on them, dares say "no" to these previously-unconstitutional searches.

▲   ▲   ▲

Tomorrow's News

GENI Out of the Bottle, Pt. II

Bucky Fuller's Global Energy Network (Note: See *articles in Chapter 6 and elsewhere in this volume —Ed.*) continues to move forward on many fronts. In recent developments:

• The American Society of Mechanical Engineers sponsored a conference on the global grid in Manitoba, Winnipeg, Canada July 10-13. Ontario Hydro, Manitoba Hydro and Teshment Consultants provided funding, and presenters came from as far away as the Soviet Union.

• GENI (Global Energy Network International), has acquired a prestigious Board of Directors and stepped up their fund-raising activities to finance further publicity for the global grid idea. Among their current promos: a GENI T-shirt, an educational video, a Dymaxion map showing the grid in place, and informational brochures. For details: GENI, P.O. Box 24455, San Diego, CA 92124.

• Arab nations have asked consultants to draw up plans for a grid that would connect Istanbul, Turkey to the southern tip of Saudi Arabia. Additional plans may extend the grid as far west as Morocco and as far south as Zaire; Egypt has also expressed interest.

• Japan's Sanyo Electric has developed a $14 trillion program, "GENESIS" (Global Energy Network Equipped with Solar Cells and International Superconductor Grids). This plan follows Fuller's general outline but also includes blanketing four percent of the world's desert areas with solar panels.

• *POWER International,* a magazine read by utilities engineers in 110 countries, did a major article on the world grid idea in their issue for First Quarter, 1991, pointing out the growing trend for local networks to link up into larger and more economical trans-national grids.

• In one major but unsurprising setback the U.S. Department of Energy has refused to give any support to GENI; the Bush administration still pins its hopes on nukes and oil.

The Decline and Fall of the American Empire

A new United Nations study ranks Canada and Japan as leading the world in "human development"—a composite index including education, life expectancy, political liberties and economic well-being. The United States ranked seventh, trailing not only Canada and Japan but also Iceland, Sweden, Switzerland and Norway.

Ranking nations in terms of 40 indicators of civil liberties, the UN study found Sweden and Denmark tied for first place and Iraq in last place. The U.S. finished 13th.

On equality between the sexes, Finland, Sweden, Denmark, France and Norway topped the list. The U.S. finished 10th.

The U.S., however, still leads the world in homicide and rape.

(Source: LA Times, 23 May 1991)

Geodesic Desalinator

A new device, based on geodesics and the dymaxion principles of R. Buckminster Fuller, promises a method of distilling and desalinating potable water from any source by purely solar means. Its triangular segments may construct dome enclosures of unprecedented size, and each segment may include thermoelectric cooling wafers which accelerate condensation. These silicon wafers cool without compressors or ozone-eating CFRs, and may be powered by photovoltaics. As an alternative to such energy-and-hardware-intensive schemes as reverse osmosis plants, the nonpolluting solar desalinator dome uses the least energy and materiel to produce the most pure water.

Variations of this device may operate on land or, alternatively, float on water surfaces. (J. Baldwin of *Whole Earth Quarterly* has reported that Bucky once said California would eventually turn to desalination and that the desalinators would not stand on land but float on the ocean.)

According to the World Game Institute, the single largest global need is clean water.

You can obtain specifications on the geodesic desalinator by sending $5.00 in stamps to Gary Vincent, Write-On Communications, 3671 Vinton Avenue, Los Angeles, CA 90034.

City of Angels

"(J. Edgar Hoover) would have scared hell out of them. He has a file on everybody." — Richard M. Nixon

In the wake of the widely-publicized Rodney King beating, the Los Angeles Police Commission suspended Police Chief Daryl Gates, the City Council quickly re-instated Gates—and the battle now proceeds through the courts as Angelinos wait to learn who (if anybody) controls their police force.

Not so widely publicized: an April 5 press conference at which Ramona Ripston, Executive Director of the Southern California ACLU, asked pointedly, why the City Council has lined up in solid support of Chief Gates "when so many members [of it] have been privately and publicly critical of the Chief for a number of years?" Ripston added, "This curious response raises questions of what kind of information may have been gathered over the years on city officials by LAPD intelligence operations."

In 1979 the ACLU successfully sued the LAPD for "intelligence operations" (i.e., spying) involving 113 individuals and organizations whose politics Gates opposed. In recent statements, Gates seems to convey veiled threats that he has damaging information concerning Mayor Bradley and Dan Garcia (president of the Police Commission) which he might release if the fight gets dirtier.

(Source: ACLU Open Forum, May/June 1991)

In a related story, a jury has awarded Black activist Michael Zinzun $3,840,000 in damages in his libel suit against the LAPD. Zinzun had charged that the police circulated defamatory "information" about him, during his campaign for office, even though they had the evidence on file to prove the stories untrue.

Jurors told the press, after the Zinzun trial, that they doubted the testimony of both Chief Gates and his aid, Robert Vernon.

(Source: LA Times, 15 May 1991)

Since Gates took over as Police Chief, successful law suits against the city alleging police brutality have steadily increased. In the 1970s, before Gates' reign began, the city paid out an average of about $500,000 per year to settle such suits; after three years of Gates' command, this had increased to $2,652,000 in 1982; the figure has continued to climb steadily, reaching $8,069,431 in 1990. (The total for 1991 stands at $12,000,000 as of June.)

(Source: Santa Monica *Outlook,* 11 March 1991 and 29 June 1991*)*

In a June 11, 1991, press release, the LA chapter of the ACLU announced that their office has been burglarized three times since they called for Gates' resignation, and stationery was stolen. The ACLU asks members to report any strange or suspicious mailings on their letterhead.

As we go to press, Chief Gates has announced that he will definitely resign next April, maybe.

Ah, it does bring back memories of the "mean streets" in Raymond Chandler's Los Angeles novels—but where the hell is Philip Marlowe now that we really need him?

Cold Fusion: Dead Or Alive?

Cold fusion, pronounced dead several times, continues to show some peculiar signs of possible life. Edmund Storms of Los Alamos, in a recent review of 40 "cold fusion" experiments, notes that 21 of them indicated more heat coming out than electrical energy going in. Storm also listed 13 experiments in which scientists claim to have found tritium—an unlikely result if no fusion had occurred. Simultaneously, Robert Bush of Cal State Polytech reported an experiment in which "cold fusion" gave out more heat than the electrical energy going in, for 54 days before he shut it down.

Many other experiments have failed to duplicate these results and the scientific community as a whole tends toward skepticism.

(Source: Wall Street Journal, 3 July 1991*)*

Psychedelic Renaissance

At the November/December, 1990, meeting of the Multi-disciplinary Associations for Psychedelic Studies (Berne, Switzerland) delegates from the US, the USSR, Switzerland, Germany and Czechoslovakia reported "a sense of optimism that has not existed for many years." Highlights:

• Researchers from the US and USSR report hopeful signs that their governments will allow research on MDMA in the treatment of depression caused by terminal illness.

• US researchers reported that the FDA has shown new willingness to consider some LSD research again, for the experimental treatment of addictions.

• Dr. Albert Hoffman, discoverer of LSD, encouraged scientists to oppose the "fanaticism" of the war on drugs when it becomes a war on scientific drug research.

In related stories:

• Stanford University instructor Stuart Reges brazenly flouted the terrified silence that has fallen over academia ever since Dr. Timothy Leary's imprisonment in 1970. Writing to Drug Czar Bob Martinez, Reges mocked the whole "war on drugs" and announced that he often had psychedelics in his possession while on campus. Stanford promptly fired Reges, after the Czar threatened their federal funding.

• A few weeks later, UCLA philosophy professor Michael Gehman wrote a similar letter to Czar Martinez, declaring he had a whole "filing cabinet" full of grass, once gave a lecture while tripping on "some righteous Acid," kept his lunchbag full of psychedelic mushrooms and often shared a joint with a student during explorations of epistemological philosophy ("I think it definitely enhances the discussion"). When all hell broke loose, Gehman described his letter as a hoax and encouraged University officials to search his office. They found no drugs, and Gehman then announced that he has taken an appointment to teach at Vassar College next autumn. "I advocate the right use of certain drugs, like marijuana," he added. *(Source: L.A. Times,* 21 May 1991)

• Confirming rumors which had previously appeared only in counter-culture magazines and sleazo tabloids, historian Thomas J. Reeves states, in his new *A Question of Character: The Life of John F. Kennedy (Macmillan, NY, 1991)* that JFK experimented with methamphetamine, cocaine, marijuana, hashish and LSD while in the White House. Reeves also records 30 visits to the White House of Mary Pinchot Meyer, named in

Tim Leary's *Flashbacks* as Kennedy's LSD connection; Reeves reports that insiders called her "Lady Ottoline of Camelot."

(Some people playing Dr. Leary's "Mind Mirror" game on their computers, claim that occasionally—probably at random— they confront evidence that the CIA murdered Meyer; the screen then goes blank and a window comes up telling them that this file has been erased in the interest of National Security.)

"I don't like sience becaws..."

After *Parade* magazine published an article by Dr. Carl Sagan about the decline in the quality of science education in the U.S., Sagan received a lot of mail on the subject. In a follow-up article, he quotes from some of the more memorable epistles he received. Highlights:

• "Not all Americans are stupid. We just rank lower in school big deal."

• "I really didn't understand the point of that article. I thought it was very boreing. I'm just not into anything like that."

• "If we are so far behind, how come Michael Gorbachev came to Minnesota and Montana to Control Data to see how we run are computers and thing?"

• "All the smart kids are looking for the fast buck these days, so they become lawyers, not scientists."

• "I don't want you to improve education. Then there'd be nobody to drive the cabs."

• "Science has discredited itself. It works for politicians. It makes weapons, it lies about marijuana hazards, it ignores about the dangers of agent orange etc."

(Source: Parade, 6 February 1991)

FIJA Update

The Fully Informed Jury Amendment would compel courts to inform juries of their right to nullify oppressive laws—a right guaranteed since Magna Carta but often deliberately hidden by judges and prosecutors *(Note: See "Jury Nullification" in Chapter 8 —Ed.).* This proposed amendment has now received publicity—favorable and otherwise—in literally hundreds of newspapers coast to coast, and recently received the endorsement of Col. James "Bo" Gritz (the most decorated soldier of the Vietnam war) in two speeches in the Los Angeles area.

Also in LA County, according to Westside *Libertarian* (May, 1991) police arrested FIJA activist Ron Tisbert for "soliciting" on county property. (Ron had circulated a FIJA petition outside a Lancaster courthouse.) In a similar case, Sacramento cops arrested an unnamed woman for circulating FIJA material outside a court-house there, while her son stood trial for possession of LSD.

The *FIJA Activist* (dated only "1991") lists four states as already having laws compelling judges to inform juries of their right to nullify laws that they find morally repugnant: Maryland, Oregon, Indiana and Georgia. 24 other states have limited jury nullification provisions in their state constitutions—only regarding free speech cases. As FIJA points out, in all 28 of these states, judges still usually attempt to convince juries they have no choice but to convict if the defendant violated the law— no matter how unjust or unreasonable the law may seem to them.

The FIJA Amendment, as some activists have pointed out, doesn't even need to become law in order to change the courts. Since jury nullification already exists as a common law guarantee, when the publicity about FIJA reaches a suitable "critical mass" jurors will know their rights on entering the court room and judges can no longer deceive them.

Agnosticism Rising

Agnosticism now holds third place among religious attitudes in America, with 21.7 million adherents (as compared to 79.3 million Protestants and 57 million Catholics). This places the Agnostics way ahead of fourth place Buddhism (7.5 million), fifth place Judaism (5.9 million) and sixth place Islam (4.6 million) Rounding out the Top Ten, in descending order: Mormons (4.2 million), Atheists (1.2 million), Hindus (750,000) Sikhs (around 250,000) and Quakers (around 200,000.)

(Source: Santa Monica *Outlook,* 21 March 1991*)*

Night of the Hunter

Fundamentalist preacher Roy Alan Yanke, 37, confessed to robbing 14 banks of $50,000, saying he needed the money to hire whores to satisfy his "tremendous appetite for sex." A female parishioner defended Yanke, calling him a "wonderful man," and said the Devil made him do it.

(Source: L.A. Reader, 10 May 1991*)*

Garbage Security

Has the New World Order got you down? Worried about the Supreme Court's increasing animosity against the Bill of Rights? Thinking of emigrating? Well, an answer has appeared to at least one of our vanishing privacy rights—the Court's recent ruling that the police may search your garbage without a warrant. Joan Cook Housewares now offers a handsome desktop paper shredder for only $45.95. With this nifty document-chewer installed in your kitchen, you can shred incriminating letters, sensitive memos, checks, etc., just as fast as Ollie North, and walk tall again, secure in the knowledge THEY can't find a paper trail to incriminate you.

(Source: Joan Cook Housewares, 3200 SE 14 Avenue, Fort Lauderdale FL 33350*)*

▲   ▲   ▲

Alvin and Heidi Toffler
In Praise of Our
Kinder, Gentler War Machine

In the May, 1991, issue of *World Monitor*, Alvin and Heidi Toffler have published a hymn of praise to the marvels of "Third Wave" (computerized) warfare, under the title "War, Wealth and a New Era in History." You literally have to see this article to believe in it, otherwise you will suspect me of writing satire here.

The Tofflers' war-lust transcends even the recent Hollywood blockbusters glorifying bigger and bigger orgies of destruction on wider and wider screens with louder and louder soundtracks. Nobody since Bruno Mussolini (Ben's son) has expressed so much unabashed joy in the art of killing, maiming and crippling human beings.

Nobody since de Sade has stated the case for "value-free science" so eloquently or proclaimed its implications so blatantly.

And nobody since Machiavelli has shown such total contempt for the notion that morality should play some role somewhere in human affairs.

The Toffler's conversion to the Rambo-esque notion that modern technology makes killing people more fun than ever rests upon their enthusiasm for the recent Gulf War, which they describe with all the pulsating purple prose of D. H. Lawrence writing about copulation. The Tofflers have little interest in Lawrence's Super-Orgasm; they get the hots from "smart tools," "smart weapons," the "precision and customization" that reduces "collateral damage" (e.g., dead children), "precision-targeted weapons," "speed and movement," "rapid deployment," "surprise," "war...choreographed in time" (like a ghoul's ballet?), "incredible orchestration" (the *dans macabre*)—and so on, and so on.

The more efficiently the military machine kills people, the more aesthetic it all seems to Alvin and Heidi. You might think they had discovered a new art-form more exquisite than *haiku*.

The Divine Marquis could not have written a better rhapsody to the mathematical science of burning people and blowing holes in them. At the famous *soiree* that led to his arrest, Sade kept a precise tally (remember?) of how many times

249

a whore flogged him and how many times he flogged her; he marvelously anticipated the New World Order's entire mental set, with all its anal-compulsive counting of wounds and cost-efficient analysis of pain and time-and-motion studies of torment. Before the Gulf War and the lyric ecstasies of Mr. and Mrs. Toffler, the closest approximation to Sade's dream appeared in the smoothly functioning Nazi annihilation camps, where the gas ovens worked with what the Tofflers would call "incredible orchestration," where every arm had a precise number tattooed on it, and even the gold fillings in the victims' teeth got counted, weighed and preserved for the State treasury.

Naturally the Tofflers tells us that the super-brains behind this lovely little war really did minimalize "collateral damage." Total Iraqis killed, they cheerfully inform us, number "several hundred or at most several thousand." How marvelous, I think. Perhaps next they will write a glorification of Jack the Ripper, reminding us that his victims totaled "six or at most eight."

I'll bet a lot of Americans believe that "several hundred or at most several thousand" figure, or at least want to believe it. As Abbie Hoffman once said, "There seem to be a lot of different realities going around these days."

According to the *Washington Post,* U.S. losses numbered 55 killed, 155 wounded, 30 missing, and 9 prisoners of war, while Iraqi losses numbered 2,085 tanks, 962 armored vehicles, 1005 artillery pieces, and 103 aircraft destroyed *(chart reprinted from* Extra, *May/June 1991).*

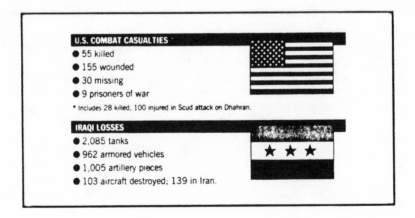

U.S. COMBAT CASUALTIES *
- 55 killed
- 155 wounded
- 30 missing
- 9 prisoners of war

* Includes 28 killed, 100 injured in Scud attack on Dhahran.

IRAQI LOSSES
- 2,085 tanks
- 962 armored vehicles
- 1,005 artillery pieces
- 103 aircraft destroyed; 139 in Iran.

Either the *Post* believed nobody got hurt on the Iraqi side, or they don't count Arabs as human beings, I guess.

However, according to the BBC on March 3, the Iraqi death toll reached 65,000 to 100,000.

The *London Observer* for March 5 set the death-toll at 100,000.

The *Christian Science Monitor,* March 15 (when more details became known) set the total at 100,000 to 200,000.

According to the International Red Cross/Red Crescent, Iraqi casualties numbered at least 200,000, including 70,000 children.

According to Dr. Helen Caldecott of Physicians for Social Responsibility, the Iraqis lost 250,000. A quarter of a million, in one month, staggers the imagination. Hitler's death camps never achieved that "speed," "precision" and "choreography."

Considering the hour-after-hour bombardment for more than a month, which figure seems most plausible?

And, despite all the Tofflers' rhapsodizing about "smart weapons," Paul Rogers of the University of Bradford, England, estimates that only seven percent of the munitions fired at Iraq qualify for that description. Mostly, the Iraqis got hit by conventional bombs of the sort Bucky Fuller memorably described as "delivering more and more explosive power over longer and longer distances in shorter and shorter times to kill more and more people." As Rogers points out, a lot of the tonnage dropped on Iraq consisted of cluster bombs, of which he says:

"Cluster bombs have several advantages over napalm—now considered obsolete in most circumstances. Without the negative overtones of napalm in the public mind, they cause destruction and death on a larger scale with more control." (*Covert Action Information Bulletin,* #37, Summer 1991.)

Oh, well, those poor people had to die, in the logic of *Realpolitik,* because we had a moral duty to destroy a "new Hitler." Ah, now I see; it all makes sense, after all.

But how come the new Hitler remains in power? Why did we destroy the economy and industry of Iraq, murder maybe as much as a quarter million people, and leave "Hitler" in office? I feel confused—especially since the State Department finds a new "Hitler" every two or three years lately, always in a Third World country whose resources our corporations happen to covet.

Most of the American press preferred and still prefers not to discuss the number of victims at all. This whole mindless cult of weapon-worship, for which the Tofflers serve as "intellectual" fronts, might collapse if we actually knew how many men, women and children our not-so-"smart" bombs stupidly killed, blinded, burned or crippled forever.

It reminds one of Panama. The press told us, at the time, that "only a few hundred" Panamanians died in that merry escapade. Since then, the pitiful handful of dissident little journals still surviving here, and Pacifica Radio, have asserted the existence of mass graves in which thousands lie buried, and even the mainstream "60 Minutes" (CBS) has shown one of the mass graves, holding at least 4000 corpses, and let us hear the voices of the Panamanians who claim to have seen many other mass graves, about which the U.S.-installed new Panamanian government remains, to say the least of it, evasive.

To an unprecedented extent, the government and the media now act as partners-in-disinformation (e.g., General Electric, one of the chief war contractors—pardon, defense contractors— owns NBC, one of the major news sources for most people; McNeil/Lehrer gets its funding from petroleum companies; etc.) The propaganda machine becomes increasingly blatant, as indicated by that crazy (or self-satirizing?) *Washington Post* chart. Now, thanks to the Tofflers, Futurism and/or Future Studies and/or whatever one calls our field, will appear to the intellectual minority as just another part of the War Machine's propaganda mill.

One wants to weep when thinking of this: the Tofflers have now become the best-known "Futurists" in the U.S. Readers of their ode to mass murder—who must number millions, since shorter versions of the *Monitor* article have appeared in several newspapers—now have the conditioned association "Futurism= killing Third World people" as firmly implanted in their neurons as "dog=bark," "night=moon," "birthday=gifts," "Picasso=modern art" "bacon=eggs", "Rock=drugs," or the advertisers' "new car= hot sex.."

I can't imagine why every Futurist in the world hasn't gone to hide in a cave for at least a year; I myself have seriously considered changing the mast-head of this newsletter to "The Magazine of Heresy" until the word "Futurism" loses the stink of death the Tofflers have given it.

And the war-propaganda machine (of which the Tofflers have made Futurism a part) does seem, to the thinking minority, increasingly dishonest and dishonorable. For instance, the Tofflers do not mention any "dissident" attitudes toward the Gulf War, or any of the facts that support such attitudes.

They do not attempt to "refute" the opposition, anymore than the media did. Like the media, they merely pretend that no opposition exists. They assume, without argument, that the "official" propaganda line represents the only reasonable view of the war.

And the "official" line never changes. Over 50 years ago, in *As We Got Marching*, John T. Flynn described it in terms that fit exactly the view that the media and the Tofflers wish us to take of the Gulf conflict: "The enemy aggressor is always pursuing a course of larceny, rapine and barbarism. We are always moving forward with a high mission, a destiny imposed by the Deity to regenerate our victims while incidentally capturing their markets, to civilize savage and senile and paranoidal peoples while blundering accidentally into their oil wells and metal mines."

The enemy leader always gets identified as crazy; the people of the country get murdered accidentally, as we nobly seek to liberate them from this monster; and all facts that cast doubt on this fairy-tale quickly become non-facts because they cannot get published or broadcast in the major media.

To take one glaring example, none of the mass media has ever mentioned—nor do the Tofflers mention—that most of the oil in Bahrain belongs to a company largely owned by George Bush Jr. Bahrain coincidentally adjoins both Iraq and Kuwait, and coincidentally a permanent U.S. Army post now exists there, in the wake of the Gulf war. While Jungians may interpret those astounding coincidences in occult terms, cynics will see a more mercantile explanation. But the Tofflers, like the mass media, do not "interpret" these coincidences at all. They simply do not mention them. George Bush Jr.'s oil interests in the war area have become a non-fact—vanished down "the memory hole," in Orwell's metaphor.

(The only publications that have mentioned George Jr.'s oil interests, as far as I know: *Common Cause, Extra, New Jersey Libertarian*.)

The Tofflers, like the major media, don't think we should know such things, anymore than we should know the exact number of human beings murdered in the course of what Dan Quayle so aptly called "restoring the illegitimate government of Kuwait."

Or—take the matter of the "gigantic" Iraqi military build-up in Kuwait, "poised to attack Saudi Arabia," as the media constantly told us. The *St. Petersburg (Fla.) Times* (6 January 1991) had former government analysts examine satellite photos of Kuwait, and these experts could not find any evidence of this Iraqi build-up. This story of the army that didn't exist got picked up by Pacifica Radio, *In Our Times* and *Extra.* The mass media blacked it out entirely. Our government had told us an enormous lie, but the media no longer sees its role as exposing government lies when it catches them; its role now seems only to help in the cover-up, so the lie can circulate uncontradicted. As whores or camp followers of the War Machine, the media bend any way their Client wishes and licks whatever the Client tells them to lick.

Of course, sometimes a little truth still finds its way into the major media. The *New York Times* for April 8 quotes a Lieutenant Bill Feyk as comparing the ruin of Iraq to a journey through Hell: "It was like driving through Dante's Inferno," he said. I guess he lacked the techno-aesthetic sensibilities of the Tofflers, and couldn't appreciate the delicate "orchestration" of the burned flesh and bloody bodies.

In the same story, the *Times* quotes a Sgt. Larry Porter: "We have all had a chance to call our wives and most of the guys could not talk about it to them. I don't think my wife needs to know what took place over here. I do not want her to know that side of me." It sounds like Sgt. Porter couldn't groove on the "orchestration" and "choreography" of mass murder either. Maybe the Tofflers should try re-educating him.

I remember a time—some of our readers must remember a time—when Futurism did not serve just as another whore or camp follower for the Military-Industrial machine. In that long-ago age (over a decade ago...) Futurists saw visions and dreamed dreams. They spoke of possible Utopias. They designed alternative positive scenarios, instead of glorifying the dismal "official" New World Order scenario. Above all, the spoke frequently of Bucky Fuller's distinction between weaponry and "livingry," and of the wonderful "Utopian" things we could do, as a species, if we spent less on weaponry and more on livingry.

Some Futurists still think that way—the folks at the World Game Center in Philadelphia, for instance. But the mass media has no interest in such odd ducks, out of step with the Reagan-Bush Era. Those who glorify weaponry, like the Tofflers, become the "official" Futurists—the only Futurists the public gets to hear about. The very word "livingry" has vanished down the memory hole, along with the first, fourth and eighth amendments and the idea of an independent press.

Ach, Dr. Goebels, you should have lived to see this hour. I remember the great propaganda film you financed, Leni Reifenstahl's lyric *Triumph of the Will,* containing some of the most superb montages since *Potemkin,* showing how happy the Germans felt after bombing hell out of a smaller country: how they walked with a "new pride" and a "new sense of national dignity." George Bush and his kept Ideologues have stolen all your great ideas from that film, and they have done it even better than you did.

They've tied it up in yellow ribbons.

▲   ▲   ▲

Weaponry and Livingry:
A Cost Analysis

Bucky Fuller's World Game Institute, now under the capable leadership of Medard Gabel, has published a new summary of what the majority of the world's people say they want, and what it will cost. Major investments include:

- Providing clean water for everybody: $50 billion
- Ending starvation: $19 billion
- Providing clean, nonpolluting energy: $40 billion
- Ending soil erosion: $24 billion

Other housekeeping needs included in the World Game budget:

- Decent health care for all humans: $15 billion
- Stabilization of population: $10.5 billion
- Abolishing illiteracy: $5 billion
- Stopping deforestation and ozone depletion: $12 billion

Together with a few other goals (such as ending acid rain and global warming), the Grand Total needed to make the planet "work" well for all: **$252 billion.**

Current worldwide expenditures on weaponry every year, the Institute notes, equals $1 trillion—or approximately four times the cost of the "livingry" of the above program to provide the world with what people actually want.

Zine Review

Army Man

(P.O. Box 1620, Boulder, CO 80306. $15 for six issues)

Despite its title, this remarkable and delightful little mag does not represent the U.S. Army; it doesn't even devote its pages to parody or satire on the U.S. Army, as you might surmise next. I guess the title represents just another of the editor's whimsies.

Not that *Army Man* has an editor. A list of contributors appears in each issue (at the back, of course) but no editor's name is given—and most of the contributions have no author's name attached. (Perhaps only the contributors' friends know who wrote what in each issue...)

If this sounds a bit fey, the contents do little to re-establish traditional (conditioned) notions of what a magazine "is" or "should be." The features seldom run longer than 5 or 6 lines, and you can consider them jokes, poems, prose poems or cries of existential anguish, as you see fit. Startling freshness and bezonked originality seem the only thing these flying bits of gonzo wisdom have in common.

Ezra Pound once called for a magazine "where important writers (e.g. Joyce, Eliot, myself)" could contribute short insights instead of having to inflate every perception into an essay. 70 years later, *Army Man* seems the answer to Ez's dream.

But judge for yourself. Over the next couple of pages, I offer a few of my favorite bits from this totally unique little mag:

When your ears ring, say hello
and a small voice will tell you what to do.

Dragnet Haiku
Eleven fifty-seven p.m. –
The white chrysanthemum

I went to see "Clean and Sober,"
starring Michael Keaton.
I don't remember too much about it, though.
I was pretty wasted.

Dad always thought laughter was the
best medicine, which I guess was why
several of us died of tuberculosis.

Probably the earliest flyswatters
were nothing more than some sort of striking surface
attached to the end of a long stick.

I KNOW THIS WON'T MAKE MUCH SENSE TO YOU, SON,
BUT WUBBA WUBBA NUK NUK NUK.

BRIDE (quietly, tearfully): Ladies and gentlemen, I'm afraid there won't be a wedding after all. Because, you see....my finance has...has died.

HECKLER FROM BACK PEW: Louder!

BRIDE (louder, almost hysterical): My fiancé has died!

ANOTHER HECKLER: Funnier!

Today's Scripture:

"Now it came to pass in the third year of Hoshea, the son of Elah, king of Israel, that Hezekiah, the son of Ahaz, king of Judah, began to reign."

–2 Kings 18:1

You can make fun all you want,
but when a zebra talks
people listen.

Why doesn't life happen all at once?

That'll give you an idea of *Army Man*. You either love this sort of off-kilter writing, or you probably can't stand it at all. I love it.

▲   ▲   ▲

Weirdness Updates

"What started as a legitimate effort by the townspeople of Salem
to identify, capture and kill those who did Satan's bidding
quickly deteriorated into a witch hunt."
—Army Man

You may remember that a while back Jim Moseley of *Saucer Smear* accused CSICOP crusaders Phil Klass and Zan Overall of sleazy behavior—trying to suppress a book on the Gulf Breeze UFOs by one Ed Walters. *(Note: See "High Weirdness" in Chapter 9—Ed.)* Klass then wrote Moseley a letter denying the charge—but Overall wrote Moseley a letter admitting they had done what Moseley claimed but attempting to justify it. Moseley printed both letters, leaving his readers to decide if they did it and Klass lied in denying it, or they didn't do it and Overall (inexplicably) lied in admitting it.

Now Klass has printed a broadside against Moseley with such brilliant polemic as:

"Is it true that Moseley applied to Alcoholics Anonymous but was turned down as incurable?

"Not really, AA told him their quota was filled and suggested he re-apply in 50-100 years."

And:

"Is it true that Moseley's daughter has had an illegitimate child?

"She's had so many that Moseley has lost count."

Moseley printed the whole diatribe in *Saucer Smear*, Vol. 38, No. 5, commenting only that Klass's claims were "libelous, untrue and not all that funny."

Elsewhere on the libel front, CSICOP has other troubles. As noted in Chapter 1 of this volume, one of their affiliates had already lost one libel case in 1988 (in Oregon) and their Hawaiian affiliate has a libel suit pending against them. Now more cases will soon come to court.

• Dr. Eldon Byrd has sued James Randi and CSICOP for statements Randi made as a CSICOP spokesperson, alleging that Byrd had served a prison term for child molestation. Byrd claims he was never convicted of such a crime and that Randi lied maliciously.

• Uri Geller, the Israeli psychic-or-charlatan (take your pick) has started four suits against Randi for alleging that he, Geller, associated with Dr. Byrd, knowing Byrd to be a child molester;

and also for claiming that Geller "drove" an unnamed scientist to suicide (Geller says medical records show the scientist died of complications resulting from diabetes and a heart attack); and for calling Geller a "psychopath" and a "social disease"; and for claiming that Geller has committed the felony of blackmail; and finally for claiming that Geller's metal-bending feats have no original feature about them. Geller insists that Randi lied on all these counts, and that he will prove it in court.

(On the metal-bending issue, Geller's suit claims only that his feats possess originality, contrary to Randi; Uri does not attempt to bring the vexed question of "paranormality" before a court. English and American courts have traditionally ducked that issue, even when it seems central to a libel case, and ruled only on whether the defendant acted with or without "malice" in the legal sense.)

Two of Geller's suits were dismissed on technicalities (he was late in filing the first, and filed the second in the wrong jurisdiction); two remain pending.

• Randi has sent out a press release saying he "won" the two cases that never got to court, but complaining bitterly that his legal expenses have bankrupted him. Randi ringingly asserts that the libel suits represent "harassment" and an insidious attempt to destroy the First Amendment. He begs for funds to continue the battle, saying he "knows" he is right.

• Randi has resigned from the Board of Directors of CSICOP.

• *Fate* magazine (August, 1991) asserts that the new edition of Randi's book *Flim Flam* contains many alterations of passages which they had earlier labeled inaccurate, especially regarding his early career as astrology columnist for a Canadian tabloid.

• CSICOP's libel insurance has been canceled, according to two independent sources I consider reliable.

On another front, Al Seckel, former executive of the Los Angeles CSICOP affiliate, continues to face serious charges against him made by CSICOP member Tom McIver.

McIver asserts that Seckel lied in claiming a degree from Cornell University, which he did not have, and also lied in claiming to be enrolled in post-graduate work at Caltech, when he was not. Letters from Cornell and Caltech seemingly confirm these charges and have been widely circulated by McIver and others. McIver has also been sending open letters about these alleged frauds to the Board of CSICOP and all interested parties since 1987. Nobody from CSICOP has ever answered McIver—

until one recent letter from Phil Klass which did not deny the charges against Seckel but attempted to dilute them.

Klass said Seckel "almost" had a degree from Cornell, and McIver answered that that was like being a little bit pregnant. Klass also asked, with heavy sarcasm, if McIver expected CSICOP to conduct a full FBI-style investigation of every member, and McIver answered, no, he merely expected them to take some official notice after evidence of fraud has been made available to them for four years.

• McIver also charges Seckel with financial improprieties, and Seckel has threatened McIver with a libel suit.

• A George P. Hanson has entered the case, supporting McIver's charge that Seckel fraudulently claimed his group had tax exemption long after they lost it. (*Fate, op. cit.*)

Although CSICOP has still not yet taken official notice of the Seckel controversy, Seckel, like Randi, has recently disappeared from their published Board of Directors.

• On the other extreme of the spectrum, Martin Cannon claims in *Saucer Smear (op. cit.)* that Bill Cooper (whose UFO conspiracy theories we satirized in our Gulf Breeze report) uses the alleged threat of "Aliens" as a new pseudo-scientific rationale for racism. "According to Cooper," Cannon writes, "the real aliens, the ones who control all the banks, are recognizable by their big noses... Cooper has a drawing...depicting what these extraterrestrial *bar sinisters* actually look like. The drawing resembles the sort of crude anti-Semitic caricature once found in *Der Stuermer.*"

• Cannon adds that both Cooper and "Ramtha" (J. Z. Knight) peddle a racist/occult conspiracy theory that originated with Dorothy Martin, the UFO "contactee" whose exploits inspired the classic sociological study, *When Prophecy Fails.*

• *Saucer Smear (op. cit.)* reports that citizens of Gulf Breeze continue to report UFOs "on an almost weekly basis." However, most current reports describe red lights or red objects, rather than the silver disks in Ed Walters' dubious photos. TV newsperson Mark Curtis told of a red UFO he had seen personally and said he had no idea what it was.

Fear and loathing also haunt the Christian Fundamentalists:

• Despite James Randi's novel interpretation of the first amendment, judges continue to uphold the libel laws. In an aftermath to the McMartin Pre-School "Satanism" case (*Note: See "Sex, Satanism and Sodomized Dogs" in Chapter 8 —Ed.*), three of the accused teachers have won a libel action against one of the parents. Superior Court Judge Keith Wisot awarded the plaintiffs only $1, saying that the defendant, Robert Currie, although guilty of "inaccuracy," acted without malice, since he really believed a Satanic coven existed in the McMartin school.

Commenting on the low $1 award, Virginia McMartin, 84, said "I got what I wanted—the truth to come out. I didn't care a snip about the money."

McMartin and her son and daughter had been among nearly 100 teachers accused in a 1982 "rumor panic" of sexually molesting children and engaging in Satanic rituals. The police could not find evidence to indict most of the accused; only McMartin and her son stood trial and juries failed to convict either of them. (*Source:* L.A. *Times* 8 May 1991)

• Similar charges of "Satanic" child abuse, and "ritual murder," widely circulated in other parts of the country, have inspired increasing skepticism among law enforcement officials. Sandi Bargioni, a San Francisco police officer, says she has investigated "scores" of cases of alleged Satanic child abuse and none of them could be proven. Kenneth Lanning, of the FBI's Behavioral Science Unit, expresses similar skepticism after investigating many cases of alleged "mass graves" and finding no mass graves.

However, sociologist Jeffrey Victor, of Jamestown Community College, reports that 33 "rumor panics" similar to the McMartin case have occurred in 24 states in the late '80s, and both Radical Feminists and Protestant Fundamentalists seem prone to believing any accusations of this sort. (*Source:* L.A. *Times* 23 April 1991)

• The latest "Satanism" uproar, in Guthrie, OK, involves the grave of Elmer McCurdy, an outlaw killed in 1911. McCurdy, although not as famous as the James boys or the Youngers, has the distinction of traveling more extensively after his death than any other Western outlaw. After he got shot by a posse, McCurdy's corpse went on display in Pawhuska, OK, for several years, but then two men who identified themselves as McCurdy's brothers gained possession. They then took the body on tour all over the west; many years later, it ended up in a museum in Long Beach, CA; by then it had acquired so much lacquer that it passed for a dummy—until an arm broke and L.A. coroner Thomas Noguchi pronounced it a human cadaver. Further investigation identified it as the wandering McCurdy. The remains then finally received what we call "a decent burial" in McCurdy's home town of Guthrie.

263

The grave caught the attention of a Mrs. Rebecca Luker, previously convicted of S&L frauds in New Mexico. Mrs. Luker began one of the popular "mystery games" now fashionable, including a visit to McCurdy's grave at night; rumors of "occultism" quickly spread through the town, and the game became the target of heckling by Fundamentalist religious groups shouting "devil worship" at the players.

After negotiations with the city council, the game continues. The Fundamentalists still follow the players to the cemetery, but keep a respectful distance and only sing hymns. (*Source: Wall Street Journal*, 11 July 1991)

1994 Update

Final Updates and New Fuckups

1. Well, it took a little longer than I expected to get this anthology whipped into shape.

2. Parapsychologist Elden Byrd got his libel suit against Randi and CSICOP into court before Uri Geller's suit. The jury found that Randi had libeled Byrd, but that CSICOP bore no responsibility for Randi's lies. CSICOP, however, still has Geller's suits pending.

CSICOP now admits no association with Randi and has adopted the attitude of Prince Hal toward Falstaff: "I know thee not, old man."

3. Naomi Wolfe, of all people, has now launched an attack on the hate-filled ladies I have called "Radical Feminists" or "androphobes." Wolfe, in her new book, *Fire with Fire,* calls them "victim feminists," and scorns them for becoming professional victims—wallowing in self-pity and refusing to accept adult responsibilities. She also says a few harsh things about their male-bashing, but does not explicitly join me in comparing them with other bigoted hate movements. Well, however you slice it, I feel happy that Wolfe at least agrees with my verdict that those ladies have *something* seriously wrong in their logic circuits...

Meanwhile, another heretical Feminist, Camille Paglia, has lambasted the androphobes at great length in two fine, scholarly books, *Sexual Personae* and *Sex, Art and American Culture*. Paglia finds the androphobes guilty, chiefly, of substituting mythology and dogma for sound scholarship, and of male-bashing extremism.

And Warren Farrel, once the only male officer of NOW, has published *The Myth of Male Power,* statistically refuting most of the androphobic stereotypes.

At last I feel less alone out here, defending the "indefensible" male human from unscientific slander.

...But this still remains an uphill battle. The San Jose *Mercury News* for January 4, 1994, says that many women quietly "smile" with satisfaction at a new heroine, Lorena Bobbitt, who cut off her husband's penis with a knife. I suspect,

265

or at least I hope, that when they write "women" they just mean the more rabid Feminists on their own staff, who usually scare hell out of liberal, wimpy males, and insist that the males pretend to believe these loonies represent all women.

Fortunately, all the women I know find the bloodthirsty Ms. Bobbitt as horrifying as I find Jack the Ripper (who engaged in similar mutilations on women a hundred years ago.)

And in Hitler's heyday, almost all rational, educated persons argued that a sane mind would judge Jews *One. At. A. Time.* and not all in one lump, but today those who apply the same judge-one-at-a-time standard to males still remain a minority whose opinions still usually get ruthlessly suppressed in most of the major media—and in most of the underground media, too. The power of the androphobes still terrorizes the men in both ends of media into pretending to believe what nobody with more brain cells than a hamster can ever believe: "They all look alike to me."

4. Well, whatever you or I think of the Gulf War, "democracy" triumphed when the Sabbahs returned to their palace with golden toilet bowls in Kuwait. Or at least our major media still says so.

Of course, Kuwait now has more journalists in prison than any other nation except China, according to Amnesty International. But maybe this just shows the Kuwaitis know how to please our government. China, with the greatest number of political prisoners in the world, enjoys "most favored nation" status with the Clinton administration as it did with the Bush administration.

I suppose this has *some* rationalization. I just can't figure out what the hell such a rationalization could possibly argue that would make more sense than Orwell's "Freedom Is Slavery."

5. The newspapers, radio and TV this week have resounded with "moral" judgments about new techniques of inducing pregnancy suddenly appearing in Europe. "Test-tube babies" seem primitive as the horse and buggy compared to these new developments, which in combination allow a woman to bear a child to which neither she nor any lover/husband she has ever known has contributed any of the genetic material. A "black" woman and her Chinese husband can now have a "white" (perhaps Celtic? Danish? Serbian?) baby, if that choice appeals to them.

Women of 59 (or older, it appears) can now have children. Terribly shocking, to those who think only men of that age should embark upon parenthood...

Whatever "moral" judgments one passes on this technology, it will come into wide use, in at least some nations, and some women will travel there to use it.

All the old rules and laws of life continue to break down and new rules and laws continue to appear, as information doubles faster all the time. No "morals" based on religions or philosophies created before current technology will have any relevance to our situation by next Tuesday after lunch.

6. When I first attended a World Game workshop, Medard Gabel told me the World Game Institute had presented 33 workshops in 1987. In 1993, they presented 220 workshops, all over the world, many of them to government officials. I calculate that as a growth rate of 660%.

The World Game date base has grown at an even faster rate, and with the passage of NAFTA and the movement toward GATT, the World Game will probably begin to have real impact on our lives in the next decade—just as Bucky Fuller expected when he invented the Game.

7. The Information Superhighway proposed by the Clinton-Gore team will blow the minds of absolutely everybody who hasn't kept up with the most recent breakthroughs in computer/FAX/Virtual Reality technology.

Rush Limbaugh thinks he has started a lonely, heroic struggle against President Clinton. His fans—the pathetic "ditto-heads," as he accurately (if cruelly) calls them[1] —share this delusion. Actually, poor old Rush devotes all his energy to attacking ideas originated by Tom Jefferson and Franklin Roosevelt, the old radicals of the 18th-19th and early 20th centuries. Rush doesn't have a clue, one year after Clinton's election, of what the new radicals intend and what technology they will use to accomplish it.

8. America and Russia will soon begin collaborating on a permanent space station—something I first predicted around 1973, I think. Or maybe 1974.

---

[1] Cf. Hitler: "The masses are female" (by which he meant compliant.)

Chaos and Beyond: *The Best of Trajectories*

In *Cosmic Trigger I,* I predicted that by 2028 more people would leave Earth every year than currently fly out of Kennedy International in New York—i.e., more than 200,000,000. Even though the laws of chaos indicate I should expect the unexpected, and even though I have learned the wisdom of Robert Heinlein's aphorism, "It does not pay a prophet to be too specific," I'll stand by that date and that estimate of yearly space colonists.

Robert Anton Wilson

CERTITUDE

belongs

ExcluSiVelY

to those who

Only Look

in ONE

ReFErenCE Book

—R.A.W.

Contributors

D. Scott Apel
Managing Editor of *Trajectories* and the world's most prolific unpublished novelist. For nearly a decade, he has written the video column for the San Jose *Mercury News*, and hosts Sunday Science Fiction Night on KTEH-TV, the PBS affiliate in Silicon Valley. Scott publishes *Popular Mythology* magazine and wrote *Philip K. Dick: The Dream Connection* (Permanent Press, 1985). While he has not yet attained the status of cult figure, he has become a cult figurine.

George Carlin
Absolutely the funniest man alive on planet Earth.
If you have any doubts about that, try his videos *Playing With Your Head, Doing It Again, What Am I Doing in New Jersey*? etc., all available at any high class video store catering to that special, select audience that the FBI keeps under 24-hour-a-day surveillance.

Barbara Marx Hubbard
One of the pioneers of Futurism and one of the wisest people we've ever met. She knew Korzybski personally! (You'll find more details at the beginning of our interview with her.)

Edward Kellogg III, Ph.D.
Almost certainly knows more about lucid dreaming than any other researcher, and has published extensively in the fields of psychology and electronics. Ed has also written in E-Prime for so long that he now claims he even *thinks* in E-Prime.

Timothy Leary, Ph.D.
Author of about 40 of the most innovative books on psychology and philosophy written in our century. One of the most original thinkers of *any* century, Leary naturally always appears portrayed as some sort of loony or monster in the mass media. Try one or two of his books and then see what you think of the accuracy of the mass media.

271

Ed McMahon
Made a fortune by laughing loudly at jokes by Johnny Carson that nobody else in the world would possibly laugh at.

Robert Newport, M.D.
Orthomolecular psychiatrist, Libertarian activist and one of the nicest guys we know.

Linus Pauling, Ph.D.
If you don't know what Dr. Pauling did, or why he won two Nobel prizes, refresh your memory by looking back at Chapter One. Certainly, a man that the future will remember as one of our greatest scientists and one of our greatest humanitarians. Naturally, treated as a quack by the A. M.A.

Peter Russell
Holds degrees in both physics and psychology and has spent years studying meditation in India. Among his more astoundingly original books: *The Awakening Earth, The Black Hole in Time* and a new translation the *Upanishads* into modern and startling English.

Arlen Wilson
We asked the opinion of an objective observer, who testifies, "The most beautiful, the brainiest, the funniest and the most compassionate person I have ever known. That's why I have stayed married to her for 37 years."

Robert Anton Wilson
You know. . .the dim figure in the bushes on the Grassy Knoll, holding that thing that looks like a broom handle with smoke coming out of it. . .

Production Information

Chaos and Beyond:
The Best of Trajectories

was created on a Macintosh Quadra 610,
using Microsoft Word 5.1a.

Fonts packages used include
Microsoft TrueType Master Set
and
Casady & Greene's Fluent Laser Fonts.

The majority of the text
is set in 10 pt. Bookman Old Style.
The title and chapter titles are done in Ransom.
Headers and Footers are set in Lucida Bright,
just because.

The printer-ready copy was printed out on a
300 dpi Hewlett Packard LaserJet 4ML.

The book was designed by the Trajectories Team:
Robert Anton Wilson, Arlen Wilson
and D. Scott Apel

This whole book was proof-read twice by three
people. But you know what? Scott says he'd bet
money that there are *still* mistakes to be found!
He says they call English a "living language"
because it's *alive*—and it changes
when you're not looking.
But then again, he's insane.

What CRITICS
have said about

ROBERT ANTON WILSON's

other books:

A SUPER-GENIUS...
He has written everything I was afraid to write.
—Dr. John Lilly, psychologist

...stupid...
—Andrea Antonoff

One of the funniest,
most incisive social critics around,
and with a positive bent,
thank Goddess
—Riane Eisler, author of
The Chalice and the Blade

...a very funny man...
readers with open minds
will like his books.
Robin Robertson,
Psychological Perspectives

**...a male feminist...a simpering,
pussy-whipped wimp...**
—Lou Rollins

Robert Anton Wilson
is a dazzling barker hawking tickets to the
most thrilling tilt-a-whirls and
daring loop-o-planes
on the midway of higher consciousness.
—Tom Robbins, author of
Even Cowgirls Get the Blues

**...the man's either
a GENIUS or JESUS...**
—*Sounds* (London)

**The most important philosopher
of this century...
scholarly, witty, hip and hopeful.**
—Timothy Leary

...does for quantum mechanics what Durrell's
Alexandria Quartet did for Relativity, but
Wilson is funnier.
—John Gribbin, physicist

...malicious, misguided fanaticism...
—Robert Sheaffer, CSICOP

...while pretending to amuse, Wilson actually rids the
reader of important fictions necessary to the
conduct of life as we know it.
A very dangerous book!
—Dr. Nick Herbert, physicist

**...like swallowing a hand grenade
coated with LSD:**
it will either expand your mind
or blow it to Kingdom Come.
—Victor Koman, author of
The Jehovah Contract

...a profound book that reveals with raw humor the intrinsic inconsistencies in the thought systems underlying much of the craziness in our society.
—Peter Russell, author of
The Global Brain

The man's glittering intelligence won't let you rest. With each new book, I look forward to his wisdom, laced with crazy humor.
—Alan Harrington, author of
The Immortalist

...a master satirist who views history as an open question...
—Brad Linaweaver,
Atlanta *Constitution*

The
Trajectories
Catalog

Number 2 — September, 1994

The merchandise below is *not available in any store.*
This catalog is your sole opportunity to order these
one-of-a-kind goodies, direct from the source.
How can you possibly navigate the '90s without them?

In addition to the items below, we also offer a variety of
paraphernalia like coffee mugs, T-shirts and bumper stickers.
And we're adding new audio and video tapes on a regular basis.
Drop us a card and we'll send you a full catalog and order form!

<u>VIDEOCASSETTES</u> *(VHS only)*

• "Fear In The Night:
Demons, Incest and UFOs" (1993)

An hour-long talk by Robert Anton Wilson, wherein he
discusses perception, memory and reality in his inimitable style.

$19.95

• "Twelve Eggs in a Box:
Myth, Ritual and the Jury System" (1994)

If you've never been to a lecture by Robert Anton Wilson, here's
your chance to discover what all the excitement is about. And if
you *have* been to one, here's an opportunity to re-experience the
intellectual excitement. Caught "live in concert," Dr. Wilson
delves into the mystic significance of the dozen in myth,
literature and "real" life.

Available November, 1994   **$19.95**

AUDIO CASSETTES

(Each audio cassette runs between 55 - 60 mins.)

• "An Hour with Robert Anton Wilson"

Originally released as the first audio edition of RAW's
Trajectories Newsletter (#11; Autumn, 1992), this favorite is
now available without a subscription. RAW speaks about films,
the New Feudalism, the Men's Movement, and much more.

$6.00

• "Another Hour with Robert Anton Wilson"

Originally released as the second audio edition of *Trajectories*
(#13; Winter 1993/94), now available as a "back issue." RAW
discusses filming a movie in Portugal, the War Between the
Sexes, his experiences serving on a trial jury, and much more.

$6.00

• "Uncle Bob Explains Everything, or Poor Old Bob Exposes His Ignorance"

RAW regularly appears on radio KAZU in Santa Cruz, CA, in
conversation with ace interviewer Pat Ferguson. Their hundreds
of hours of dialog have been distilled into this massive project,
projected to reach some 20 hours of recorded material on 20
cassettes. For convenience, we've broken the existing releases
into sets of three cassettes:

* **Volumes 1-3:** **$15.00**
  * "Politics"
  * "Crowley"
  * "Religions"

* **Volumes 4-6:** **$15.00**
  * "Disinformation"
  * "Men? (& Sex)"
  * "Current Events"

* **Volumes 7-9:** **$15.00**
  * "Strange Days"
  * "Stranger Nights"
  * "We Could Tell You, But Then We'd Have To Kill You"

HOW TO ORDER:

1. Tear out or photocopy the previous page and circle the prices of the items you just can't live without. Or merely write down the titles and prices of these items on a separate piece of paper.

2. *Please add $1.00* **per item** *shipping and handling charge.* (Every penny of this, and more, goes directly to Office Depot, for envelopes, and to the U.S. Postal Service for delivery. Trust us, the struggling small businessentity groused cynically, you're getting off easy on this one.)

3. Total it all up. It's OK to use a calculator or a supercomputer.

4. Fill out a check or money order (sorry, no credit cards) for the Total amount.

5. Be sure to include your name and mailing address.

6. Stick the order form with your mailing address, and your check or money order, in an envelope and mail it to:

The Permanent Press
Dept. MB
P.O. Box 700305
San Jose, CA 95170

Our Guarantee:

If you are not completely satisfied with your merchandise, we will refund your full purchase price, including all shipping charges, if you just mail the stuff back with a note telling us why you're not absolutely delighted.

Please allow 6-8 weeks for fulfillment of your order. Thanks!